Dyn-o-mite!

Dyn-o-mite!

Good Times, Bad Times,
Our Times—A Memoir

Jimmie Walker

with Sal Manna

Da Capo Press
A Member of the Perseus Books Group

Set in Goudy Old Style by the Perseus Books Group

Library of Congress Cataloging-in-Publication Data
Walker, Jimmie, 1947–
    Dyn-o-mite! : good times, bad times, our times—a memoir / Jimmie Walker ; with Sal Manna.—1st Da Capo Press ed.
        p. cm.
    ISBN 978-0-306-82083-0 (hardcover : alk. paper)—ISBN 978-0-306-82110-3 (e-book)
    1. Walker, Jimmie, 1947– 2. Comedians—United States—Biography. 3. Actors—United States—Biography. I. Manna, Sal. II. Title. III. Title: Dynomite.

PN2287.W24A3 2012
792.702'8092—dc23
[B]
                                                                    2011049684
First Da Capo Press edition 2012

Published by Da Capo Press
A Member of the Perseus Books Group
www.dacapopress.com

Da Capo Press books are available at special discounts for bulk purchases in the U.S. by corporations, institutions, and other organizations. For more information, please contact the Special Markets Department at the Perseus Books Group, 2300 Chestnut Street, Suite 200, Philadelphia, PA 19103, or call (800) 810-4145, ext. 5000, or e-mail special.markets@perseusbooks.com.

10 9 8 7 6 5 4 3 2 1

To my mother

and to my friend who I miss
every day of my life,
Steve Landesberg

Contents

Foreword by David Brenner ix

1. Our Times 1

2. I'm from the Ghetto 5

3. Stand-up for the Panthers 31

4. Making It in New York 55

5. Kid Dyn-o-mite! 83

6. I Am Not J. J. 111

7. The Whipping Boy 129

8. Freddie, Richard, Andy, Mitzi, and Budd 161

9. A Black Sheep among Black People 185

10. The Late-Night War 213

11. The N-Word 233

12. On the Road 253

Acknowledgments 265

Foreword

By David Brenner

IN 1969 THERE WERE MAYBE TWO HUNDRED PEOPLE IN AMERICA WHO earned their living solely as stand-up comedians—that is, doing stand-up paid for their shelter, food, clothing, and other necessities. There hadn't been a new face for about six years. But then, in New York City, a group of fresh, young men and women appeared on the comedy scene, including yours truly.

The members of this small wave of uniquely funny people met each other while performing in clubs in Greenwich Village, the West Side, the Upper East Side, Brooklyn, and wherever someone would let us tell jokes for no money, just for laughs, or, oftentimes, for no laughs. Some became stars; others didn't. One of those who did was Jimmie Walker.

I met Jimmie in an Upper West Side club named the African Room. I had gone there in hopes of doing a set. On stage was someone I had not seen before in the few months I had been doing comedy. After he came off stage, we talked. I invited him to come with me to other clubs to work out and to meet and join our little clique of stand-up comedians.

Now, here's the never-told-before story of the dyn-o-mite advice I gave him. (Yes, he heard me say that word in my act, often with that strange inflection. It's okay. Time heals.) You see, Jimmie was then a very short, very fat, very white man, but all he talked about on stage was what it was like to be black and live in a black neighborhood. It made no sense. Audiences hissed and threw things at him, usually hard-boiled eggs. It was disheartening. He was about to give up comedy. That's when I stepped in to put him on the road to stardom.

We were leaving the Camelot, an open-all-night, greasy-spoon restaurant where comedians would meet for breakfast and commiserate about bad sets we had that night or try to borrow money from the hookers. After breakfast, everyone split. As Jimmie and I stood outside asking passersby for spare change, I turned, put my hand down on his fat shoulder, looked down at him, straight into his bright, blue eyes, and said, "The problem with you is your physical presence. You want to be a star?" He nodded. I continued, "Then lose the whale blubber, add inches of height to that dwarf-sized body of yours, and, most importantly, get dark! Become a black man! They're coming into style. Join them!"

He did everything I told him to do, sometimes to exaggerated lengths, such as overdoing his little, upturned nose, making the mouth too big—and let's not get into the too loud laugh. Ugh! He dropped way too much weight, and he went way, way overboard on the darkening. But he was now a tall, thin, black comedian—and now his jokes killed. He didn't remain a one-trick pony either, like so many comedians today do. He was too smart, too well versed, and too funny to be limited. A black star rose in the comedy heavens.

What has pissed me off over the years is hearing black comedians make fun of Jimmie, referring to him as a Stepin Fetchit type. Totally unfounded. What they should acknowledge is that if it weren't for Jimmie Walker busting through, thanks to *Good Times*, TV's white, glass ceiling, they would still be black, but they wouldn't be comedians.

Now, turn the page and read about one of my funniest and most beloved friends.

Dyn-o-mite!

1

Our Times

I'm from the ghetto. I'm here on the exchange program. You can imagine what they sent back there.

THAT WAS THE FIRST JOKE I EVER TOLD ON NATIONAL TELEVISION, on *Jack Paar Tonite* in 1973. Fortunately the audience laughed. That was all I needed, and for the rest of my performance I killed—as comedians say when they do very well. Little did I realize how much truth there was in that one joke.

A few years earlier I had opened community rallies around the country for the Black Panthers. But I was considered "too black" for television.

Then, a couple years after *Paar*, I became the first young black sit-com star in TV history—the Black Fonzie. But soon after the revolution was televised, I was accused of "cooning it up." In the end I became too black and not black enough, too funny and not funny enough—all at the same time.

They were good times and bad times. They were my times. They were our times.

In 1975, I had this bit:

> *I think pretty soon there is going to be a black president. Inaugural*
> *theme be playing the "Theme from Shaft." Prez pulls up—white*
> *El Dorado, white bucket seats, bubble top. Prez gets out, tilts his*
> *beaver-skin hat to the side, braids flowing down his shoulders, looks*
> *at the crowd, and says, "Ladies and gentlemen, brothers and sisters,*
> *I am very happy to be elected president of these great United States.*
> *But moreover, I am even happier to be elected the first black pres-*
> *ident of these great United States. Right now, I'd like to give you*
> *the Inaugural Address, but first . . . the number for today: 7-5-6.*
> *You got it? Then you the vice president!"*

It only took thirty-three years for my "prediction" to come true, though our first black president did not come from the streets and was not running a numbers racket—other than the federal budget. I would have loved to see him on Inauguration Day in a beaver-skin hat and braids though.

America, it is time to get real. The time has come to blow up the myths, the stereotypes, the political correctness, the hypocrisy of our modern life. And it is time to once again laugh at ourselves and at each other. That's right, *at* each other.

> *Lots of new thangs coming out about black history. Found out*
> *there were black cavemen. They dug up a three-million-year-old*
> *Cadillac . . . two payments still due.*

Years after first telling that joke (when it was cool to say "thang"), black people still laugh at those lines. White people just feel guilty because they want to laugh. But we should all be laughing at that joke—especially when I'm on stage telling it! Am I right, people? As comedian

Godfrey Cambridge once said, "If two men are laughing at each other, nobody gets stabbed."

What I have understood my entire life is that I am an individual. Each of us is an individual. Each of us makes choices in life, and we are responsible for those choices. Blaming our race, our parents, our economic status—whatever—is common today. But they are all excuses for not coming to grips with our own lives and our freedom to choose.

I had a violent father and grew up in the ghetto, but I did not become a drug addict. I was the son of folks from Selma, Alabama, but I did not hate white people. I was a child of the '60s, but I did not put flowers in my hair. I enjoyed sudden enormous fame, but I did not do a celebrity crash and burn. Why not?

Because of the choices I made. I believe that, ultimately, every one of us is free to choose. Even though I am black, I am free. I believe that each of us is free, free at first and free at last.

I'm from the ghetto. I'm here on the exchange program. You can imagine what they sent back there.

2

I'm from the Ghetto

I WAS ABOUT TEN YEARS OLD WHEN MY FATHER WALKED INTO OUR apartment in the Melrose projects with his girlfriend. His wife, Lorena, my mother, was sitting in the living room with me and my younger sister, Beverly.

"See, this is what you're supposed to look like," my father said to my mother, proudly showing off the other woman, well dressed, light skinned with ruby red lips, her hair black with fashionably blonde streaks. "You need to look like this," he told my mother. "That's why you're not worth anything."

My mom did not object. Instead, she offered the other woman a cup of coffee.

When the visit was over, my father and his girlfriend—I never forgot her name: Faye from Fayetteville, North Carolina—got in his '56 Buick, which we were never allowed to ride in, and drove off for a golfing vacation down South.

I'm sure moving north to New York City seemed exciting and promising when my parents moved there after getting married in Selma. But by the time I was born in 1947 at New York Hospital in Manhattan, dad was already "Daddy Dearest." Even a child knows that you do not hurt people like he would my mother. Even a child like me knew that

5

my father, James Carter Walker, the man after whom I was named—I was a Junior—was a horrid person, a real nasty guy. But there was little anyone could do to help. White people had money to get marriage counseling. Black folks just tried to survive.

My first memory is of being three or four years old and standing on a stool in the kitchen when we were living in Brooklyn before moving to the projects. My mother was boiling water on the stove to make grits or boil tea, and I watched her. Then one of the legs of the stool broke. I reached up to grab hold of something and pulled the pot of hot water onto me. I screamed and cried as the water scorched my left leg. I didn't go to a doctor. White people had money for doctors. Black folks just tried to survive. My leg still bears the scars.

My father, a man of small stature—only about 150 pounds—worked as a Red Cap baggage handler at Penn Station. He must have experienced a demeaning feeling of servitude, of always having to smile and ask white folks, "Carry your bags, suh?" and gratefully reply, "Thank you, suh"—especially for a man who grew up in Alabama. Red Caps were not unlike the Pullman porters on the trains themselves, who were so anonymous that customers called every one of them "George." They were not even worthy of individual names. Still, being a Red Cap was one of the better jobs available to black men at the time, with most of their income from tips.

The highlight of his life was when the Count Basie or Duke Ellington bands came to the train station on their way in or out of town and he handled their baggage. He would rave about them—how they dressed and how generous they were, giving him a huge five- or ten-dollar tip. Those were the few times I saw him happy, and those were among the few extended conversations I remember ever having with him.

My mother had to fight to move us from Brooklyn and into the Melrose projects in the South Bronx. The projects were a step up. They didn't take everybody. That's right, people, there was a waiting list to get into the ghetto! The neighborhood was mostly black and Puerto

Rican but with a couple of white families too. They probably got lost and just couldn't find their way out.

My father was a Red Cap for more than thirty years, yet he did not support us. Mom had to pay the rent—$53 a month—for the three-bedroom apartment on the top floor of the fourteen-story housing project on 156th Street and Morris Avenue in one of the country's poorest ghettos. She worked three minimum-wage jobs: during the day as a school cafeteria aide and cleaning houses and then the night shift at a printer, where she collated pages for books. Despite all that labor, we were on and off the welfare rolls and taking government handouts of cheese and powdered milk. I did not know what welfare was, but I could tell from the looks on the faces of the other people waiting in line for "government assistance" that to be there was embarrassing. As a kid, I didn't know we were "poor" because everybody I knew was in the same boat. But I was always happy when those months would come along that I would not have to stand in that line holding my mother's hand. I knew even then that welfare was a train to nowhere.

One day when I was about nine years old I ran out of my bedroom to find my father pounding my mother, his fists to her face, to her body, like a boxer. I didn't know what happened to instigate the situation. When she was on the floor, he stomped on her with his shoes. He was in a rage. She pulled herself up and ran out of the apartment. I watched as she reached the stairwell and then he followed her down the stairs. He hit her every step of the way, one punch breaking her jaw. He yelled at her as she cried and struggled to escape from him. My sister wanted to fight him, but she was too little, just seven years old. So she ran to him and hung on to his leg, trying to stop him from going after my mother anymore. I was scared, not knowing what I should do. My mother was getting beat up! I ran after them as they headed down the stairs. When they reached the building entrance, he finally stopped, got into his car, and drove away.

The police came. One of them was a white cop, and it was the first time I ever heard a white person be nice to a black person. My mother was bleeding and in bad shape, and he felt for her. He wanted to help. He said, "Tell me where he is and I will go get him. Tell me where he went."

She wouldn't tell him. Then she went to the emergency room and they wired her jaw shut.

Later, during another incident, my father broke her jaw again. Again, the police came.

"We're not going to file charges if you're not going to cooperate," one of the cops told my mother. "We want you to tell the truth and not back out when we go to court."

My mom was silent. I too said nothing. I wasn't shy, but I wasn't outgoing either. My sister did all the talking and explained everything that happened.

They were used to seeing domestic abuse in my neighborhood, most of it because of drunken husbands. Strangely enough, despite my father's terrible violence, he wasn't an alcoholic and he didn't do drugs. He was actually sober when he did these things, which made his behavior even more vicious because he was completely coherent. Understandably, the cops did not want to waste their time on this case if my mom was not going to press charges and testify and go all the way.

She said she would not. Back then, even when wives were pounded and paralyzed, women rarely left their men. But there was more. This is hard to believe—and it was hard for me to believe even then—but she loved him.

That did not matter to me. I hated him. I wanted him gone. Though he never struck me or my sister, I dreaded every moment he was there. Thankfully, he was not home most of the time. Every now and then he would stay a day or so. Usually he came by on Sunday night to watch the *Ed Sullivan Show*. If I had known I would never see him again, I would have been a happy child.

With him not around much and my mother working almost around the clock, my sister and I were latchkey kids, spending a lot of time in the apartment by ourselves. I wasn't into reading or studying, but I loved watching television, from news programs and interview shows like David Susskind's to comedy shows like *The Honeymooners* and listening to the transistor radio for music and other talk shows. I was never into wild fiction or fantasy. Even a sitcom like *The Honeymooners* had its grim and gritty edge.

With summer, when we otherwise would be around all the time while on vacation from school, my mother got us out of the house and out of the line of fire of dad's rampages. She'd send us down South to Birmingham to stay with one of her sisters—my four-foot-six, drinkin', smokin', pistol-packin' Aunt Inez. Even my father would get shaky when Inez visited us in New York. Right in front of the kids, Inez would tell my mother, "You're a fool putting up with that man." She was tough.

When we stayed with her in Birmingham, Aunt Inez would have me and my sister walk two miles to the grocery store in ninety-degree heat for a carton of Camels—every single day. The grocer was a white man, so if there was a white person there, even if he or she was behind us in line, we had to wait until that person was served first. That would never happen in the Bronx!

Going South, the culture shock was enormous. When I first saw "Black Only" drinking fountains, I didn't even know what that meant. What I did know was that they were dirty, so I drank out of the white fountain. When Aunt Inez caught me, she slapped the shit out of me.

"Do not ever do that again! You're lucky nobody saw you! People would kill you for doing that!"

"Why?"

"It's not for you."

"Water's coming out. What's the difference?"

"You drink out of this other one, you hear me?"

The most shocking thing was when Aunt Inez crossed paths with white people in public. In New York you would tell someone what you thought right to their face. Even my mother would tell me, "Why don't you tuck in your lips?" or "Lighten up, why you so dark?" She didn't mean to be funny; she was telling the truth. But in the South a woman like Aunt Inez, who despised white people like only someone raised in Alabama can, transformed into the sweetest of angels in front of them.

"Miss Jones, we sho' happy to see you," Aunt Inez would say. "You are the nicest people to us."

Out of earshot, she would warn us, "These are the Joneses. You got to be nice to them and you got to know how to speak right to them."

Aunt Inez was some sort of housekeeper, and sometimes she would take us along when she had to go to a white person's home to watch over their kids. The white kids would talk to us in the kitchen—we weren't allowed into the rest of the house. They wanted to know about New York and what it was like living there.

Afterward, we'd tell Aunt Inez we were talking to them and she'd be so excited. "Oh my God, you got a chance to talk to the Jones kids! They will be going to the University of Alabama, and they are going to be big people around here."

I didn't want to hear any of that. I was from New York! The Joneses were just people—nothing special, even for white people. But I could never say that to Aunt Inez. She has been dead these many years, and even now saying something against her, I am afraid she still might come after me!

I met a few white people back in New York during my first job— shining shoes outside nearby Yankee Stadium in the Bronx when I was ten years old. A little later I delivered newspapers, the *New York Post*, mainly to Italian families, on a route just outside the projects. But I never really knew white people until I became a vendor at the stadiums when I was fourteen years old, beginning with Yankee Stadium but also at Shea, the Polo Grounds, Madison Square Garden, and so on. Most black people, including myself, were not especially interested in them or their culture. What surprised me was that they, especially the Jewish kids I worked with, were interested in mine. They wanted to know about our music, our lives, everything.

They were the first people I ever met who had drive, who wanted to do something with their lives. They weren't working selling peanuts and soft drinks to buy a new $12 pair of Flagg Bros. shoes. They were working to earn money to go to college so they could become doctors or lawyers or open a business. To them, if you didn't go to college—even a lousy college—it was nothing short of shameful. Growing up in the projects, I could not conceive of such a plan—few of us could. Education? That was for someone else. In the projects you didn't think about the future. There was no future; there was just today.

They were white and Jewish, guys like Gary Cohen and Alan Marcus, but we became friends. They had cars and would come into my neighborhood to pick me up to go to work. They introduced me to the Stage Deli and invited me to the Huntington Townhouse, an iconic banquet hall on the Jericho Turnpike that hosted bar mitzvahs and weddings. I would put on the inscribed yarmulke and—this is probably not a shock—still stand out in the crowd. These were progressive people, and to some extent I was a trophy: "Hey, look at us. We got a black person here! We're not racist!"

I used to have a bit in my act about going to the Huntington Townhouse on Saturdays.

> Gary Cohen would get dressed up in a nice powder-blue suit, put on his yarmulke, and I'd go with him. With twenty bar mitzvahs going on, he'd just walk around and pop into a room every now and then. Inevitably, some woman who hadn't seen her designated bar mitzvah boy since he was a child and could not possibly identify him would say to her husband, "Harry, that must be him. Give him the envelope and let's get the hell out of here." We'd take in a couple grand a weekend!

That was only a joke, but I bet that scam would work today.

The extent of my criminal life involved the Great Candy Caper. About a mile away from the projects was a candy factory. Talk about temptation. I loved Chunkys. A Chunky was a candy made of milk chocolate and filled with raisins and peanuts. They were originally made in New York and had been around since the 1930s. They were beautiful and delicious, and when I was a kid, one Chunky cost only five cents. This factory had lots of other candies, but the Chunky was my pot of gold.

One night several of us kids broke in. It was not difficult. This was the late '50s—a very different time in our country. There were no razor-wire barriers or security dogs or burglar alarms. We crawled in through an open window. We weren't exactly criminal geniuses. We didn't realize until we were inside that we hadn't brought anything with us, like shopping bags, to help carry out the loot. So we took only what we could put in our pockets or carry in our arms. Still, a few dozen boxes of Chunkys, and Clark and Hershey bars were a good haul, and we ran happily home.

By the time I reached the lobby of our building the word was out that the police were looking for the guys involved in the "candy heist." How they found out so fast, I didn't know—maybe the police tracked us down following the candy we dropped along the way, a sort of Hansel and Ghetto. When I got into our apartment, I stashed the Chunky bars under my bed and prayed the police would somehow skip my place in their search for the culprits. When you're a kid, you don't know what trouble is until you get into it.

About ten o'clock that night, the knock came. It was not a neighbor's knock or a salesman's knock; it was an "official" knock on the door. My mother answered.

Two policemen stood there. "Mrs. Walker, we have it on good authority that your son stole some candy from the factory nearby. We're here to get the stolen property back or make sure there's restitution."

Cowering in my room, I heard them, but still hoped I would not have to come out to face my mother.

She came into my room instead. "Did you steal that candy?"

At first I went with, "What? Candy? Huh?" It did not work. She walked me into the living room, where the policemen stood.

"Look, Mrs. Walker, we will take him downtown to juvie if he doesn't fess up. We know he was one of the kids."

I saw the guns in their holsters and the billy clubs in their belts.

"Um, but it wasn't my idea," I said. "It was John Westbrook." He had stolen my baseball glove, so I figured he was fair game.

"Do you have any of the candy? We'll look if you don't show us."

I pulled out the boxes from underneath my bed.

"Alright. We might come back again for more information."

As they took away the Chunkys, I was quivering.

My mom said, "Why did you do something like that? You know that was wrong. No, I can't buy you a dozen Chunky bars, but I can get you two. How many do you want? Because you're not going to get a dozen. Now go back into your room, and I don't want to hear anything more from you."

The next day, when all of us kids got together, we were tough guys once again.

"Yeah, the police came, but I told them I didn't know nothing! I don't know if anybody squealed, but it wasn't me!" That's what each of us said. Of course, every kid had ratted out at least one other kid. Nobody was going to admit how really frightened we were. Maybe I just learned life's lessons really fast, because the Great Candy Caper scared me into never stealing anything again.

I hung out with a group of guys in the projects, but we never called ourselves a gang. My buddies had nicknames like PoPo (the funniest of the group), Head (very quiet, but we listened when he spoke), and Gooie (the best looking of us). There was also Irving Lipscomb, who was black even with a name like that. I know we were not really a gang because there has never been a gang with a member named Irving. In any case, Irving was two sandwiches short of a picnic.

We were barely teenagers, but we thought we were pretty tough, at least when we were together. The Melrose, Patterson, St. Mary's, and Highbridge projects as well as neighborhoods such as St. Anne's—each had their own turf. At Melrose, John King was our leader. He was the fastest and the strongest. Once, we were on St. Anne's turf, and they came after us. We ran and we ran and we ran. They targeted King and somehow caught him. They beat the crap out of him. Today, an inner-city gang would probably just shoot the other gang member dead without a second thought. But for us back then, they subjected King to the ultimate insult—they made him say, "Mommy." Only then did they let him go.

When we next saw John King, who we thought could kick anybody's ass, he was a beaten lad. Seeing that happen to someone was frightening and sad.

Another time we went to the Highbridge projects at night for a dance at somebody's apartment. When the Highbridge guys heard we were there—and hating that we might be dating Highbridge girls, which we were—they busted in. One of them had a machete.

He yelled, "I am going to kill anyone from Melrose or anyone I don't recognize!"

I jumped head first out the two-story window and into the bushes below. My buddies followed. The Highbridge guy then swung his machete out the window hoping to hit one of us. I figured he was then going to rush downstairs and intercept us as we crossed in front of the main building. Scared and scratched up from the jump, we hauled ass. Through back alleys, with dogs chasing us, we never stopping running for the entire eight miles home.

We had trouble at Patterson too. When you got off the subway one stop before ours for Melrose, you had to walk through the Patterson projects. If the Patterson guys saw us, they would chase us back to the border with Melrose. Conversely, when they came to our projects, we did the same to them. The lines were pretty well drawn. The problem was that at junior high school you met girls from Patterson and elsewhere. If you wanted to go out with one, you would have to venture into enemy territory to pick her up because her parents wouldn't allow her to come to your neighborhood alone.

Then there were the Italian guys, who had a real advantage because they had cars. We would sit on the stoops in front of our buildings and see them drive into our neighborhood. Someone would yell out, "Dagos on the way!" We would duck behind a bench or run behind a building because they would shoot at us! I guess that was their sport—hunting niggers in the projects. We were the targets of their drive-bys. Today, a gang would blow you away with firepower. Back then they were playing with BB guns or .22s. Nobody was likely to get killed.

But when my friend Ronald Wiley scooted behind a building, a bullet ricocheted off the bricks near him. A piece of the broken brick hit him in one of his eyes, ripping it out of the socket. The eyeball hung by the nerve as he held it in his hand. There was blood everywhere. We took him to the hospital. They took the eye out and put a patch on. Eventually they gave him a glass eye.

I admit it—I was never a fighter. I only got into one fight. I didn't want to be involved, and when I was, I wanted it over as fast as possible. The only detail I remember is that the guy sprained his back and screamed. That was all. That was the end of my career in street violence.

Despite the turmoil at home I managed to avoid getting into drinking or drugs. In fact, I have never done any drugs and I have drunk alcohol only once in my life. I know what you're thinking: "Oh yeah! You are telling me that someone in show business, a comic on the road for hundreds of days a year, doesn't drink, do drugs, or smoke? What is he, some religious freak, someone on a morality crusade?" Neither, my brothers and sisters. I did not follow the Ten Commandments as written in the Bible. I followed the Ten Commandments as seen in the reality show. I saw what not to do by watching the people around me. I was influenced by good examples of bad examples.

For example, there were my mom's younger brothers, Cornelius and Herbert. They would drive down from Connecticut to visit on a

Thursday and they would stay drunk through Sunday. Cornelius had a reason to drink: When he was a child in Alabama, the Klan threw a torch under their house. Turned out that was where the kids were hiding. His shirt caught fire and burned one of his arms to the bone. It was a shriveled, hideous-looking thing that was puffy and sometimes oozed a yellowish pus.

Before he would visit, a well-meaning person would tell everyone, "Do not say anything about the arm. You understand me? Do not say anything about the arm." Cornelius would enter and, of course, someone would be so shocked they'd blurt out, "Oh my God, what happened to your arm?"

He was taunted and laughed at and made miserable all of his life. He drank to numb the pain, both physical and emotional. Herbert kept up with his brother's drinking too. Both of them were short men and had a Napoleon complex. They would challenge people to fight at the drop of a hat. If you looked at Cornelius's arm, Herbert would get in your face and say, "What the hell are you lookin' at, man?"

"Nothin'."

"Bullshit!" And the fight would be on. With just one arm, Cornelius wasn't much help. Most of the time they would get their heads kicked in.

When they arrived on Thursday, I liked Herbert and Cornelius. By Saturday night, with all of the fighting and drinking, seeing them laying in their own vomit, I wished they had never come. I saw people such as them change, get totally out of control when they were drunk or high, and that never seemed like fun to me.

My mother would ask them to take it easy with their drinking. But they could not.

"Mom, they're drunk!" I complained.

"They're your uncles. Shut up."

My mother loved her brothers, no matter what. She loved her kids too. She was always good about talking to us about drinking and smoking.

For her brothers and herself, she kept a stash of Canadian Club whiskey and cartons of Chesterfield cigarettes. "If you want to drink, you want to smoke," she told us, "it's right there. Do whatever you want. Go right ahead. I'll leave it right out for you. But here's what's going to happen when you drink. You'll feel good for awhile, but then you are going to get sick to your stomach and throw up. You're going to have headaches, get splotches on your face, and start to look really old. Your eyeballs will turn red. You're going to stumble around and fall down."

Nothing good about any of that, I thought to myself.

"If you smoke," she went on, "this is what's going to happen to you. You're going to have bad breath. Your teeth are going to get yellow. And you're going to cough all the time. If you want that, go ahead."

No, really, thanks anyway.

The only time I ever drank was when I was fifteen. We were at the YMCA. Someone brought Ripple wine and I kept drinking from the bottle. It tasted terrible. Then, just as my mother said, I got sick. My friends pushed me into the bathroom. I put my head into the bowl and vomited. Someone then flushed the toilet with their foot. I took my head out and then put it back in—and passed out. I became so ill that my friends had to carry me home. I stayed in bed for two days. My mother never asked why I was sick. She didn't have to.

I never drank again—even when I went to bar mitzvahs and they would always have Manischevitz wine there.

"It's just wine, not hard liquor," they would say.

"That's okay. Is there any Dr. Brown's soda?"

My mother was the same when it came to curfews. The rule for many kids in my neighborhood was that when the streetlights went on, that was the signal to come home. My mother told us, "I will be at work. I can't watch you. Come home when you come home. Try not to get into trouble."

I did not get into much trouble at school. After all, I was hardly there. When I was, I sat at my desk, looked out the window, made paper airplanes, and shot spitballs. I don't blame the teachers for their lack of interest in guiding me. Almost all of them were white, and most of them did not want to be there either. But if you were a teacher, you could avoid the draft. So here they were in the ghetto wondering, "How the hell am I going to get my car out of here in one piece after class?"

I took a twisted pride in the fact that I handed in the same essay in English class from the second grade to the ninth grade. It was about Jim Gilliam, a black infielder with the Brooklyn and Los Angeles Dodgers. It never got any better either—always earning a B or C.

One day I was in front of Yankee Stadium shining shoes, and there was my hero! He was dressed in a brown tweed suit, driving a brown Caddy, and on his arm was a beautiful brown-skinned woman. I thought he was the coolest dude I had ever seen. He handed me a buck to shine his shoes and I told him all about himself, quoting my essay. When he gave me his autograph, it was one of the biggest thrills of my life.

I found out why the Caucasians are better at school than we are. Because y'all are better cheaters! The white kids had the answers to the tests all written up and down their arms. I tried that one time and almost went blind!

The only class that appealed to me when I was at Broncksland Junior High, JHS 38, was music. I fell in love with the saxophone when I was nine years old and I begged my mother to buy me an instrument, the only thing I ever wanted her to buy me other than baseball gloves. I don't know how she did it, but she bought me a Selmer sax, the best on the market, at a pawn shop. I was in heaven. I took that Selmer Mark VI alto sax to school and they put me in the band. For a while music was the only reason I went to school every day. I thought that when I grew up, somehow my life would involve playing the sax, like Paul Desmond in Dave Brubeck's band. But I never got the hang of actually reading music. I probably sounded terrible, but I didn't care—I loved to play.

The girls loved it too, and that was a very good thing. After one talent show in the assembly hall, the audience applauded my solo. I went into the hallway, and a crowd of girls gathered around me.

"My God, you are incredible!" they said.

No one beyond my mother had ever said I was incredible doing anything. I'm sure I was awful, but it didn't matter. The girls thought I was incredible. I was one cool thirteen-year-old boy, all dressed up in a white shirt and black pants. I looked like a clarinet playing the sax.

"What's your name?" they asked.

I said, "Sax." And that's what I began calling myself.

I was in every band in the school and lots of groups outside school—jazz, classical, pop. I wasn't very good, but I was enthusiastic. One teacher gave me some valuable advice I still believe to this day: "If you're going to be wrong, be wrong and be strong. Play it, don't fake it. Play it!"

I so wanted to get better, but we couldn't afford private lessons. In fact, there were times I didn't even have a sax to play. We would have to pawn it for extra money. My sister would say, "He can't play that thing. He's never going to do anything with that. He's never going to *be* anything. I'm going to go to college." She would want the money for French tutoring or classes to help pass the SAT. My mother would agree and hock my sax at the local pawn shop for $50 or $100. When it would get close to the 120-day limit at the shop, we would get that note saying if we did not pay the loan with interest, the sax would be put up for sale. I'd hustle, working more stadiums to make sure I did not lose the sax forever. That sax was in and out of the same pawn shop time and time again. Every time I had to give it up was painful.

The All-City band was selected from the best junior and senior high school players after an audition in front of Mercer Ellington, Duke's son. I was so determined to try to get in that for the only time in my life I asked my father to drive me somewhere. Because he thought Duke might show up, whom he adored and had met at Penn Station, he agreed to drive me to the audition downtown in the '56 Buick he had never allowed us even to sit in.

In the auditorium there were hundreds upon hundreds of kids—the cream of the musical crop. I had battled to keep my one horn, and here were fourteen-year-olds with three or four saxes. When they went on stage to play, they would put down a music sheet and actually read it. I knew I was in trouble.

I said to my dad, "We can't stay. I have to go."

"What?"

"I'm not on the same level as these guys."

"You've been playing. You're in your room practicing. What's up?"

"I'm not good enough."

And we left.

They probably would have laughed me out of the room if I had played. The memory of that disappointment, of the realization that I just did not have the talent, pains me to this day. Even though I went on to play in bands while at DeWitt Clinton High School, I knew I wasn't good enough—and before long "Sax" was no more.

My life with women—or I should say "girls"—did not start out very well either. I was hopelessly in love, as hopeless as a twelve-year-old could get, with Colonia Porter. She was a year younger and had beautiful, smooth, charcoal black skin, big brown eyes, and sparkling white teeth. She also had a boyfriend, a sixteen-year-old named Gerald. He didn't go to our junior high, but he would always be in our schoolyard at lunch time. He talked to Colonia the whole hour. At the end of the day he would walk her home.

Colonia, who was rather shy and quiet, had no idea I even existed. I knew I did not stand a chance competing for her against a sixteen-year-old. Besides, it was pretty obvious that she was in love with Gerald. But a boy could still daydream. Then one winter day she came to school without a coat. I gave her my sweater to keep her from getting cold—and she put it on! I was so incredibly happy. After school she gave it back to me. I took it home and slept with that sweater for a month.

Later that year she came to class totally distraught, crying uncon-trollably. Her girlfriends tried to comfort her, but they couldn't. Gerald had broken up with her and she was devastated. She was so upset that she went home early. I decided that because Gerald was now out of the way, this was my big chance. When school let out, I walked to her apartment, hoping to comfort her and, not coincidentally, make a case for being her new boyfriend. I was finally going to get my shot at the beautiful Colonia!

When I arrived, there were dozens of people at her home. I walked in and asked for her. People were crying. Everyone was very sad. I asked for her again. No one would tell me anything. But I overheard what the adults said to each other.

Colonia had come home and hung herself. An eleven-year-old girl. Her whole life ahead of her.

I didn't completely understand all of what happened. In some selfish way, I thought she had hung herself rather than go out with me. But her death did not change me. I already knew life could be hard. I also knew, even then, that you could not give up, that you had to keep on keeping on.

I don't say I "graduated" from high school; I say I was "evacuated." For the next three years at Clinton I hung out with my classmates, which did not involve going to many classes. The teachers moved me ahead without caring that I wasn't passing any subjects. As I was about to enter my senior year a guidance counselor called me in to check on my progress toward graduation. I was stunned when he told me that I had so few credits that my chance to graduate high school on time was nil.

"Aren't I a senior?" Nobody had ever said anything to me that I was in trouble.

"I'm sorry but you're not even a freshman."

So I just stopped going to high school. The way I figured it, I was bored of education and the Board of Education had decided to give me early retirement. That smart move qualified me to become a clerk at the

Grand Union market in Manhattan, where I hoped to get an advanced degree in delivering groceries. The Grand Union was right by the East River, so I told people I had a job with a river view!

My mother was not happy. She insisted I take night classes at Theodore Roosevelt High School. She too took a step toward improving her life. Two of her sisters, Aunt Lavaida and Aunt Birdie Mae, staged what we now call an intervention. They sat her down and told her that she needed to get out of her marriage before she lost her life. Finally, she agreed, and after seventeen years of marriage, my parents divorced. My father would no longer be around, and though we stayed in the Bronx, we moved out of the Melrose projects.

I was eighteen and a half years old when I earned my diploma from night school, which officially allowed me to graduate from DeWitt Clinton. But I had no aspirations, no hope for the future.

My best friend, Jimmy Underdue, the Big Do, and I would stand outside an appliance store and watch the large console TVs in the window. On the screen were all of these ads about joining the military. We saw guys marching and running, but what really impressed us was that they showed them at a mess table eating oranges. We went, "Wow, free fruit. That's great. We need to get into this, man."

We went to a recruiting office, where a uniformed man was stunned that anybody was actually walking in to enlist during the height of the Vietnam War. He looked at us like we were insane. He said we had to take an aptitude test first.

"Let me give you the first ten answers," he offered, obviously not wanting to lose these two fools, no matter how dumb we may be.

But just as he was about to tell us the answers, his superior showed up. "Sorry, can't do it now," he told us.

"You guys joining up?" asked his boss, not quite believing his own eyes.

"Yeah," I said, "we're comin' in."

We took the test and handed it to him. As he marked it, he kept looking up at us.

"Nobody fails this test," he said. "But both of you did."

That wasn't going to stop him or us, though.

"Why don't you come back," he suggested, "and we'll figure something out."

I guess we had nothing better to do, because we did go back. There was a different recruiter in the office.

"You joining up?" he asked, just as surprised as the first recruiters. "First, you'll have to take this test."

"Ah, forget it." We left.

Later, Jimmy did enlist in the Marines. He was sent over to Vietnam in the summer of 1967. Private First Class Underdue was a radioman with an eight-man scout patrol when a helicopter dropped him onto a hill overlooking the Co Bi Thanh Tan Valley north of Phu Bai in South Vietnam on the morning of January 2, 1968. His patrol noticed a few North Vietnamese soldiers nearby, but the Vietnamese disappeared into the high grass.

As soon as night fell, under cover of a grenade barrage and heavy machine gunfire, a dozen or so enemy soldiers rushed the Americans. Most of Jimmy's comrades were hit immediately. Jimmy spotted an injured soldier nearby and rolled toward him. The action may have saved his life because, as he rolled, a bullet only grazed his temple.

The patrol leader yelled for whoever was left to get out the best they could. "I moved away from him," Jimmy remembered, "and as I did, a grenade blast killed him."

The only two survivors were Jimmy and another black private, James Brown from Louisiana. They crawled down the hill and through the jungle and hid in a bomb crater. With US helicopters flying overhead, Jimmy tried to attract their attention by taking off his green woolen undershirt and waving it. "One chopper landed briefly, and I thought they had spotted us. But they took off again." The jungle canopy was too thick for them to be seen.

Safety was at a US base called Camp Evans (strange that the name Evans would later play such a part in my own life). But neither man had a compass. If they ran into the enemy, they would be killed or, perhaps worse, captured. They heard artillery firing in the distance and, during the night, attempted to follow the sound they hoped would signal the location of the camp.

"It was raining and I was cold and scared," Jimmy later told reporters. "We had no water and hadn't eaten for two days. I had a terrible ache from my head wound. The most we stopped was for a minute to catch our breath. We couldn't forget six of our buddies had died."

Around noon of the following day they spotted soldiers moving along the crest of a hill, but they could not tell if they were friendly or enemy. For hours they stayed where they were. Finally, they decided to ford a stream—and came face to face with the point man of a Marine patrol. Just as nervous and wary as the tired men, for a moment the Marine considered firing on them. Luckily, he did not. Underdue and Brown were rescued. Jimmy received a Purple Heart.

When he came back to the States, Jimmy was not in good shape. While in Nam he got into smoking marijuana and doing heroin, and he brought his drug problem back with him. He was also quieter and wouldn't talk much about what had happened over there. As if what he had been through was not enough, after he came home he got married and fathered a child who was autistic. Raising an autistic child is difficult now; it was near impossible then because no one knew how to handle that condition. When we would meet, Jimmy was obviously not the same guy I had known. He was always depressed. Seeing him was tough.

People always talk about the wasted lives of people in the ghetto. Nobody wanted to stay in the ghetto; everyone wanted to get out. Nobody wants to stay poor.

I grew up with Rodney Dawson in the projects, and he was so poor that his single-parent mother was never able to keep up the prescription for his glasses to correct his really bad eyesight. And because he could not afford new sneakers, whenever they got wet, you could hear them squeak. He would put newspapers in the bottom to keep down the noise. But at six-foot-five, he was still on the junior high basketball team. Without being able to see properly, his shooting was pretty bad, but he could block shots and sometimes dunk.

We had a full gym for a game against one of our main rivals. You could feel the tension in the air. Rodney was ready to take the jump ball to start the game, and his mom ran into the gym, screaming that her son was not going to be playing basketball on a Saturday. Maybe they were Jehovah's Witnesses. A stunned gym watched his mother drag Rodney away. We didn't see him for awhile, and finally he dropped out. He became a heavy drinker and was only in his twenties when he was stabbed to death in a bar fight.

There were friends of mine who died from heroin and many more from alcohol, no doubt about it. But I also had friends at Melrose who grew up and did well, became firefighters, had businesses, went to college. Some of them went to war for us too. We should never forget those from the ghetto who fought in Vietnam, including friends of mine like Jimmy Underdue and Willis "Butch" Reid, who came back damaged, or Stanley Jackson, who did not come back at all.

Stanley was huge; at fourteen years old he was well over six feet tall and 250 pounds. He was a man-child. His family was intact but even poorer than the rest of us, even poorer than Rodney Dawson's. At one time his brother had to wear his mother's dress because he had no clothes. That's how poor they were. Hearing that the Army paid $96 a month and gave you free uniforms, he enlisted as a teenager. When he came back after his first tour in Nam, he sure did look great in his uniform.

"And we get all the fruit we want," he said proudly. "We even have papaya." I didn't know what papaya was, but there was definitely something about the availability of fruit that brought in recruits from the ghetto.

He signed up for another tour, and when he came back he looked even better. I remember saying to him, "Stanley, those Cong will never get you. Those bullets will bounce off you, brother." That was the last time I saw him.

One day I came home after work and saw his mother in the stairwell. She was inconsolable, beyond tears, pulled up in a fetal position. The story that went around was that Stanley and another soldier were sitting in a Jeep, passing a joint between them. A Vietnamese kid came up, saying, "American GI, American GI" and dropped a hand grenade in the Jeep. And that was that.

A couple months after the Big Do returned to the Bronx, I enlisted in the US Army Reserves, as a private in the 518th Maintenance Battalion at Fort Totten in Flushing. The enlistment would be for six years. But I never served. When the Army looked over the results of my physical examination—I was over six feet tall and just 115 pounds—they determined I was medically unfit and gave me an honorable discharge. Yep, I had even flunked a physical.

Then I found SEEK—Search for Education, Elevation and Knowledge—a government-funded program with the City College of New York designed to prepare low-income students for college. The government would pay me $50 a week to go to class at a learning center off campus on the West Side. Leaving my career in grocery transportation at the Union Market was an easy decision.

Despite graduating high school, it was not until I went to SEEK that I read my first book—Dick Gregory's autobiography, *Nigger*. That was SEEK's plan of attack; get us interested in reading by appealing to our sense of Black Pride—and it worked. I could relate to Gregory, who grew up dirt poor and with an abusive father who was unfaithful to his mother. Yet he had overcome and become a famous comedian.

I have never forgotten a couple of the jokes in that book: Gregory walks into a segregated restaurant down South, and the white waitress tells him, "We don't serve colored people here." Gregory answered, "That's all right, because I don't eat colored people. Bring me a whole fried chicken." Then a trio of rednecks walks in and says, "Boy, we're givin' you fair warnin'. Anything you do to that chicken, we're going to do to you." Said Gregory: "So I put down my knife and fork, and I picked up that chicken, and I kissed it."

I had never been shy in school, but I certainly was not a class clown either. Gregory's book planted the first seeds in my mind about becoming a comic.

Also at SEEK, I came upon Langston Hughes, who wrote about black life in Harlem in a way that was honest and real without being harsh. His main character was the funny and folksy Simple. He wasn't complicated; he was simple. I loved Hughes's entertaining style and that Simple talked like we talked—and without apology. Simple said, "I ain't ashamed of my race. I ain't like that woman that bought a watermelon and had it wrapped before she carried it out of the store. I am what I am."

I knew what I was, but I wasn't sure what I wanted to be. Most of the kids I knew growing up were trying to beat the system, including me. Now, at SEEK, I was around kids who wanted to become part of the system so they could raise themselves up.

Around the same time, the push for Affirmative Action kicked in across America. There were always people trying to save us: What can we do for these poor Negroes? Being black worked for us, including me, and put us to work. I was given a job at Johns-Manville, a company that manufactured insulation. Fortunately, I didn't work with the asbestos; I was in the mailroom. After a few months I became a "middle manager." I had stationary printed that read: J. Carter Walker, Head of Mailroom, New York City. I was sleeping in the ghetto, but now I was working at 40th Street and 5th Avenue. Look out, world, here I come!

Donald Beckerman, an instructor at SEEK, asked me, "What do you want to do in life?"

I told him about my job at Johns-Manville. "I have my own stationery!" I said proudly.

He told me they called my position "middle manager" for a reason. I can spend my whole life in the middle—or I can do something I really love to do.

"No bullshit. What would you *really* love to do?" he asked.

At night, I'd sit in the park, chasing chicks, watching guys playing basketball, and listening to Frankie Crocker on the radio. Crocker was one of the coolest cats around, and every black person in New York tuned in to his show on WWRL. He was flashy and flamboyant. He would say of himself, "For there is no other like this soul brother—tall, tan, young, and fly. If I'm all you've got, I'm all you need." His show would start with a woman saying, "Do it, Frankie! Do it to it!" He'd end with, "Ladies and gentlemen, I've done my time, I've got to continue my prime. Frankie's got to go." Then a woman's voice would be heard pleading: "Frankie, please don't go!"

"Gotta go, baby. Time is up!"

I told Beckerman, "I'd love to be a disc jockey." I thought my answer would end the discussion.

Instead, he said, "Okay, I know some people in radio."

He took me to a station and asked his friend what I would need to do to get into radio. Was he serious? I wasn't. But I couldn't say no.

"It's hard," he admitted, "especially in your case, being from the ghetto." He was referring to my accent, part New York, part black. "You'll have to lose that if you want to be on the air." I hesitated. He went on: "Or you can be an engineer and do all the stuff behind the scenes."

That seemed easier, so I said, "Okay."

"But you'll need to get a first-class radio operator license."

Geez, I thought, there is a complication every step of the way when you take this "career path." I was ready to bail. But again Beckerman refused to let me. Not only did he know someone who ran a radio announcing and production school, the RCA Institutes, but he arranged to get me a grant to attend.

I left my job at Johns-Manville and went through the months and months of training. The exam for the first-class license was not easy, and lots of people wanted to have one. I failed three times.

With money getting tight, I needed to pick up another job. Somehow I passed the civil service test and landed work at the post office. They assigned me to a parcel post station, where each night I and another employee had to load a semi-truck with packages, from small, light ones to large, heavy ones. Along with the physical exertion, there was the mental strain. Today, they use computers and scanners to log in the packages. Back then we had to record each package by hand. I remembered those days in a joke I later used:

> *They have drug testing for employees of the post office. But there is one drug you will never hear about at the post office: speed.*

We worked from midnight to eight in the morning. After a while I put a big couch in the back of one of the trucks and would try to get some sleep (during the day I was going to school at SEEK). That winter was brutally cold, and of course, there was no heat in the back of the truck. So my partner had the bright idea to build a small bonfire on the ramp into the truck! We were sure nice and warm while we were working. But then we left to take a break to get some food. The fire swooped into the truck and packages began burning up. The foreman ran out, yelling at us as we put out the flames. They suspended us for eight days.

I could not wait to leave that job. Thankfully, on the fourth try, almost two years after my first attempt, I passed the first-class radio operator license test. Doors opened up. White radio stations were under public pressure to hire blacks, but they did not want a black disc jockey. An engineer, however, would fit the bill, and there were very few blacks with that valuable first-class license.

I was hired almost immediately at WRVR, the radio station of Riverside Church. In those days radio stations went off the air during the night, and an engineer had to open the doors and turn the transmitter back on every morning. I landed the gig to arrive at 5 a.m. It didn't matter if there was a snowstorm; I had to be there or else there would be no broadcast. I finally had a good excuse to quit the post office—and I did.

After a year at WRVR a job opened up at WQXR, the radio station of the *New York Times*. When I showed up, so young and so black, the man at the station skeptically asked if I had a first-class license. I showed it to him. I wasn't even finished filling out the application when he said, "You're hired." I became one of the first blacks to work in downtown radio outside of janitorial departments. Almost all of the on-air blacks, including Frankie "The Loveman" Crocker, were uptown.

During my second day at WQXR it was raining, so I bought an iridescent raincoat on the spot. I was so proud of having a great new job. I was so happy about my good-looking slick raincoat. Everything was looking as good as that rainbow-colored raincoat.

When I got home that day, I bumped into a friend.

"Did you hear about Jimmy?"

"No," I said, remembering only that he was having money problems and I had loaned him $20 the week before. "What's happening with the Big Do?"

"He jumped off the subway platform and threw himself in front of a train."

We call each other brothers all the time. But Jimmy and I—we were *brothers*.

3

Stand-up for the Panthers

REVOLUTION WAS IN THE AIR. BUT WHEN I STOOD UP IN FRONT OF my freshman Oral Interpretation class at SEEK, I had no idea I would soon be in front of crowds who were shouting "Black Power!"

I had to speak for three minutes on the spot without any notes. All I knew were a few Dick Gregory jokes, such as:

> People would stop smoking if the warning on the side said, "Caution: Cigarette smoking will make you Black."

The way I figured it, if no one liked my speech, I could blame him for the material. But the class dug what I did. They laughed, so I kept rapping. That really "turned me on," as we used to say in the '60s. I started to think that maybe standing up and telling jokes was something I was good at.

One teacher, Alice Trillin, disagreed. She saw an original story I wrote and called me into her office.

"Not funny," she said. "Your ideas are weak and your grammar is the worst I have ever seen. You think you're good and you're not. You need to reconsider what you're doing." She gave me a copy of a *New Yorker* article. "*This* is funny."

I quickly looked over the magazine piece. "This is different from what I'm doing," I said. "I'm doing stuff about the street, from the street."

"This is how you should write," she said, handing me another dozen or so *New Yorker* articles. "My husband wrote all these. He's a great writer and someone you should follow." Her husband was rising journalist Calvin Trillin.

She sensed that I was rejecting her criticism, which only made her more vehement about stopping me from what she saw as embarrassing myself. "You're not going to try to submit this anywhere, are you?"

"If I can, I will."

"This will never sell. You're just not good at this."

I was still working as a radio engineer, now at WMCA, one of the major AM stations, and I wasn't able to be part of the SEEK talent shows at night. But I continued performing my jokes and bits in class. I was even invited to perform in front of other speech and drama classes. Students would see me in the hall and say, "Hey man, you were funny." Their encouragement kept me going. After all, nobody in my family had ever been in show business. The only thing I knew about being a comedian was what I had learned from Gregory's book.

In the projects word would spread like wildfire when a black act was going to be on *Ed Sullivan* or some other big television show. We made sure we were home to watch the Jackson Five, Supremes, Four Tops, or comedians like Godfrey Cambridge or Flip Wilson—each of them were one of us. So, too, were the first blacks on local TV news. Bob Teague on WNBC and Gil Noble on WABC were probably the first black anchormen in the city in the late '60s. But to become one of those blacks, a black man on television, was not on the radar for any of us in the projects. I never even fantasized about that possibility.

Then, one day in 1968 someone at SEEK suggested I go to a gathering place in Harlem called the East Wind where a group called the Last Poets might let me on stage. I said to myself, what do I have to do with poetry? Don't comedians like Gregory play nightclubs?

When you're young, you don't know any better. Sometimes that can be a good thing, but sometimes that can send you in the wrong direction. Instead of going to the East Wind, I went to the Club Baron, a down 'n' dirty black club at 132nd Street and Lenox Avenue.

A haze of smoke and the smell of reefer overwhelmed me. People were drinking. There were hookers. There were transvestites. And this was during the day! I had never been in a place like that in my entire twenty years of life.

"Frank Schiffman at the Apollo told me to come over and see you about a gig," I lied confidently to the manager, dropping the name of the owner of the famous Harlem theater.

He looked skeptically at me. "You know Frank Schiffman?"

"Yeah! I work the Apollo all the time." I plowed ahead—with energy! "My schedule is really busy, but I have next week open and he told me you could squeeze me in." Of course, I had every week open.

"Frank Schiffman told you to come here?"

"Yeah! He wants me to do some time when Joe Williams is here. I work with the Count Basie band all the time. Joe knows me." Joe Williams, who I had never met, had been the singer for Basie for ages and was truly one of the greats.

"Okay, okay," said the manager. "Come by next Friday and you can do those sets. We don't need you for the whole week."

"No problem," I said nonchalantly. "What kind of money we talkin' about?" I never lacked for chutzpah, a word my Jewish friends taught me.

"We'll see."

"But I need to know the money."

"We'll see." He would not budge.

"Alright, I'll be here."

When I arrived for my first out-of-the-classroom performance, I saw Williams at the bar doing shots. He wore a tam and an ascot, and he smoked a cigarette in a holder. Other than Jim Gilliam, he was the most famous person I had ever met. But that did not stop me from interrupting the conversation he was having with someone.

"Mr. Williams, I'm Jimmie Walker. I'm your opening act."

"What?" he asked in his unmistakable baritone voice.

"Yeah, I'll do my fifteen or twenty before you."

He looked perplexed at this goofy-looking, skinny kid standing in front of him.

"Have you ever performed before?" he asked suspiciously.

"I work the Apollo all the time," I boasted.

He knew I was lying, shook his head, and returned to his conversation.

"I see you talked to Joe," the manager said.

"Yeah, we're buds. We go way back. What time do I go on? Eight o'clock?"

He looked at me with a smirk. "No."

"Well, when does the show start?"

"Eleven-thirty."

"That's almost midnight!"

"That's right, three shows—eleven-thirty, one-forty-five, and three." He looked me over. "Can you drink?"

"I don't really drink."

"Let me put this another way: Are you old enough to drink?"

"No."

He told me I could sit in the supply room in back. I waited there alone for hours. Finally, the emcee came to me and asked for my intro. Naturally, I told him to say I work at the Apollo all the time.

"You work at the Apollo?"

"Yeah! All the time!"

I nervously walked onto the stage, which was elevated above the seventy-five-foot long bar. I had heard that if the crowd didn't like you, they would throw shot glasses up at you—if you were lucky. Because looking down from the stage, I could also see guns and knives in the belts and jackets of men at the bar.

My "act" was what I had done in class. But here, after the first minute everyone in the club went back to their conversations or whatever else they were doing. It was like I wasn't even there. I did another minute or two before thinking that maybe I should just leave. Not that anyone would notice. So I walked off the stage.

The manager came to me. "You're a comedian, huh?"

"Yeah! I do a show at . . ."

"Show? You didn't do five minutes. From what I heard, I'm glad you didn't do your show."

"I'll be better at the one-forty-five."

"Let me tell you something. The one-forty-five show is going to be great—because you won't be on it."

I was disappointed, but I plugged onward.

"I'm going to get paid for this show, right?"

He stared at me without saying another word. At midnight I walked to the desolate 125th Street subway station and contemplated my failure all the way home.

I needed a new plan.

I had yet to even get a shot at being a disc jockey in the city. I spent months auditing a speech class at the New School that SEEK paid for to help me get rid of my regional accent. But I was still behind the board. So when a friend said there was a DJ job available at an R&B station in Norfolk, Virginia, I left WMCA and headed south. Jim Walker was on the air!

I had the early afternoon shift, a couple hours every day, on WRAP, 850 on your AM dial. That's right, people, I was rappin' on WRAP. This being my first job behind the microphone, I guess I wasn't very good—at least that was what the ratings said. Personally, I was a city boy alone in the country and had a hard time adjusting to the lifestyle, just like those summer days in Birmingham. After only a few months I headed back to New York. This time I would check out the Last Poets at the East Wind.

The Last Poets had formed on May 19, 1968, when David Nelson, Abiodun Oyewole, and Gylan Kain teamed up to perform in Mount

Morris Park at a celebration for Malcolm X's birthday. They were politically charged and radical. At that first appearance they walked on chanting, "Are you ready, nigger? You got to be ready!" Soon after, Felipe Luciano, Nilija Obabi, Umar Bin Hassan and Jalal Nurridin joined, creating an ensemble that many today credit as the foundation of rap and hip hop.

Revolution, creativity, and something called "ritual drama" oozed out of the East Wind and onto the streets of Harlem. I went to their third-floor loft at 23 East 125th Street, down the street from the Apollo and adjacent to the Celebrity Soul on Wax record store and Olatunji's African Drum and Dance Center, to offer my services as a comedian.

Nelson and Kain were not interested at all, saying, "This cat's full of shit. We don't have time for this. We deal in heavy revolutionary action. Who is this dude anyway?"

But Abiodun and Felipe disagreed, saying, "Come on, it can't hurt. Let him get up there. If he bombs, he bombs. Go ahead, man, you can do it."

There was no admission charge the night I first performed there, but a donation was highly recommended—at least a dollar bill—"nothing jingling," as they would say. The show kicked off with someone announcing the latest news about the evils of whitey, including which black brothers had been incarcerated and why they had to be freed. The audience of a couple hundred punctuated the news with a few "Wake up, niggers!"

"Now give it up for the comedy of Jim Walker!" Uh, thanks.

My first joke was about how bad the weather was that night: "It's raining so hard, I saw Superman in a cab!"

The crowd loved it as well as the rest of my eight minutes, much of it borrowed (okay, stolen) from Godfrey Cambridge. The Superman joke might have come from Clay Tyson, a then-known black stand-up comic who worked with James Brown and had a few records out. I couldn't "borrow" from Gregory or Bill Cosby because they had a smooth storytelling persona about them. Cambridge did more traditional jokes that were easier to put in my own style. One that I did based on a Cambridge bit was:

> *What's been happening uptown lately is there's been a lot of rob-*
> *beries, man, and what's been happening even worse is black people*
> *have been robbing black people. We robbing us. This leads me to*
> *the area of nonviolent crime. Now in violent crime we doing*
> *damned good. But in nonviolent crime—I mean when was the last*
> *time you seen a black embezzler? Or a black man getting busted*
> *for juggling the bank books? I'd like to be walking down 125th Street*
> *one time and have a black brother lay a counterfeit one dollar bill*
> *on me, with a picture of Washington—Booker T. Washington!*

After the Last Poets did their chanting-rapping-drumming-political thing, someone passed a hat for additional donations for the comedian. I was paid $25, making it my first professional gig.

I went on to perform with the Last Poets for the next few years—at clubs, rallies, and black colleges up and down the East Coast, including Howard, North Carolina A&T, St. Augustine's, Delaware State, and Virginia Union. They never said, "Hey, we're going to Howard University. We'll give you a hundred dollars to come along." It was more like, "We're going to Howard University. Do you want to go? It's a benefit." A benefit meant there was no money, at least for me. But the experience was invaluable.

Hanging around the Last Poets and the East Wind taught me a great deal—and not just about show business. Often a popular activist writer such as Nikki Giovanni or Sonia Sanchez would take the stage to read their poetry. I also absorbed a lot of black history that our schools forgot to teach us. I knew who Martin Luther King Jr. was, of course, but the Last Poets enlightened me about others, such as Malcolm X and Marcus Garvey.

The Last Poets were one of the most important cultural forces in black history, and I was right there with them. At times a big talent

agency like William Morris would come by to check them out—not
with a white agent, of course, but with a black assistant. The "wolf in
a sheep's clothing" approach did not sit well with the Poets. So when
a white record producer named Alan Douglas called and said he wanted
to work with them, they were suspicious and hostile.

They told him to meet them at 137th Street and Lenox. There he
found a schoolyard with two blacktop basketball courts and a couple
dozen black guys staring at him. As he cautiously approached, the
crowd parted like the Red Sea for Moses. Revealed underneath a basket
were four Last Poets—rappers Abiodun, Jalal, and Bin Hassan, plus Nilija playing the congas. They instructed Douglas to stand at the foul
line, and right there and then they performed their best material. Douglas, who also produced Jimi Hendrix, was so impressed that he drove
them to a friend's studio and recorded an album that afternoon.

The Last Poets's self-titled debut album sold half a million copies,
largely by word of mouth, because it sure was not going to get much
radio airplay. Their whole vibe, not to mention the track "When the
Revolution Comes," had a tremendous impact on many artists, including Gil Scott-Heron and his "The Revolution Will Not Be Televised."

But the Last Poets would fall apart. Money has a way of corrupting
people. "Whitey" was supposed to be the enemy, but whitey had the
money. Some people began to consider the Poets to be sell-outs. Others,
including some of their own members, began to treat the Poets more
as a business than a movement. Mix in a few jail sentences, and before
long their moment had passed, though their legacy remains to this day.

I performed at benefits anywhere at any time for anyone who
would have me. Harlem Youth Federation for the legal defense of the
Harlem Five, billed below Askia Muhammad Toure, a pioneer in the
Black Arts Movement? I was there. The Uhuru Festival sponsored by
the Black Arts Freedom Library? I was there, billed below the Third
World Poets and Black Nation Quintet but ahead of the Universal
Messenger of Drums. Black Spring for the Afro-American Studio for

Acting and Speech? I was there. An Evening of Jazz, Films, and Poetry headlined by saxman Pharoah Sanders? Call it A Night of Blackness or Black As We Are, and I was there, baby. A Free Affair in Honor of Sayeed of the Harlem Five Out on Bail (seriously, that was the title) was held five months after the first benefit, which apparently had been successful. Black Panther leader H. Rap Brown was a guest. I was the comedian.

Occasionally someone would wonder why there was a comic on the bill. But especially on the road at colleges, even though the students wore berets and dashikis and Afros (I never could grow one), I found that audiences were still black people at heart—people who love to laugh at themselves and their lives.

One thank-you letter read, "Your performance was beautiful and it relayed to the audience the power and beauty of our Blackness." Yeah, we used to talk like that. The city of New York even invited me to be a judge for the Miss Harlem Contest! Forget friends with benefits; this was benefits with benefits.

I met most of the leaders of the movement, including those with the Black Panthers. But the Panthers were formed and strongest in California. They were from Oakland and did not translate to New York and the East Coast quite as successfully. Stokely Carmichael, however, was one of us, a New Yorker. He moved from SNCC (Student Nonviolent Coordinating Committee) to the Panther Party and was responsible for popularizing the term Black Power. Stokely was very smart. I was impressed that he had gone to the Bronx High School of Science, where you had to pass a test to get in. Some of us rarely passed a test when we were *in* high school.

Stokely started out believing in integration, but by the time we crossed paths he was into his "Back to Africa" phase.

"You know, Stokely," I told him with a straight face. "There are a lot of white people who would love to see this 'Back to Africa' thing happen."

He did not find that amusing. He got pissed and said, "Walker, maybe you are not relevant to the revolution." He was probably right.

Stokely was a very serious guy, taking everything so hard. Life to him was black and white—and everything white was evil. He was the kind of radical who objected to using white toothpaste. But he was one Panther who said what he meant and meant what he said. In 1969 he did go back to Africa.

The Panthers earned a lot of good will in the black community because of their free-breakfast program for kids. Though launched in Oakland, the program soon had kitchens operating in cities across the country, feeding more than ten thousand children every day before they went to school. The Panthers helped instill self-worth in the black community too. They talked about standing up for ourselves, that sometimes we can't turn the other cheek. They talked about not looking for a handout; sometimes we need to do things for ourselves. I could not disagree with that. Power to the people!

The rallies I performed at were very militant affairs, with the Panthers blaming all of the problems of the black man on white society. After one rally in the rain, when I used my Superman joke, I heard one Panther say, "The white man made it rain!"

Another common saying was "The telephone is for white people. A black person uses the drum!" When someone yelled during a rally, "Down with the white devil!" the Panthers' white lawyer, William Kunstler, would stand up and scream, "Right on!"

My act was definitely antiwhite as well, though I have—excuse the expression—"blacked out" most of those particular jokes from my memory.

> I love to see white folks who don't work. Make me feel so good on the inside. "Why don't you go get a job? Pull yourself up by your bootstraps! I'm tired of paying taxes for people like you!"

But all I wanted was stage time. So did everybody else. When Stokely would get going, he'd speak for an hour and a half. He was a star, as was the incendiary Rap Brown. The women were strong too. In truth, I thought Kathleen Cleaver was sharper than her husband Eldridge. And when Angela Davis was there, she would close the show. She was young, pretty, flamboyant, and a Communist. Whites had Jane Fonda; blacks had Angela Davis. They would wait hours on a hot day in the park to see and hear her finally. But they would first have to see and hear me:

> The brothers tell me that our women, our black women, should always be ready to have sex with us so they can populate the world and there will be lots of us when the revolution come. The other day I get into a fight with my girlfriend. She tells me, "Jimmie, when it comes to you, I think I'm gonna take time off from the revolution."

There were some in the movement I had my doubts about—opportunists who believed a little of what came out of their mouths but also knew what to parrot in order to get through. They hopped on the Black Power train for the chicks and the cash, and make no mistake about it—there was a lot of both. Not for me, of course. I was just the comic.

In the summer of 1968 the Panthers invited me to entertain at a series of seminars and workshops in Chicago. I was given the title Official Comedian for the Black Panthers in the East. I didn't know if anybody else had a title, but I had one. Much of the leadership was there: Bobby Rush, Elaine Brown, David Hilliard, Fred Hampton, and the Cleavers among them. They were getting ready for the Democratic Convention. And all the talk was about how "The Man" was after us, about conspiracies and spies. I didn't think I was that significant or important for J. Edgar Hoover to care about. But I was there, and I'm probably still in an FBI file today.

One night after a rally a group of us went to Fred Hampton's apartment in Chicago. We knocked on the door and waited a couple of minutes. A woman cracked it open as if we might be burglars. She recognized a few of the others and let us in. The place was barren—a few chairs and a couple of lamps without shades turned on. Incense was burning.

Hampton was young, just twenty years old, but he had a commanding presence. When he brought together a number of militant groups, including the Black Panthers, Brown Berets, and Red Guard Party, he coined the term "rainbow coalition" long before Jesse Jackson borrowed it.

I sat with a couple of folks in his kitchen while he and others went into the living room. After more than an hour they rejoined us. Fred said matter of factly, with no fear or panic in his voice, "I don't know how much longer I'm going to be around. I think they're going to kill me." "They" was the FBI, CIA—the US government. I was shocked. Why would they want to kill this guy? As we got up to leave, Fred hugged everybody, including me. It was a goodbye hug. I thought he was crazy about being targeted for death, that he needed to take a chill pill.

Later that summer, along with the rest of America, I watched the riots at the Democratic Convention on television. I would see certain Panthers get arrested and I would think, "Wow, I know that guy!"

A year later I was back in Chicago, opening at a club or theater, and I turned on the TV for the news. They said a Black Panther leader had been killed—it was Fred Hampton. They reported that the Chicago police had gone to Fred's apartment and been attacked. The police then shot him dead. When I returned to New York and went to the East Wind, the story was different. They said Fred and his pregnant girlfriend were sleeping as the cops busted in. They shot him more than fifty times.

The truth was hard to find. Race colored everything. But Hampton turned out to have good reason to be paranoid. Uncovered later was the fact that the FBI was keeping tabs on him and the others, tapping their phones and infiltrating the group. I did not know it at the time, but William O'Neal, Hampton's bodyguard and the head of security for the Chicago chapter of the Panthers, was actually working for the FBI.

I, however, was not a militant. Nor was I a "Negro," which was a putdown. A Negro was someone like Aunt Inez. Her older generation, though they had experienced abuse from whites and talked about it all the time in private, would personally apologize to white people about the Freedom Riders and those in civil rights marches. When I was in Birmingham, Aunt Inez would tell white people, "I'm sorry. I don't know about these young people today. They have nothing to do with us."

Call me a Negitant. I was where most blacks were, like most people usually are—in the middle. I was just not that angry. Why would I be? I had not been around many white people to start with and had truly never witnessed whites treating us badly because of the color of our skin. The black people I was around didn't spend our time wondering what the white people were doing to us. I didn't believe white people were out to get us; I figured they had other, more important things to do. In fact, the whites I had come into contact with—my friends from the ballpark and teachers at SEEK—had actually helped me.

I heard what the Panthers and the Poets said, and I took it all in. But what they were yelling about was not part of my reality. As Godfrey Cambridge joked,

> You people aren't going back to Europe, and we aren't going back
> to Africa. We got too much going here.

I believed in Satchel Paige's line: "Don't look back—somebody might be gaining on you." I wasn't looking back.

The Last Poets finally got me to the Apollo. Frank Schiffman, the owner, and his son Bobby didn't want them to perform there because they felt the Poets were too antiwhite and the crowd might get out of control. Even Honi Coles, the famed black tap dancer who had become production manager at the Apollo, objected. But the local community put on the pressure, and the Last Poets were booked—and so was I as their opening act.

My mother had first taken me to the Apollo when I was a child. I remember seeing Frankie Lymon and the Teenagers, the Harlem singing group who had the massive hit "Why Do Fools Fall in Love," and later Sam Cooke and then James Brown when he truly was Mr. Dynamite. For someone in the ghetto, going to the Apollo was like a Jew going to Jerusalem or a Muslim going to Mecca. I never dreamed that someday I would be on that legendary stage. Although my mother had been upset with me about my career path ever since I quit the post office, she got over that disappointment in her son on the night I played the Apollo.

Well past midnight, long after the show was over, I hung around after everyone else had left. I walked on stage, still wearing the khaki safari jacket that was becoming my trademark. The one small lamp traditionally kept lit was the only illumination. I stood at center stage and thought about where I had come from and where I was now. Pure joy washed over me. I reveled in my moment, and, well, the moment was cool.

Soon I would get used to being on that stage—not as an opening act but as an emcee. I became one of two regular emcees, along with the unrelated and bald Roger Walker. But I wanted to do more than introduce acts. So I'd do my jokes too. Some artistes did not appreciate that.

The first night I worked as emcee was for a show with Wilson Pickett and Joe Simon. I did my bit, got my laughs, and then introduced Pickett with as much flair as I could muster.

"Now, ladies and gentlemen, you know him, you love him—welcome Wilson Pickett!"

Pickett, who was hugely popular, did his show, including hits like "In the Midnight Hour" and "Mustang Sally." Immediately after he exited to his dressing room, the stage manager found me and said, "Mr. Pickett wants to see you in his dressing room."

I thought, "Great, he probably liked some of my comedy and wants to compliment me." First I returned to the stage for some more jokes and to introduce Joe Simon: "Ladies and gentlemen, you know him, you love him—welcome Joe Simon!"

Then I went to Pickett's dressing room.

"I thought you were the emcee," he said coldly.

"Yeah," I said, "but I'm a comic too."

"You emcee, right?"

"Well, yeah."

"You're the guy who brought me on?"

"Yeah."

"What the *fuck* was that?!"

"What?"

"'Ladies and gentlemen, Wilson Pickett'?"

"That's it, right?"

"No, that's not it. I'm the Wicked Mr. Pickett, and you say it at least three times, and you tell them all my hits. Forget the jokes. Then 'Ladies and gentlemen, the Wicked Mr. Pickett!' Then you get the fuck off."

I walked out somewhat shaken, and the stage manager pointed me to Joe Simon's dressing room.

"What was that?!" Simon yelled. "'Ladies and gentlemen, Joe Simon'? Forget the jokes. This is what you say: 'All the way from Louisiana, the man who gave us 'Let's Do It Over,' 'Teenager's Prayer,' '(You Keep Me) Hangin' On,' and his million-selling smash hit, 'The Chokin' Kind.' Then you walk to one side of the stage and say, 'Joe Simon!' Then you walk to the other side of the stage and say, 'Joe Simon!' Then you walk to the center of the stage and say, 'Joe Simon! He's back there! He can't hear you! Joe Simon!' Then I come out."

"I'll be happy to do that intro, Mr. Simon," I said. "But after I do my jokes."

I stood up for my stand-up. Once, when I heard the Delfonics tuning up their voices behind the curtain while I had a couple of minutes left as an opening act, I yelled on stage for them to shut the hell up! But my attitude did not sit well with Honi Coles. He and other Apollo folks wanted me fired. But Bobby Schiffman liked me, so I stayed. I kept doing my jokes, every show, five shows a day, a couple days a week. I would close my time on stage with a joke about an algebra question my teacher supposedly asked me in school:

> *If Farmer Brown took five hours to plow his field, how many hours would it take Farmer Brown if he had Cousin George do half the field in one-third the time it took Farmer Brown, and if one of Farmer Brown's horses was ill, slowing Farmer Brown down by 18 percent? Now, showing all work on a separate piece of paper, how long would it take Farmer Brown to plow his field? Give the answer in FEET!*

I always managed to get the audiences laughing. That was not easy. Apollo crowds were notorious for being tough on performers who showed any weakness. One comic, Danny Rogers, got into it with a heckler, and the guy pulled out a gun and shot him.

So I went into Bobby's office one day and asked for a raise from $400 a week. Honi was there. They looked at me like I was a Klansman at an NAACP convention.

"You're lucky to be on that stage!" said Honi. Ever since the Last Poets, who he did not like, he had tagged me as an arrogant punk who did not know his place.

"I think I'm doing a good job."

"Are you insane?" said Bobby. "You're not an act. You're an emcee. You don't make the people happy. The acts make the people happy."

Honi piled on: "You're making a lot of trouble around here for a guy who ain't shit and ain't funny. Who the fuck do you think you are?"

"I'm Jimmie Walker!" I said, thinking that should be answer enough.

"Who the fuck is that?" said Honi.

Bobby waved his hand at me. "Get out of here!"

So I went to Frank, Bobby's father.

"You really think you deserve a raise being an emcee at twenty years old?"

"I'm doing comedy too. That counts for something, doesn't it?"

"Let me talk to Bobby."

They gave me a $25-a-week raise.

My mom was probably never prouder of me than when she saw me at the Apollo. I heard that she would stand in the lobby and somehow subtly announce to the people walking in that her son was the emcee. I did consider myself lucky to be there, and I took advantage of it too. Every now and then I would spot a girl in the audience I knew from junior high, a girl who never noticed me back then, and I would get to impress her with a tour backstage and an inflated rap about how I knew Gladys Knight and the Pips, the Dells, Harold Melvin and the Blue Notes, the Emotions, Jerry "Ice Man" Butler, and on and on.

I became so familiar to the music acts that I was often booked for their shows on the rest of the "chitlin' circuit." Along with the Apollo, these were predominantly black theaters, such as the Uptown in Detroit, Regal in Chicago, Uptown in Philadelphia, and Fox in Detroit as well as clubs deep in the inner cities of America throughout the East, South, and Midwest. The unofficial circuit developed because at white theaters black acts were rarely allowed to perform and black audiences were hardly welcomed either.

One day at the Uptown in Detroit, a man and a woman came backstage and said they liked what I was doing. They asked if I would be interested in emceeing a tour around the country. They were from Motown Records, which was about to send out the Motortown Revue (aka Motown Revue). I met them again the next day at the Motown offices, where they told me more about the "truck and bus" tour—which meant everything we would need would be coming with us either by truck or bus.

Coincidentally, the first Motown act I had already worked with was Motown's first act ever. In 1959 Marv Johnson recorded "Come to Me" for Tamla, Berry Gordy's predecessor to Motown. Marv had several major hits over the next couple of years, such as "You Got What It Takes," and he was Gordy's first star. But when I opened his show at Detroit's legendary 20 Grand nightclub, he was near the end of his Motown career.

The 20 Grand, my first genuine club gig outside of the New York area, was a club where Gordy would go to see potential artists he could sign for his fledgling record company. Gordy sat in a booth along with an associate or two as well as his sister Anna, who would later marry Marvin Gaye. The artists worked their asses off trying to impress him.

Everyone from Smokey Robinson and the Miracles to the Supremes to Stevie Wonder had played there. A hard-core joint filled with sleazy lowlifes in the middle of the ghetto, the 20 Grand packed more guns than any place I have ever been. It made the Club Baron look like a convent. Everybody packed a piece, brother. How do I know? Because they were out in the open! They showed them, Chuck Berry style! (As a teenager, Berry famously flashed a handgun to steal a car.)

Everybody had a gun because fights were constantly threatening to break out. Every night I was at the 20 Grand there was a gun incident. The antihandgun folks won't like to hear this, but gun proliferation actually stopped greater violence. If there was a fight brewing and someone pulled a gun, usually people said to themselves, "Well, maybe I will reconsider whether this fight is really worth continuing." Fights did not start with guns, but showing a gun usually ended them.

Even the artists, such as Marv, would carry guns, sometimes to threaten whoever was supposed to pay them.

"Hey, where's my money?" the musician would say.

If the club owner hesitated, the musician would show his piece. "I want my fuckin' money!"

On occasion a friend of the owner would see what was happening, come up behind the musician, and pull their own gun. That was just business as usual.

After I exited the stage renowned Motown choreographer Cholly Atkins—who gained fame in a tap dance act with Honi Coles before he taught those great dance steps to the Temptations and all of Motown's artists—loved to bust my chops: "Hey man, I heard those jokes you were doing. You'd better keep moving because I don't have choreography fast enough for you to dodge a bullet!" Cholly taught me that you should work hard in show business, but don't take the business so seriously that you don't have all the fun you can along the way.

Playing the Regal in Chicago was just as dangerous as the 20 Grand. I never felt safe there. We came in on a Monday and played through Sunday. Everyone in that rough ghetto knew what day we would be paid—and most acts, especially black ones—were always paid in cash. We worked hard for that money: shows at noon, three, six, nine, and midnight on weekdays, and then another 2 a.m. show on weekends. We had to be careful walking to and from the theater, though the theater itself wasn't secure either. Wardrobe would be stolen from backstage, and musicians were lucky to get out of there with all their instruments.

Marv Johnson was also set to be on the Motortown Revue. The schedule had us hitting the road across the South with the Temptations, Edwin Starr, Marv, and myself on the boys' bus—called the Funky Bus—and the Marvelettes, Martha Reeves and the Vandellas, and Mary Wells—though she had left Motown Records—on the girls' bus. But first we heard a speech in the parking lot of Hitsville, USA, the Motown headquarters on Grand Avenue, about our code of conduct:

"We are going south, to Tennessee, Arkansas, Mississippi, Alabama and so forth. When we get to the concerts, you will see sections roped off. The white kids will be in the middle. On either side there will be the black kids. We do not want you associating with the white kids, especially the white girls. No touching, no nothing. Nothing. Because if you do, there will be trouble."

Rightly or wrongly, "trouble" in the South sounded a whole lot more ominous for black people than "trouble" in the North did.

"When the white girls rush the stage, go to the other side of the stage. When the show is over and everyone is in the field or parking lot, there will be white girls there from the audience. You are not to speak with them. And Lord knows there will be no white girls on the bus."

We were on the road for four or five weeks. If we didn't stay at a boardinghouse at night, we slept on the bus. Finding food could be difficult. We would have to go to the black side of town for a restaurant or, when we pulled in too late at night, find someone willing to cook for us at home.

Traveling on the bus was crazy and it was loud. Everybody talked about music. Every guy talked about chicks. Some guys argued over sports: Who was better—Denny McLain or Satchel Paige? Singers worked on their harmonies. Musicians practiced on their instruments— Little Stevie Wonder always blowing on his harmonica. On a scale of one to ten, the noise would be at thirteen. And through all of this there would inevitably be one guy sitting up in his seat and stone-cold asleep.

There was a lot of smoking and drinking too, but there were very few problems. For the most part people were just happy to be working. If there was trouble, those at the center of it knew they would be off the tour.

That nearly happened many years later to Johnnie Taylor, who had two huge hits, "Disco Lady" and "Who's Making Love." Long after the Motortown Revue I emceed the Kool Jazz Festival across the country. On the bill were an all-grown-up Stevie Wonder, Aretha Franklin, Natalie Cole, Tavares, Mighty Clouds of Joy, Wild Cherry, and Taylor, who had a big alcohol problem. Sometimes he would not show up or, when he did, would go way over his time allotment on stage. A drunken Johnnie would go on and on. I would have to hustle on stage and dance him off. The promoters finally went to him and said, "Hey man, if you don't show up or you show up and stay on stage too long, we're going to let you go." Johnnie was worried.

Next up was Riverfront Stadium in Cincinnati. I was in the dugout doing press for the show as the workers set up the stage at second base. Johnnie arrived, wearing a nice royal blue suit and a derby on his head, all dressed up and ready to go for his performance. "I told you guys," he said soberly, "I'm not missing any more shows. I am here on time for today's show."

The stage manager looked at him and said, "That's great, Johnnie, but the show is tomorrow."

Back on the Motortown Revue, Edwin Starr wasn't satisfied with simply getting on stage and singing. He had scored with the Vietnam protest song, "War," and he was into putting on a major production. However, to cut down on expenses, he did not travel with a band; instead, he hired bands in each town to back him up. He then would go to a black church and donate money to get the choir to join him. He'd also visit local schools and donate money if twenty students would join him that night and, during "War," run from each side of the stage to the center and pretend to attack each other, as if they were in battle.

Edwin was also a major-league conniver of women, along with Smokey Robinson and David Ruffin of the Temptations. What was surprising was that the women were not lowlifes; they were solid black citizens—schoolteachers, nurses, bank tellers. When our tour came through, these small-town girls decided they were going to grab a "star" and do something wild for once in their lives. Me? Occasionally, when there weren't any band guys left, a young lady might settle for the emcee.

Detroit had its Motortown Revue and other cities had their hometown stars on the chitlin' circuit too. I emceed the Philadelphia show with the Delfonics ("Didn't I (Blow Your Mind This Time)"), Stylistics

("Betcha by Golly, Wow"), Harold Melvin and the Blue Notes ("If You Don't Know Me by Now"), Blue Magic, and the Intruders ("Cowboys to Girls"). The Chicago package tour brought together the Dells ("Give Your Baby a Standing Ovation"), Chi-Lites ("Have You Seen Her" and "Oh Girl"), Emotions ("Best of My Love"), and Jerry "Ice Man" Butler ("Only the Strong Survive"). Many of these acts are still around today, though they have gone through large-scale personnel changes. As comic Carol Leifer has said, "I went to see the Drifters, and they had changed so much they were now white!"

The days of the police in the South setting dogs on blacks were gone, but they were not forgotten. We would overhear adult whites at the shows say, "We're gonna hear some nigger music tonight!" or "I can't stand that nigger music. I took my kids here because they wanted to. But I told them don't touch any of them and don't let them sweat on you." Their best compliment was "These are white niggers, the ones you hear on the radio. They're alright." But the kids, both black and white, loved the music, and to some extent that music helped change the attitudes of whites for the better—eventually.

But after a tour in the South with any of those shows, just like after a summer with Aunt Inez in Birmingham, I was always glad to get back to New York City.

There, again at the Apollo, I opened for Marvin Gaye and Tammi Terrell. That was such a strange relationship. You might think they were lovers, but they were not. They were just the most amazing best friends—unbelievably tight. They had hits together like "Ain't No Mountain High Enough," "Your Previous Love," and "Ain't Nothing Like the Real Thing." Then in March 1970, at the age of twenty-four, she died of a brain tumor. I worked with Gaye about three weeks later, and you could see backstage that he was crushed. He was in such heavy pain. On stage he dedicated a song to her and began to cry. He completely broke down and could not continue. Two years would pass before he would perform again in public.

Many years after my first Apollo appearance I opened for Gladys Knight and the Pips at the Westbury Music Festival on Long Island. I ordered a limousine to chauffeur my mother to the concert. She came backstage afterward. The first thing she said?

"You're still doing the algebra question!"

4

Making It in New York

FROM THE EAST WIND TO THE APOLLO, I WAS PERFORMING IN FRONT of almost wholly black crowds. I was spinning in place so fast that I hardly knew I was not moving forward. Then someone said, "You're not bad. Maybe you could be a more commercial act. There's this room downtown run by a guy named Frankie Darrow who puts on comedians. He'd probably love to see what you do." Appropriately for a black comic, it was called the African Room.

Near Times Square, on 44th Street between Sixth Avenue and Broadway, the African Room was a nightclub that, despite its name, featured limbo contests and calypso music from a Caribbean steel band led by a singer named Johnny Barracuda. On Monday nights though, Darrow hosted a showcase, attracting upward of twenty acts—singers, comedians, jugglers, dancers, whatever.

The audiences were still basically black, but there were also whites, and many of the showcase performers were white too. Comedians David Brenner, Steve Landesberg, and Danny Aiello, and singers Bette Midler and Melissa Manchester were a few of the unknowns trying to get on stage to do their thing. One of many acts who would never be heard from again was Three Is Company, a trio of brothers from Long Beach, New York. They tried to be a new Marx Brothers, I guess. Uh, not good.

But one of the brothers did go on to fame and fortune, by the name of Billy Crystal.

Usually you had to audition to get a spot, but I came in with such energy and a different flavor that Frankie put me on right away. It was either that or he was scared I was going to shoot somebody—because I came on very strong and very ghetto.

I was far more street than the other black comics at the African Room—Stu Gilliam, Scoey Mitchell, Joe Keyes and an older comedian named Jay Bernard. He had an odd opening: "My name is Jay Bernard. That's J-a-y B-e-r-n-a-r-d. That's Jay Bernard. Just in case you can't remember it, it's Jay Bernard. J-a-y B-e-r-n-a-r-d." He went on like that for three minutes. If a comic did that today, it would be called deconstructing comedy à la Andy Kaufman. Back then it was just stupid funny, for the first minute anyway.

Next to the stage in the African Room was a giant, eight-foot mechanical gorilla that slowly rotated back and forth and would growl as its green and yellow eyes rolled around in its head. The gorilla would continue its antics even while someone was on stage. It distracted the audience and annoyed the performer. But Darrow would only turn it off during the most popular acts.

Here was a new audience for me—the somewhat racially mixed downtown crowd. But I did the same material as I did at the Apollo, the same edgy racial humor labeled Black Only. Such as a routine about pitching pennies—about how the guys in the projects talked as they gambled, flinging pennies onto the cement, trying to land them as near as possible to a wall. The end came when someone threw a "leaner," a rare feat in which the penny stands on its edge and leans against the wall, beating everything. I had my characters arguing and cursing like cousins at a Harlem barbershop.

If a heckler kept interrupting my act, I would use an old Redd Foxx line: "If you keep on, I'm gonna have to come out there and cut somebody!" If it was a white guy, I would hit him with "Hey man, what's wrong with y'all? This is great shit. Oh, you're white! Now I know why you don't get it." If they were black: "Ever notice how in a whole crowd of black people, a nigger always stands out?"

The problem was that even the black people in this audience wore leisure suits. These blacks had stuff, and people with stuff like having stuff and don't want to lose their stuff. This was not the militant crowd of the East Wind who didn't have stuff to lose. And the white people in the audience were liberals not particularly wanting to be attacked as though they were notorious Alabama police commissioner Bull Connor.

The audience would turn on me. People came up afterward and said, "What's with the anger, man?"

One of those was Brenner. He was an Army veteran, a college graduate, and a television producer in his hometown of Philadelphia. He was smart, savvy, and had substance. He was also a very funny stand-up who you knew was going to succeed in a major way. He was white and Jewish, but he had grown up in the only Caucasian family in a black neighborhood, so he knew the black experience.

After watching me, Brenner introduced himself.

"What's your name?"

"Jimmie Walker."

"I'm horrible at remembering names, but I'll remember yours," he said, "because that was the name of a famous mayor of New York."

He sat me down. "Have you ever worked in front of a white crowd?" he asked.

"No, not really."

"Well, you can be a star in the black community doing what you're doing, but if you want to be a big star, you have to learn how to make white people laugh."

James Brown had said it was "a man's man's man's world," but most of all, it was a white world—and that was a world different from the projects and pitching pennies.

"I think you have talent," he said. "You're young, you have the energy, the look. But none of that will get you anywhere if you can't get on the floor in a white club."

He said I needed to tone down the racial rhetoric. "Hey, I understand there are problems," Brenner explained. "The Italians have had problems, the Irish have had problems, the Jews have had problems, the Puerto Ricans, the Chinese, everybody has had problems. Jews have been persecuted for thousands of years. But you don't hear me talking about that on stage. If you're going to do stand-up, you need to worry about being funny. Bringing up that five thousand blacks died in Biafra today isn't funny. You'll have a better chance of getting a following— of being heard—if you go more middle of the road. If you keep doing what you're doing, you will never be heard by anyone except blacks because no one else will hire you."

When Brenner spoke, you had the feeling you should listen. And if you didn't, he told you that you should. Brenner befriended me, and he was right. This was truly a career-changing conversation, and I knew it immediately. I wasn't that angry young man off stage even though I played one on stage. I was never nasty, but I did have a sharp edge. If I wanted to achieve universal appeal, I now realized, my material had to relate to white people as well as black people.

That did not mean I had to become Bill Cosby. I had gone by myself to see Cosby at Carnegie Hall a year or so earlier. I brought some jokes with me, naively thinking I could lay a few on him and he would take me under his wing. But then I saw his act—in front of an audience of a lot of white people, not many black people. He told stories—like his routine about Noah—not badda-bing jokes, and nothing racially charged. They gave him a standing ovation.

I recognized that Cosby was the best comic rolling and that there has never been anyone better as a stand-up—or sit-down—comic. But what he did was not me, not my style, not my thing. I knew that my jokes were not for him, so I never approached him.

I learned that blacks and whites are different audiences. White crowds give you a few minutes to win them over. Black crowds—you have to get their attention right away. For them, I would stand on the bar. I would stand on tables. I would take a drink in my hand and yell, "Don't think I'm not going to nigger lip this!" That would turn their heads toward me.

"You're offending people when you say that word," Brenner said disapprovingly of "nigger." "People can't laugh when they're uptight."

"But black people say it to each other all the time."

"You know, white people get offended hearing that word too. People have to like you."

I continued to use "nigger" and "whitey" or "cracker" but only when I did black gigs (I was still with the Last Poets and the Panthers). At mixed shows they became "black folks" and "y'all."

I had a mixed act and a black act, and the mixed one was starting to succeed at the African Room. After about three months they gave me a regular spot. Then, one night as I was about to go onstage, Frankie pulled the plug on the gorilla. To this day that remains one of the highlights of my career. "I'm on my way," I said to myself.

I began to play increasingly white crowds at clubs downtown and in Greenwich Village—from Café Wha? (where I first met Richard Pryor) to the tiny Apartment, with its wall-to-wall carpeting; from hootenanny nights at the Bitter End to Gerde's Folk City (opening for the likes of folk stars such as Eric Anderson, Dave Van Ronk, Karla Bonoff, Bonnie Raitt, and the McGarrigle Sisters); from the Gaslight to Upstairs at the Downstairs (where Joan Rivers ruled).

At the Bitter End, if you won the Tuesday hootenanny night, determined by audience applause, your prize would be the opening-act gig for the star headliner the following week. The crowd was with me one of those Tuesday nights and I won, much to the chagrin of co-owner Paul Colby, who was not a Jimmie Walker fan. He couldn't believe I had won, couldn't believe anyone ever laughed at my jokes.

Nevertheless, I opened at the Bitter End for Labelle, which went very smoothly because I had earlier worked with them in upstate New York when they were Patti LaBelle and the Bluebelles. We did three performances a night, at seven, nine, and eleven, from Monday through Sunday, and all twenty-one shows sold out.

I must have done okay because a writer for *Variety* gave me a review I still have, from 1970: "Jimmy Walker, 23-year-old black comic, is drawing yocks. . . . Material is usually ghetto-based, quite pointed and always funny. . . . When response is lukewarm, he quickly shifts gears with resulting guffaws."

After the last of the twenty-one shows I hung around to get paid. Colby paid everyone, from the wait staff to the busboys. I think he even went outside and gave a couple bucks to the homeless guy in the alley before he finally got around to me.

He was about to hand me $50 but then stopped.

"Oh, you had two chocolate shakes," Colby said. "That's $1.25 a piece. Here's $47.50." Then he tagged it. "I'll see you on hootenanny night!"

I was happy I could put the Bitter End on my credits and happy that I had done well, but it was clear that this comic was the low man on that totem pole.

Gabe Kaplan was a comic who insisted on getting respect, even if it was in only a token way. At the Gaslight the opening act might be a magician, followed by a comic, then a poet, and finally a headliner such as singer José Feliciano. Kaplan asked the club manager how much the comic was usually paid for the three shows a day, seven days a week.

"Fifty dollars."

Gabe said, "Then if you want me, it will cost you $51."

The most important club for a comic was the Improvisation on West 44th Street in Hell's Kitchen. The Improv was a showcase club where the bookers for national television shows such as the *Tonight Show* would scout new talent. You were not paid, and there was no lineup for the acts. You showed up, and when owner Budd Friedman felt it was the right time for you, he'd say, "You're next." Some nights you might hang around for two hours and never get on stage.

Budd also insisted that comics not perform back to back. He would put a singer or some other act between them. Mike Preminger, a comic in our group, said that he dreamed one night that he had died and all of us, including Budd, were at his funeral. Suddenly Budd stood up and stopped the funeral. "Wait," he said, "first we bury a singer and then Preminger."

I auditioned for Budd, but apparently he wasn't impressed—he put me on at one in the morning. So I stopped going. After all, I was killing downtown. But Danny Aiello, who was also a doorman at the Improv, said he would put in a good word for me. When I did go back and did well, Budd finally gave me better times.

The Improv featured many of the same people I was working with at the African Room but also others, such as Robert Klein, Richard Lewis, Stiller and Meara, the Ace Trucking Company, and Andy Kaufman. The waitresses, including some who later became stars such as Midler, Liz Torres, and Elayne Boosler, doubled as singers, breaking up the comedy acts.

Klein was highly respected and an important influence on many comedians of that day and today. He graduated from DeWitt Clinton High School like I did, but we were polar opposites. He was very serious—even wanted to be a serious actor—and I was very loose and had no interest in acting. Klein considered himself better than anyone else and acted like it. But like Brenner, he knew what he was doing.

Until I met him and Brenner, my material was pretty much kept in my head, barely written down, and I never knew what I had performed where. I learned the stand-up's work ethic from them. Every joke of theirs was written down and arranged by subject into "chunks" that were TV-ready for appearances on the *Tonight Show* or *Ed Sullivan*. They audio taped every show and knew when and where they told every joke. They worked very hard, and comedians like Jay Leno, Richard Lewis, and, later, Jerry Seinfeld picked up on their way of working. So did I.

That stage at the Improv was where we honed our craft and paid our dues. That stage was the only place we could get exposure, where we could get discovered, where we could try out new material, where we could get better.

I would come off stage after a bad set and say to Budd, "That audience was terrible." Budd would answer, "It's a poor workman who blames his tools, young man." I did not like it when he said that, but it was true; almost every time the fault lays with the comic, not the audience. Even if the set is not going well, you must look like it is and plow through. At some point, hopefully, the audience thinks, "Wow, maybe we're wrong." Then they loosen up. Lessons like those were hard earned.

To any stand-up, those moments on stage provided our oxygen, kept us breathing. We performed for free, but we fought for stage time. So when Klein would take our spots in order for him to hone his act before a Sullivan or Carson shot, the other comics were not happy. One of us would be about to go on stage and Budd would rush in and say, "Oh, Klein's here. He's going on now." You were bumped out of your spot and into a later time.

Sometimes a much later time. Klein would pass us as we stood in what we called the "bullpen"—where we would gather before taking the stage—and say, "I'm just going to do a quick ten." Thirty minutes later he'd still be on, wailing away.

Every evening beginning about 7 o'clock, I would do seven to ten showcase gigs, ten to fifteen minutes each, running from the Improv on the Lower West Side to Catch a Rising Star on the Upper East Side. I walked, I took the subway, sometimes I jumped in somebody's car, sometimes Brenner would pay for a cab for us.

At each place I and every other comic struggled to get a spot. Fifty acts or more might show up every night for those precious twenty slots on each stage. Not only did we perform for free, but we also paid for any food or drink we bought, just like any other customer.

On some winter Saturday nights the performers, not the customers, at the Improv were the ones standing outside in line. We usually waited in the bullpen holding area next to the showroom. But when it was snowing hard, Budd would let in the audience for the second show as soon as we finished the first show. The club would get so crowded that the audience would spill into the bullpen.

"Grab your coats, guys," Budd would tell us. "Go outside."

We weren't getting paid or fed, and now we were standing outside in the snow. We kept telling ourselves, "We're paying our dues."

Every now and then at a club a customer would see me standing around and offer to buy the comic some booze. When that first happened, because I don't drink, I said, "No, thanks." Then club owners clued me in: "If you're offered a drink, take it! And order something expensive, like Crown Royal or a brandy. The customer pays for it. So I get the money. You don't have to drink it. Just bring it back to the bar." In other words, Jimmie, just like at a party, if you are not drinking, that means there is more for everyone else!

The first showcase club to give us free food and drink (not alcoholic) was Catch a Rising Star, run by Rick Newman. After your set you could get a hamburger or hot dog with a soda or, if you did really well, a bowl of pasta. That forced Budd to throw a free soda our way every once in a while at the Improv.

After our night of shows the comics would all meet at about two in the morning at the Camelot restaurant at 49th Street and 8th Avenue. We would hang out, have breakfast, throw jokes back and forth, tear apart everyone else's act, and talk about our experiences on stage.

I probably learned as much about comedy at the Camelot as I did at the Improv. One late night/early morning I ordered my usual orange juice (the fruit thing again!) and a fly landed nearby. Brenner swatted it away. Then he took out a piece of paper and started writing.

"What are you doing?" I asked.

"I have an idea for a joke."

"What are you talking about?"

"I swatted a fly."

"What kind of joke is that?"

"I don't know, Jimmie, but there's something funny in there. Like, you never see flies die of natural causes. We're always killing them with something. Maybe that's the seed of a joke." Brenner later did expand that idea into a killer routine in his act. When it came to observational humor, anything might be the beginning of a joke—even the flies at the Camelot.

After the Camelot we would get a cab to drive Brenner to his apartment at 69th Street and 3rd Avenue and then drop me off at 85th Street, where I could catch the subway. But it was hard for black people to hail cabs in Manhattan. The cabbies, afraid of getting robbed, did not want to go to the ghetto. They would ignore you and drive past. So Brenner would wait on the sidewalk and signal for one to pick him up. When the taxi stopped, he would open the door and I would run out of the dark and jump in with him.

"When I host the *Tonight Show*," Brenner told me one day, "I'll have you on and we can do a joke based on the cab story: 'Cabdrivers don't want to go to places like the Apollo at 125th and Lenox. But Jimmie and I got a cab and I told the driver, 'We're making two stops: First, 69th Street and 3rd, and then 125th and Lenox.' When the cab stopped at 69th Street, where the white people lived, Jimmie got out. 'Now,' I told the driver, 'take me to Harlem.' The cabdriver thought we were nuts.'"

Okay, David, whatever. At the time he was nowhere near hosting the *Tonight Show*, and I could only dream of being a guest. But that was Brenner: He had a plan and he would be ready.

Jerry Stiller and his wife Anne Meara were probably the biggest act playing the Improv, having appeared on the *Ed Sullivan Show* thirty-six times in the '60s and '70s. He was Jewish, she was Irish, and thus domestic stand-up comedy from a married duo. They were the only comics I know who successfully pulled that off.

Maybe the reason they were able to stay married in real life is that off stage they did not act like celebrities; they were more down to earth than anyone in their lofty position. If I said something nice about seeing them on *Sullivan*, they deferred to me, saying, "Thanks, but that was a funny bit I saw you do the other night." When Anne was cast in a summer replacement sitcom called *The Corner Bar*, she said she was going to put my name in to play the black cook. I told everyone that my big break had arrived—I was going to be on a TV series! Next thing I knew, *The Corner Bar* was shooting without me. You learn to get used to disappointment if you are going to survive in show business.

However, success could also strike out of the blue. The Improv had a house piano player who had been on the road forever and would play for singers as well as Andy Kaufman for his Tony Clifton lounge character. Performers who were new to the Improv would come in and ask, "Are you the piano player?"

Insulted by the anonymity, he would answer, "I'm not 'the piano player.' My name is Raymond J. Johnson, Junior. I happen to play piano."

During an improvisation sketch Billy Saluga of the Ace Trucking Company comedy group imitated him on stage, exaggerating Raymond's annoyance by saying, "My name is Raymond J. Johnson, Junior. Now you can call me Ray, or you can call me J, or you can call me Johnny, or you can call me Sonny, or you can call me Junie, or you can call me Junior. You can call me Ray J, or you can call me RJ, or you can call me RJJ, or you can call me RJJ Jr. But you doesn't hasta call me Johnson!"

Saluga made the character bigger and bigger, adding a nasal voice, then a cigar, then a zoot suit. Then he pulled the character out of the sketch to spotlight him even more. Audiences loved Raymond J. Johnson Jr., and Saluga took off, becoming a national sensation on television, everywhere from variety shows to commercials. But the real Raymond hated it!

Among those Raymond J. Johnson Jr. accompanied at the Improv was Bette Midler. I first saw her at the African Room when she billed herself as Midler of Fiddler because she was performing in *Fiddler on the Roof* on Broadway. After she began appearing at the Improv Budd became her manager.

One night a customer approached her about working that weekend at the Continental Baths, a gay bathhouse that he owned. There would be a lot of gay men sitting around in towels, but he would pay her $500. She happily accepted. But Budd was not pleased. He needed Bette to work those nights as a singing waitress. "You go sing at the Baths, don't come back here!" he threatened. Bette held her ground. She pointed out to him that she was a singer first, a waitress second.

Naturally, she asked Raymond J. Johnson Jr. to be her piano player. He knew how talented she was and that her career would take off. If he ditched the Improv and committed to her, his life would change.

"I was on the road thirty years," Raymond told her. "I'm not going anywhere anymore."

So Bette enlisted Raymond J. Johnson Jr.'s substitute piano player at the Improv, a guy named Barry Manilow. She left the Improv as well as Budd as her manager. Not too long afterward Midler became a major star, as did Manilow.

I never played a bathhouse, but I performed anywhere someone wanted me. A dance studio at 96th and Broadway regularly hired comics from the Improv for $50 for a twenty-minute set to entertain senior citizens. But Budd refused to recommend me, saying he didn't think my humor would go over very well in front of that elderly white crowd.

One night the guy in charge of booking their entertainment saw my act. He told Budd, "Geez, I've never seen him before. Let's have him perform next week."

The dance studio was filled with old people—really old people. I just did my thang.

I'm thinking of moving to the suburbs. Riverdale. Scarsdale. Get myself a house with a black picket fence. Have a little white jockey

on the front lawn. Maybe put out a fluorescent watermelon. I want
to let my neighbors know I'm in the neighborhood!

I killed! The old people loved it. Even today people are stunned that
with the material I have that I get laughs from senior citizen audiences.
What they don't understand is that some of those old people are hipper
than the young audiences at comedy clubs. They have seen and been
through a lot of life. They don't look like they know what's happening,
but they do. Their outside covering may be shaky—having the walkers
and the thick glasses—but what's inside them is solid. They take a
minute to get settled in and there is a percentage not completely aware,
but most of them will be right there with you. They are old enough to
appreciate that you can have too much of some things in life but you
can never have too much laughter.

Obviously, I did not lack confidence. I knew that if I did not believe
in myself, no one else would. I pushed for more gigs, more stage time,
more money, more everything. Because if I did not, no one else would.
After I opened a few nights for the Jimmy Castor Bunch, right after
their massive hit "Troglodyte (Cave Man)," at the Cellar Door in the
Georgetown neighborhood of Washington, DC, I asked owner Jack
Boyle for more stage time. He ignored me.

That didn't stop me. I saw on his schedule that O. C. Smith, who
had hit with "Little Green Apples," would be coming in soon. I had
earlier opened for him in Chicago.

I exaggerated my status and told Jack, "I'm the opening act for
O. C. I don't know why I'm not on that bill."

"So?"

"If I'm not on with him, O. C. won't be happy," I bluffed.

He added me to the date. When I arrived, again I asked for more
stage time. Again Jack ignored me.

So I went on longer than I was supposed to. Jack came up afterward
and told me to cut down my time. I told him that not only did I want
more time, I wanted more money too! He looked at me and said, "You

are the most arrogant 'nobody' I ever met!" I didn't get either the time or the money.

But I opened for O. C. Smith many times after that, including in front of thirty-five hundred prisoners at the Cook County Jail in Chicago, Illinois. I had material for that audience too.

> *Take a black holdup man. He ain't making no money. He ain't got enough money to ride a cab to work, he gotta ride a bus. He gotta stay in that dark, damp alley, catching rheumatism in his knees. Suffocating 'cause he's got his wife's stocking over his head. Just to hit you in the head for four dollars. I mean what's the use of having a black brother on the Supreme Court if we blacks can't do crimes classy enough to get here.*

That wasn't the first time I had a captive audience either. During that period I opened for B. B. King at New York's Sing Sing penitentiary. Also on the show were Joan Baez and the Voices of East Harlem, a singing-dancing "positive message" group of teenage girls and boys I knew from gigs with the Last Poets.

Sing Sing was imposing, stark, and forbidding. We had been talking and joking, but when they slammed shut that large iron gate behind our bus, there was a little fear in all of us that we might never get out. We fell strangely quiet. I promised myself that I would never take my freedom for granted ever again. I was so nervous that I barely ate any of the chicken and mashed potatoes they fed us. B. B. and his band had no problem—they were used to playing prisons. The guards counted the knives and utensils before we left the dining room, just to be sure we did not bring the inmates anything potentially dangerous.

The hall where we were to play was cold and bare except for a stage and rows of folding chairs. When the Voices of East Harlem rehearsed, the prison officials stopped them. The girls, they told them, could not dance how they were dancing. Their movements were way too suggestive given that some of the prisoners had not been with a woman in a long, long time. The girls had to throw on some more clothes and tone down their dance moves.

As usual, I killed. Of course, some in the audience had also killed—literally.

> We got to learn how to be like all those white folk and use that little pen and paper and write down that $500,000 embezzlement. Meanwhile we're in the parking lot shooting it out for a quarter. We're spending more money on ammunition than we're getting away with.

The inmates jumped up, shouted, and laughed hard. The reviewer in the *Village Voice* slyly said I "stole" the show.

After the performance a guard said two prisoners wanted to talk to me. Earlier, B. B. had met with a few inmates who had guitars and he gave them some pointers. I figured these were inmates who thought they were funny guys and wanted some advice about comedy as a career.

The guard put me in a detention room and brought in two prisoners chained on their wrists and ankles. I knew them! We grew up together. Though we weren't friends, I knew their families, hung out with their brothers. They were happy to see me. I was shocked to see them—at least at Sing Sing.

They were both in for manslaughter from separate incidents. One said he had been with a friend who decided to rob someone. The robbery went bad and the victim was murdered. They got away with seven bucks. He told me he had no idea there was going to be a robbery let alone a murder. He was sentenced to ten to thirty years and had already served four. The other guy I knew from the neighborhood had been in and out of jail since he was sixteen years old. He had spent three years in prison for robbery when he got into a jailhouse gang fight and killed another inmate with his bare hands.

Now both of them had renewed their friendship from the Bronx—in Sing Sing. Our lives had certainly taken very different paths. When I left, I said the dumbest thing to them: "Okay, I'll see you later." Really?

Coming across them in prison was only slightly more surprising than hearing Jack Boyle on the phone so soon after our disagreement. He said he had a strange request to ask of me: Not only did he want me to play his club again, but he also wanted me to be ready to do *more* time on stage.

Miles Davis was coming to the Cellar Door after the release of his classic *Bitches Brew* album. Miles was a revered jazz musician, but he was notoriously unpredictable. I might have to do as much as fifty minutes before he would go on.

The room was packed for every show, mainly with adoring fans from the area's colleges. I would tell my jokes and wait to hear a clap from the wings to let me know Miles was ready. Sometimes he would stand outside the club smoking a cigarette or just stay in his dressing room. In the meantime I had to keep going, getting into audience participation—"So where are you from?"—when I was out of material. When I finally heard the clap, I would get off stage.

Sadly for his fans, Miles played his trumpet balls to the walls on only a few of the ten or more shows. For the others he messed around for half the show, maybe played a little piano, and cut his set short. His great band—Wayne Shorter on soprano sax, Joe Zawinul on electric piano and Billy Cobham on drums—did the heavy lifting. Many of his fans, who treated him like a god, left disappointed.

Because I was doing more time, I of course asked Jack for more money.

"Fat Jack," I said, knowing he hated to be called that, "I need $600 a week."

"You're not worth it."

"One day I'm going to come back and record an album here," I told him. "I won't be a 'nobody' then."

"Yeah, right."

Some of the clubs I played were not, well, legal. They existed for only one night, and the locations—usually an abandoned warehouse or loft on the West Side—could only be discovered through flyers or word of mouth. Yet hundreds of people would show up at about one in the morning. Years later they were called raves, but we referred to them as after-hours clubs.

They had a disc jockey and disco dancing, and at around 4 a.m. the music stopped and they brought on a comedian. I would walk into the middle of the floor—no stage—and do at least half an hour. The purpose was less entertainment than to give the promoter time to sell more drinks, all of which were very expensive. The break also gave the promoter time to begin packing up. When the "club" closed, he wanted to get out of there as quickly as possible, just in case the police finally showed up.

Sometimes the comic would not last half an hour. The sweaty, drunk, sex-charged crowd was not in the best mood to hear jokes at 4 a.m. They would boo and shout for you to "get the hell off" so they could crank up the music again. Only two of us were actually good at these gigs—me and Freddie Prinze. We were younger and hipper than most of the other comics, and we could interact with the multicultural crowd better than they could. We played it loose, brother.

When we finished, the dance would continue for another two hours, until usually right around sunrise. Unless the police arrived, in which case I quietly walked away as if I had stumbled onto the place by accident—never look like you are scared. That was good advice for a comic struggling on stage too. Another lesson learned was to get your money *before* you went on because the dude with the money might not be there at the end.

Like me, Freddie had tremendous confidence. He came from the middle-class Washington Heights area and had boundless energy. He was only seventeen years old, but he believed he was the best comic in the world. His real last name was Pruetzel and he wanted to change it to King because he wanted to be known as the King of Comedy. But Alan King already had that surname, so he chose Prinze, as in the Prince of Comedy.

I don't remember the moment I met Freddie, but I do remember what it was like every moment I was around him. He was electric. There was always something going on with him that was different from other people. He was a rarity. At the same time that he had an in-your-face attitude, he was so good looking and charming that you could not help but like him. He reminded me of Muhammad Ali, who would talk shit about knocking out his opponent but be so funny about it that you could not help but enjoy him.

> I'm leaving my bedroom late at night to go into the kitchen. A roach says to me, "Hey, Freddie, where you goin', man? Hey, you don' bring back some potato chips, we shut the door on you, man!"

Somehow Freddie made that joke work. He had enough chutzpah to get on stage and do forty-five minutes despite having almost no act. Besides a catchphrase—"Looking good!"—all he had was his Hungarican routine about being part Hungarian and part Puerto Rican. Even that was sketchy. He was hardly Hispanic from a cultural standpoint. But it was a lot easier to make jokes about Hispanics than about his Jewish Hungarian father. One of my favorites:

> My mother's always talking about her wedding. "You shoulda been there," she says. She doesn't remember. I was there, and so were my two brothers.

Freddie had no problem telling you how talented he was or how successful he was with the ladies. One night at the Camelot, he boasted, "I can get as many women as I want."

"How many?" Brenner asked.

"I can get at least five in one night."

"Wanna make a bet on that?" Brenner asked.

"Absolutely," Freddie said.

Brenner, Landesberg, a few others, and I took him up on the wager. We used Brenner's pad because his building had a doorman who could keep count for us. The next night, along with Freddie, we made our rounds of the showcase clubs. At about two o'clock in the morning we met up at the Camelot. Except no Freddie. At 3 a.m. we rolled up to Brenner's apartment and asked the doorman how many women had been in the apartment with Freddie. He told us that Freddie had been going in and out—with nine different women! In one night! He was a piece of work.

Lenny Bruce was a favorite of his, and he and I would listen to his records for hours. Coincidentally, one of those albums was put out by Alan Douglas and his Douglas Records, which released the first album from the Last Poets. We had every book about Lenny too. We would discuss everything about him. We lived, breathed, talked, and studied comedy, but especially anything Lenny. We were hooked on the guy because he just seemed to be so important, so different for his time, and we wanted to tap into that energy.

When I listen to his albums now, the material sounds to me to be more rant than comedy. From Klein and Brenner, I learned to be more succinct. They had more refined pieces, with a beginning, middle, and end, because they were writing for TV shots. Lenny rambled like a nightclub comic. He was inflammatory and controversial, which made him a hero to most comics, including me and Freddie. But we were very different in style from him.

Strangely, Freddie became intimate with Kitty Bruce, Lenny's daughter. She worked at the Improv as a coat-check girl and went crazy over him. She loved Freddie. "You are the first comic to make me laugh since my father," she told him. Freddie, as expected, quickly took her to bed. Whenever he screwed her, he would come back to us and say excitedly,

"It's like Lenny is watching us!" After we all moved to LA he told me that he made love to her on the grave of Lenny "Bruce" Schneider at Eden Memorial Park in Mission Hills—and that during the act he heard Lenny rooting him on: "Go man, fuck her! Fuck her!"

I had my first serious relationship with a woman I met at the Improv. Leah came up after a show and we started a friendship. She was about ten years older than me, had a master's degree in history or literature, and was extremely smart. She was a substitute teacher, did temp office work, and wrote articles and poetry, though she never sold any of it. She was very much into authors—from Shakespeare to Jack Kerouac to LeRoi Jones (aka Amiri Baraka). She introduced me to their writing and that of others. She was like a character out of a Woody Allen movie, except she lived on the West Side of Manhattan instead of the Upper East Side. But I didn't think of her in romantic terms, despite her great legs, because she was white. She was simply a friend who was supportive of my comedy career. She would type up my material and, because she was one of the few people I knew in the city who had a car, sometimes drive me wherever I had to go.

Finally it dawned on me that she wanted a more physical relationship. But I did not want to go out with or be seen with a white woman. I had just come from working with the Black Panthers and was very much into my antiwhite bag. I did not want a white girlfriend.

I told Brenner about my problem.

"I've gone out with all races and religions," he said. "When the lights are out and you're under the sheets, a woman is a woman. Just go for it!"

Three or four months passed before Leah and I went to bed. But I still felt uncomfortable. She was terrific to me—totally devoted—and I knew she was happy with our relationship. I, however, was not so devoted and did not treat her as well as I should have, emotionally speaking. I always had an excuse: "You're white. You don't understand." Having seen what my father did to my mother made me want to treat women decently. But that does not mean I knew how to have a relationship. Leah was my teacher in many ways, but inevitably, we grew apart.

Barbara was the polar opposite of Leah except that she was also white—Leah had forever broken that taboo for me. Barbara was aggressive and tough. She was not sweet; she was cocky as hell. I met her at a comedy club in Greenwich Village, and she looked like a young woman from the Village—tall, slim, and brunette, like a Joan Baez. She played a little guitar, sang a little, painted and sculpted a little, and had come to the city from upstate to get into show business. She was opinionated about everything. She would even be critical of what I did on stage. But if someone else said something negative, she would defend me with everything she had. Other comics would ask, "Who's that chick? She got into a beef at the bar with some people about you." Later she would tell me, "You know, you sucked tonight."

By this time the other woman in my life, my mom, had become a nurse. She worked her way up in the field, became a registered nurse, and then went to college and earned a master's degree. Eventually she was appointed the head of nursing at Montefiore Hospital in the Bronx. I'm just a comedian; my mother is the one who deserves to have a book written about her. She never complained, and she achieved so much.

She remarried—a really nice guy named William Boyce, who she met at church. A small, round man, Mr. Boyce was supposedly one of the first black guys in the laborer's union. He loved my mother very much, but she never seemed very close or affectionate to him. Maybe it was a marriage of financial convenience for her. There were times I felt my mom stayed late at her job because she didn't want to come home to him. She still loved my father.

My career was also advancing. When *Time* magazine wrote that I was "one of the finest black comics in the country," Budd framed the article and put it up on a wall at the Improv. The club had become a major magnet for aspiring stand-up comedians.

One hopeful would drive down from Boston to work out at the Improv whenever he was in town delivering a Rolls-Royce or other expensive auto for his day job at a foreign car dealership—Jay Leno. In turn, whenever any of us were in Boston, we used a crash pad he had that we called the Leno Arms. There wasn't much more than mattresses on the floor, and I don't even think there was a lock on the door. Every now and then Leno's mom and some of her friends came from Andover with buckets of disinfectant and cleaned up the place. When I landed the Playboy Club circuit—which was pretty classy—and played the one in Boston or was booked at the far less classy Sugar Shack in the infamous Combat Zone, I stayed at the Leno Arms.

Freddie also stayed there. Fascinated by guns, once he was showing off his latest purchase and all of a sudden the pistol fired—blew a hole in the ceiling of the Leno Arms. That hole was still there when Leno moved out of the place.

At the time nearly all of the major TV talk shows came out of New York—Johnny Carson, Merv Griffin, Dick Cavett, David Frost. Even Jack Paar, a late-night giant in the '60s who hosted the *Tonight Show* before Carson, was making a comeback on network TV in the early '70s. But every comic's goal was to get on the *Tonight Show* with Carson. His show could launch a career. All of my comic friends, including those who would never make it big, had by now appeared on one or more of those shows—but not me.

My first TV experience was on Joe Franklin's local show on WOR. He had been doing it for twenty years and was already a cult figure. Not only did everyone come on his show—from Marilyn Monroe to John Lennon—but anyone could get on, even me: "Big, big things for this young man. Lots of talk about him. Lots of chatter. Very funny. On the upswing. Jimmie Walker, ladies and gentlemen. Funny young man. See him at the Improvisation."

Franklin also staged a regular live showcase at Brickman's resort in the Catskills. If you did well, you might land a paying gig at one of the other major resorts, such as Grossinger's or Brown's, which catered to

Jewish crowds. I had performed at so many community halls and bar mitzvahs that I was comfortable bringing out my Jewish material.

I would open with: "I bet you're surprised to see a schvartze up here." That would always get a big laugh and break the ice. "You know, maybe you can relate to this—my mother got upset with me because she heard I was going out with a shiksa."

Not that they would always understand my jokes. I had a bit that started with "I saw this graffiti the other day," and an older woman in the front row turned to a friend and asked loud enough for me and the rest of the audience to hear, "What's graffiti?"

When Brenner became a regular guest on the *Mike Douglas Show*, which taped in his hometown of Philly, he put in a good word for me. After weeks of needling producer Ernie DiMassa and talent coordinator Vince Calandra (who had the same job for Ed Sullivan when the Beatles were booked), he finagled me an audition. In front of an audience of about forty people, all of whom were also auditioning, I did a great set—killed, destruction, even with the hard-nosed show biz crowd.

Went to an all-black school. Put on a production of Snow White and the Seven Dwarfs. *The dwarfs were black. We had to bus in* Snow White.

When I got back to the Improv, Brenner asked how it went. I said, "I think it went well but no one's called." He phoned DiMassa and asked what was up. DiMassa told him, "Yes, he was funny. But he's too black."

Brenner answered, "Yes, Ernie, that's because he IS black!"

Compared to others in comedy at the time, I *was* too black. Even with smoothing out my material and attitude from my Last Poets days, I was too caustic for mainstream TV. I also looked younger than nearly any other comic besides Freddie—I didn't even wear a suit and tie on stage. The only comic around who was younger and blacker was

Franklin Ajaye, who was far more political and scared the TV folks more than even Pryor did. One of my favorite jokes from him was:

> These police will arrest you for anything. I was in LA the other day
> with a friend and they arrested us for being two niggers on a sunny
> day. We were guilty!

I wasn't jealous of the others getting on national TV. I was happy for them. We were friends. When one of them scored, it was a celebration for all of us. We would go down to the tapings and sit in the audience to root them on. I figured my turn would come—someday. Brenner never stopped encouraging me: "Don't worry, you'll get on. I'll push for you."

Being young, black, and cool was an advantage in getting one sort of job though. I met a woman who worked for Columbia Records, which was run by Clive Davis, and she asked if I would emcee at a signing party at Max's Kansas City on Park Avenue South for one of the label's new artists. "A hundred dollars? Sure," I said.

Five guys walked on stage. They wore what we then called braids but later knew as dreadlocks. A haze of pungent smoke surrounded them, which I recognized as weed, but they called ganja. They played a style of music few people had really ever heard before—reggae. When the band finished, the crowd was stunned; no one applauded. No one knew what to think of what they had just seen and heard. Only when Clive jumped on stage and said, "Aren't they great!" was there cheering. Obviously Columbia in 1972 was not the place for Bob Marley and the Wailers.

There was a better reaction for a guy from Jersey by the name of Bruce Springsteen. His performance was so amazing that the crowd of jaded music-industry types insisted on an encore. That was strong. But Springsteen was not my style. I was more excited when Columbia signed Earth, Wind & Fire and I performed at their signing party. I could not have known it at the time, but Marley, Springsteen, and Earth, Wind & Fire would all get into the Rock and Roll Hall of Fame.

Finally, one night at the Improv Brenner accosted Tom O'Malley, the talent coordinator for *Jack Paar Tonite*.

"Hey, how about Jimmie Walker for your show?"

"I don't like him," O'Malley said. "He's too angry."

Nevertheless, Brenner persisted and arranged an audition. When I arrived at their offices, I was sent to a sterile room with only one person—not O'Malley—sitting in a chair behind a desk and eating a sandwich from the Stage Deli. His name was Hal Gurnee, and he had directed the *Tonight Show* in the Paar era and now was back with him.

I said, "Hi, I'm . . . "

He interrupted. "I know who you are. You're that Jimmie Walker guy everyone's been talking about around here."

"Okay," I said, surprised.

"Yeah, people tell us you're a pain in the ass."

"Oh," I said. "So are we going to do the audition?"

"Let's do it."

"Where? Aren't we going downstairs to the studio—where there's an audience?"

"No," he said. "Just do your bit right here. I've been in this business a long time. I know what's funny."

There is probably nothing harder for a comic than to perform for an audience of one. Laughter being contagious is a comic's best friend. But I had no choice.

I was about three minutes into my routine when he stopped me.

"That's enough."

Damn, I had failed, I thought.

"Can you do the show tonight?" he asked.

"Uh, yeah!"

"Okay, be back at five-thirty. See you then."

My reaction was less "Wow!" than "About time!" I felt I deserved this chance. I had been mentally preparing for my TV debut for more than a year. Brenner, our ringleader, had been on Carson, Griffin, Douglas, and Sullivan, and he would constantly talk about what he had done and what he was about to do. So when you finally did get on a show, you already knew what was going to happen and what you needed to do.

I called my friend Marty Nadler, who did stand-up at the Improv and elsewhere when he wasn't working at a crepes restaurant. "I got *Paar*!" I told him.

"When are you doing it? Next week?"

"Tonight!"

"Oh my God!"

"Marty, you have to take off from work and go down there with me." He said he would and called another comic, the veteran Phil Foster, and they joined me. (Flash forward about three years: Phil would play Laverne's father on *Laverne & Shirley*, where Marty would be a writer/producer.)

We arrived at Paar's studio ready for the moment that could change my life.

"Don't worry," said Phil. "You're funny. You've been doing this every night at clubs. What I want you to do is walk out and say, 'I'm from the ghetto. I'm here on the exchange program.' Take a beat and then say, 'You can imagine what they sent back there.' Open with that. It'll kill. But have a big smile on your face."

Standing backstage, suddenly I became a little anxious. Paar was walking over to me!

"I've heard nothing but good things about you," he said. "I've had many comics like you on—Dick Gregory, Godfrey Cambridge, Richard Pryor." I was relieved I had stopped using their material! He continued, "Everybody tells me you're a little bit arrogant—but funny. That's exactly what makes a good comedian. You'll do great."

Terrific. Now I had to be great!

He introduced me to the TV audience: "Here's a funny guy who was a radio engineer here in New York and now he's making his first appearance on network television. Please make him feel at home and welcome Jimmie Walker!"

I'm from the ghetto. I'm here on the exchange program.

Beat. Laughter.

You can imagine what they sent back there.

Big smile.

Big laugh! I felt like a boxer in the ring. All I needed was that first laugh and I was out there punching. I knew I did well because the laughs ate into my time and I never did all the material I planned.

I called Brenner afterward. "I already got the news," he said. "You killed!"

Marty, Phil, and I were ecstatic. I went in early to the Improv and Budd was so happy for me. We turned on the TV in the club and everyone watched the show. I was on top of the world.

Then I heard the real story about how I got the audition. Brenner, Midler, and Landesberg—all of whom were regular guests on the show—had told O'Malley that if I did not at least get an audition then they would not do the show again.

I confronted Brenner.

"You're our friend," he explained. "That's what we do."

I was glad I did not know about their effort beforehand. If I had, the pressure of not letting them down might have crushed me.

A story later went around that Landesberg was with me at the show and after Paar said I'd do fine, Landesberg quipped, "Hey, if he bombs, he can still shine your shoes." Funny line, but that did not happen.

The high from my debut did not last long. Brenner had warned that having enough good material for one shot was not enough. If you hit that first time, you would be asked back very quickly and other shows would be calling too. That first shot might not make a career if you had used all of your best stuff. Bombing the next time could undo everything.

A couple of comics from the Improv followed up with two of the worst shots in history. Marvin Braverman, one of the best stand-up comics I ever saw, was never able to overcome his Waterloo. Richard Lewis followed his first shot with an atrocious performance—beyond hideous—on the *Tonight Show*. He was a friend, so it was painful to watch. His career was set back for a while before he had another chance and eventually broke through.

You had to have six shots in the revolver, Brenner said. Some, like Seinfeld, were smart enough to wait and wait and wait until they had enough. Those forty minutes or so, not just the first six, separated the average comic from the star. Then you needed another ten minutes of material solely for the clubs, so people who saw you on TV could hear something new and different when they saw you in person.

I had my six shots ready. I was ready to fire away.

5

Kid Dyn-o-mite!

ONLY A MONTH OR SO LATER I WENT ON THE *PAAR* SHOW AGAIN.

"Here's a guy who did great last time. One of the funniest young comics around . . . Jimmie Walker!"

I killed again. Thank you.

Dan Rowan called me at the Improv. "We saw you on the *Paar* show. We love what you do. We're doing our last shows for NBC and want you to come out here and be on." *Rowan & Martin's Laugh-In* had officially ended, but they were putting together variety specials as a farewell. *Opening Night, Rowan and Martin* would be shot in Los Angeles.

"Sure, send me a ticket."

The next day at the Improv, Louie, the angry Puerto Rican cook who answered the phone during the day, yelled, "Package for you!"

Inside was a plane ticket to LA and instructions about a limo that would pick me up at the airport, about putting me up at the Sunset Hyatt House hotel on Sunset Boulevard, and so on. I thought, "I guess this is for real." Here I was, a kid from the South Bronx who grew up never expecting anything out of life, never counted on anything, and now I was getting flown to LA, the Promised Land.

I was brought to the NBC studios in Burbank and met director Greg Garrison, a pioneering television comedy producer and director who had worked on such classics as *Your Show of Shows* and the *Dean Martin Show*. Garrison had done it all—had even directed one of the Kennedy-Nixon debates in 1960—and he made sure you knew it. Oh, and he was wearing a safari hat à la Crocodile Dundee, baggy Jodhpur riding pants, and leather boots, and he carried a riding crop. Really. You cannot make this stuff up!

"I want to get this guy out of the way," he said to his crew on the set. "We have a lot to do. Let's get a few people in here for an audience. We don't need cue cards for this." He turned to me. "What's your name? Jimmie? Jimmie Walker? We've carved out a spot for you in the show to do about four minutes. We'll have you on right away." I did my shot and it went well.

> *They have different commercials for shows for black people. I'm watching TV the other day and I saw one that goes, "Are those chitlins staining your dentures? Try new Chit Off! No chit!"*

On my way to the commissary Garrison, who was chauffeured around the lot in a golf cart, drove up next to me.

"Okay, you got some laughs. So what? By the way, 'no chit'? Out!" He looked at his driver. "Move on!"

That was my introduction to crazy Hollywood—I felt more comfortable on the stage of a comedy club. But doing TV helped me get better stand-up gigs. Among the best were for the Playboy Clubs, where years earlier Dick Gregory had replaced Professor Irwin Corey to become their first black comic, which was a major breakthrough. I played them across the country. Leno did too. I often called him Ray Peno because of an early routine he did about those clubs.

You see, there would be three main acts, one on each floor of the club, and each would do two shows each night at different start times. The opening-act comic would rotate from the top floor to the middle to the bottom and then back again in the other direction. On the stage

at each room there was a sign announcing the act and a beautiful Playboy Bunny introduced you to the audience. One night, the Bunny
looked at the sign that clearly read "Jay Leno," a simple name, and said,
"Hello. I'd like to bring on our next act—Jay Seno."

After that act Jay went to the room for his next performance and
told the Bunny, "It's Jay Leno."

"Oh, I'm sorry, no problem."

She introduced him: "A very funny guy. Here he is—Bay Eno."

So then he went to the next room and told the same Bunny, one
more time, "My name is *Jay Leno*."

"Okay, I got it."

She introduced him: "One of our favorite funny people—Ray Peno."

Ray Peno and I became fast friends. When I was in Boston, along
with staying at the Leno Arms, his parents would take me and the other
comics to their favorite restaurant, the Hilltop, to chow down on steak
served on paper plates. Along with his comedy partner, a very funny
guy named Bob Shaw, we played hootenanny nights at Harvard and
the folk clubs in the area. Shaw had a bit about drugs that was so funny
that when he did it at a folk club at the University of Maryland, the
woman who booked the acts laughed so hard she really did break a rib.
I would never have thought Leno would do what he later did to Shaw
and a number of others in the comedy world—and that our friendship
would end.

Another lucrative circuit involved those colleges. The comedy team
of Joey Edmonds and Thom Curley played campuses across the country,
and they suggested I contact an agent named Lou Johnson in Minneapolis. I sent him a kinescope of my *Paar* shots and, within an hour
of receiving it, he called. I flew to Minneapolis for a showcase alongside
B. B. King and singer Michael "Bluer than Blue" Smith for college entertainment bookers from the upper Plains States (Iowa, Minnesota,
North and South Dakota). B. B. was the big winner, landing about 175
dates, but I was happy to leave with about 60. These were not fancy

Playboy Clubs, however. Sometimes in one day at one college I did a show at noon in the school cafeteria, then opened for a ping-pong tournament in the afternoon and at night performed at the rathskeller. But a paying gig was a paying gig.

You did not see many black people in those states back then. I pulled into a gas station outside Minot, North Dakota, because my car was overheating. The attendant said, "I can't believe it! You're the second black to come through here in the last year and a half. Chubby Checker stopped here when his bus broke down. You guys need to take better care of your vehicles!"

Between dates I returned to New York, where once a week I did studio audience warm-ups for a CBS sitcom called *Calucci's Department*, which starred James Coco. Not many sitcoms were still being shot in New York rather than LA, so this was a prime gig for a stand-up. My job was to get the audience revved up to laugh during the taping of the show set in a New York State unemployment office. Apparently being out of work was not very funny, because the series lasted just a couple of months. Before it folded, however, a woman came up to me after my warm-up act and said she had cast *Calucci's Department*. Now she was casting a new series starring Esther Rolle, who played the black housekeeper on *Maude*. She wanted to know if I would be interested in being on a sitcom.

I said, "Sure, let me know," and walked away. I didn't think any more about it. There are so many people in show business who say they are this or that—and aren't; who are going to do this or that for you—and don't; who say, "give me your card" and "here's my card"—and never call that you end up not believing anybody. So many gigs and TV shows had fallen through before for me that I was skeptical of everyone and everything. My line is "Everyone is a liar . . . until proven full of shit." If I had a dollar for every person who came into the Improv with a business card that said "Producer," I would already have been a rich man.

The next week I was about to do my warm-up and the woman from CBS, Pat Kirkland, was there again, this time with a man wearing a golf hat.

"Jimmie, I'd like you to meet Norman Lear." I had no idea who he was.

"Welcome aboard," he said.

What was he talking about? On board what?

"We'll begin shooting in about a month," he continued. "We're glad you're on our show."

I said to myself, "What show?" and went into my warm-up.

"You're very funny," he told me afterward. "We'd love for you to come in to help audition one of the girls too." The next day his people called my people—Louie the cook—and left a message with a day and time to meet them at CBS.

Lear had already scored with the massive hits *All in the Family*, *Sanford and Son*, and *Maude*. His new show was called *The Black Family*—at least that is what it said on the pages for the scene I did with the actresses—Chip Fields, Tamu Blackwell, and Bern Nadette Stanis— who were auditioning for the character of my younger sister Thelma. Though I never auditioned, apparently I already had the part of a character named Junior. I believe Lear and producer Allan Manings had earlier seen me at the Improv and on the *Paar* show, and they had approved my casting. But they never told me anything about how they saw the character or what I should do with him. They just said, "Do it."

That audition scene, about Thelma accusing Junior of stealing five dollars from her, would never make it into the series:

THELMA
(she snatches his painting off the bureau and goes to the open window . . . holds the painting out)
Give me back my $5.00, or I'll throw this garbage out the window.

JUNIOR
(moving toward her threateningly)
Girl, you throw that painting out the window and you gonna
hear some new sounds . . . whoosh when the painting passes the
twelfth floor and whoosh again when you pass the painting.

Meanwhile, I was happy doing my stand-up. I had gigs lined up, including the college tour. These people I did not know were talking
about taping a sitcom on the West Coast when I was doing just fine on
the West Side. Well, they could keep talking; I was going to keep working. I wasn't going to believe I was on a TV show until I was actually
there.

So instead, I was in Fargo, North Dakota, playing a college, when
the phone in my motel room woke me up at two in the morning.

"This is Tandem Productions in Los Angeles. We're looking for
Jimmie Walker."

"You got him."

"Did you get the contract for the show? You were supposed to sign
it and be in Los Angeles."

"Why?"

"We start rehearsals tomorrow. We sent you a ticket and were at the
airport to pick you up. You weren't there."

"No one told me." They had sent everything to Louie at the
Improv.

"Go to the airport. A ticket will be waiting for you. Get on that
plane."

They met me in LA and put me up at the Farmer's Daughter motel
next to the CBS studios. As soon as I settled in I called Steve Landesberg, who was in town doing Bobby Darin's variety show on NBC.
"Steve, where can I get on stage?"

I was more concerned with doing my stand-up, which might lead to
getting a shot on the Carson show, than this TV sitcom. The *Tonight
Show* was the pinnacle for a stand-up comic, but it had moved three

thousand miles from me, to Burbank, in mid-1972. If nothing else, this TV series had at least brought me to the West Coast too. I figured I would shoot the first couple shows of the sitcom, maybe get on Carson, then go back to New York to the Improv, call up Lou Johnson, and make up the college dates in North Dakota that I owed him.

That was my "plan" as I stood that night on the stage of the Comedy Store on Sunset Boulevard—the Store, as comics call it. As it turned out, none of that plan would come to pass.

The Black Family became *Good Times*. The show was a rare spin-off of a spin-off. Lear had asked black actor Michael Evans, who played Lionel Jefferson on *All in the Family*, for ideas about expanding the character of Florida Evans on *All in the Family*, who had moved on to *Maude*, in order for Esther to head her own series. He and playwright friend Eric Monte came up with a concept based on Monte's childhood in the Cabrini-Green projects of Chicago.

According to reports, Manings then did his own take on their pilot script, though Monte was credited as the writer of that first episode. The goal—bold and dangerous for the times—was to show the life— both the highs and lows—of a lower-class, urban black family dealing with the world. Importantly, the family would be solid and intact, headed by a father who worked and a mother with a moral backbone.

Florida was no longer a maid, and there was no mention of her previous employer, Maude. John Amos, who played her firefighter husband Henry on *Maude*, was now named James, a man from Mississippi with a sixth-grade education who struggled to keep a job despite his best efforts. Rather than living in New York, the Evans clan was in a housing project in a poor, inner-city neighborhood of Chicago—apartment 17C at fictitious 963 N. Gilbert Avenue. The infamous Cabrini-Green projects were shown in the opening and closing credits, but they were never referred to by name.

James and Florida were role models, strong and admirable. J. J. (as in James Junior) was their always-getting-into-trouble seventeen-year-old eldest, Thelma their beautiful-and-sweet sixteen-year-old daughter, and Michael their hope-of-the-future ten-year-old son. Though Rolle was top-billed, Amos second, and Ja'Net DuBois, who played neighbor Willona Woods, was third, the element that originally was going to make the revolutionary concept of an "urban black family" work for popular TV was young Michael. His appeal, as in many sitcoms before—from Opie on *Andy Griffith* to Ricky on *Ozzie and Harriet*—would be the hook that would bring family audiences back every week.

The difference between those earlier classic sitcoms and *Good Times* is that Michael would talk about more than family life. This "militant midget," as he was referred to on the series, would talk about society and politics right there in front of the mainstream American viewer. The audience would feel threatened hearing speeches about racism from Rolle or Amos, even—or perhaps especially—on a sitcom. But Michael saying on national TV that "boy" was a racist word was okay. After all, he was just a child.

But who was going to play Michael? The producers very much wanted Ralph Carter, the twelve-year-old who had been Tony nominated for his performance in the Broadway musical *Raisin*. But his contract committed him to a long run of that hit show. So they brought in another twelve-year-old actor, Laurence Fishburne, who had been raised in Brooklyn and had recently made his TV debut during the last season of *The Mod Squad*. They kept working on trying to sign Ralph, all the while being honest with Laurence that he might be replaced at any moment.

I did not have an agent or a manager. With contracts having to be dealt with, I needed someone who knew about the legal side. A friend recommended Jerry Kushnick, the New York lawyer for Ben Vereen, who had starred on Broadway in *Jesus Christ Superstar* and *Pippin*. Kushnick also had recently gained notoriety for winning a major case for Terry Knight, the former manager of Grand Funk Railroad, against that rock group. Jerry agreed to take me on. Louie the cook was relieved he didn't have to spend any more of his valuable time on my career!

Jerry told me I should also get an agent. I suggested Lou Johnson, who I was already working with on the college tour. He said I needed a far more powerful force in the business and approached ICM (International Creative Management) in New York, even though ICM had seen me perform many times on stage and had never expressed any interest in representing me. But now I was on a TV series; they saw dollar signs and signed me as a client.

I was not an actor and never said I was. While in New York I did a few TV commercials (Ballantine beer, Sears sneakers), but the only acting I had done were tiny roles earlier that year as a gang member in *Gordon's War*, directed by Ossie Davis, and as a street hood in *Badge 373*, a gritty cop thriller directed by Howard Koch.

Casting folks would see me at the Improv and usually reject me, saying, "You don't *sound* black." After working for years to get rid of my ghetto New York accent, ghettoese was exactly what they wanted for their films. On stage I would try to put on an exaggerated black accent. But after playing so many downtown clubs in front of white audiences who did not want to hear ghettoese, keeping that accent was getting tougher and tougher for me. The *Badge 373* filmmakers first saw me at the Improv and had the same problem—they did not think I came across as "black enough."

When I went to audition, I stopped in a store at a subway station on my way and bought a blue denim floppy hat. I figured that maybe if I wore that hat, after stomping on it and dirtying it up a bit, I would look more urban, more street. It worked. The casting people suddenly thought I was perfect and I got the role—getting kicked in the head in an alley by Robert Duvall.

My few lines in *Badge 373* ended up still being dubbed by someone who sounded "blacker." But from then on I considered that blue hat my good luck charm.

Naturally, the *Good Times* folks, from Lear to Manings, wanted trained actors. Esther had made her New York stage debut in 1962 and was enormously respected. For three years John Amos had been Gordy the weatherman on the *Mary Tyler Moore Show*—one of my favorite sitcoms of all time. Ja'Net had made her Broadway debut in the original production of *Golden Boy* with Sammy Davis Jr. Whoever played the Evans family's youngest son Michael, whether Ralph or Laurence, would also be a legit actor. Manings later said they had great difficulty finding a true actor to play J. J. When I was first suggested, he rejected me, saying, "No, he's a stand-up comic. . . . I prefer to work with actors whom I would bend."

At the first reading for the first show they realized that I might not bend.

The cast, writers, and producers sat around a table, and the actors read aloud the script for the pilot. After various lines the writers would punch them up with "ha, ha, ha." I wondered what they were laughing about. I didn't hear any jokes. At one point I stopped, turned to Lear sitting next to me, and said, "This isn't funny."

After we were done but before anyone left the table, I spoke up: "That was terrible. We have to do this over."

When I go on stage, I want devastating laughter—total devastation—until the minute I walk off. I want to always be the funniest I can be. When I did a joke at the Improv and one of my comic friends didn't think it worked, he told me. That is one reason comics are always miserable—there is always somebody who doesn't think you're funny and doesn't mind telling you. You get used to it. Or maybe someone would say, "You know what would be better?" and suggest a change. You listened and didn't take it too personally. Because if it's better, it's better.

Manings took me to the side and told me that in television you do not do what I just did.

"Look, I appreciate your input," he said, "but a lot of people have worked very hard on this. If you have a problem with what people have written, come to me or the story editors, Norman Paul and Jack Elinson, and tell us how you feel. But don't voice it like you did. That's not good."

He was trying to be nice. What he could have said was, "Just read the words, asshole!"

After two weeks of rehearsal with us Fishburne assumed he had the gig. On the day we were set to begin taping for the first time, he showed up ready to go. So too did Ralph. His contract situation had been sorted out, and he was now playing Michael Evans. Laurence was crushed. Many years down the road I would see Laurence at the gym we would go to in LA, and we wondered how his life might have been different if he had been on our show. He would definitely not have been able to land a role in Francis Ford Coppola's epic *Apocalypse Now* when he was fourteen years old. He may have thought not being Michael Evans was a blow to his career at the time, but perhaps that was the best thing that could have happened to him.

As we taped, at night I worked with Landesberg on getting more jokes into the script. The next day I would go to Ralph and Bern Nadette, who won the role of Thelma, and say, "How about we try this?" I showed them what we had come up with.

"What are you talking about?" they said, being the professionals that they were. "We have a script. No one told us about any changes."

Lear and Elinson came down together to have a talk with me. "We love the idea of you putting in new things," they said, "but try to give our stuff a little chance before you make these changes."

From then on I operated by sneak attack. Before we taped I ran my ideas by the stage manager, Buddy, and one of the cameramen, Vito, who hoped to write, produce, and direct someday. Sometimes they said, "Nah." Sometimes they said, "That's alright." Sometimes they said, "Hey, that's funny!" Then, as the tape rolled, I would throw in "funny."

The other people on stage would be surprised and maybe not happy, but the live studio audience would laugh. After the first run-through, Lear would ask me not to repeat what I had done. "You're doing something different from the rest of the cast!"

"Yeah, I'm trying to be funny!"

"That's not the point," he said, as the argument escalated.

"Did it get a big laugh, Norman?"

"Everything does not have to be a laugh. Sometimes there are just moments."

"I don't want 'moments,'" I told him, "I want jokes. I want laughs." Other cast members wanted acting "moments." That was fine with me. Just give me the jokes!

"We have messages we want to get across too," Lear said.

"If I wanted to deliver messages, I'd work for Western Union," I shot back.

Lear hated to hear that. I would win when I got a laugh, but he had me eating crow when something I tried did not work.

"This is the kind of thing that can tear a cast apart, tear a show apart," he would lay on me. "This is the kind of thing that might make writers not want to write for you." But the writers did want to write for me—because they knew I could deliver laughs.

Manings recognized that I was a different cat. He later said, "He did the first show. He heard the first laugh. He played the audience from then on in. When the show was over, I said, 'O.K., hell of a nice show, friends. Now we're going to stay and do it without the audience.' They said, 'Why?' I said, 'Because I can't edit anything because (he looked at me) you're always looking out there (toward the audience).' So I said, 'I'm going to sit here and when you (meaning me) say the joke looking at the actor, I'm going to go, 'Ha, ha, ha, ha, ha.' He said, 'Oh, I didn't know you wanted singles. I'm sorry I hit homeruns.' But he took off. I thought the young kid would take off. And he took off."

The first directors had problems too, but not with me. Perry Rosemond was hired to direct the pilot. But Esther wanted a friend of hers, Donald McKayle, to direct. McKayle was a pioneering black modern dance choreographer and stage director. Lear agreed to have them direct together. Donny directed us like a stage play, Perry as a TV production. That was doomed to fail.

After a rehearsal we would all sit down and get notes, critiques on our performances. At one such early session, Perry was there, of course. On the table in front of him was his briefcase, open and overflowing with the shooting script and other pertinent papers. Also there was John Rich, who directed nearly every episode of *All in the Family* its first few seasons. Seemingly he was present just to observe and consult.

Lear popped his head in. "Hey, Perry, I need to talk to you for a second." Perry walked out of the room.

Within a minute Lear's secretary came in, gathered up Perry's papers, put them in his briefcase, and left with them. We never saw him again.

That's show business, folks.

Rich took over as director. Even though he was officially credited on only the second episode, he oversaw the shows credited to McKayle. After just a few episodes McKayle was axed. That ticked Esther off. Accepting Rich as director was even harder for her and others in the cast because they despised him. He was in your face and brutally honest. That is probably why I loved him.

When a cameraman complained that he could not get in the right position for a particular shot, Rich spoke through the PA system, "Hold on a minute."

He came down from the booth, walked to that camera, and moved it into the correct position. He looked at the cameraman, saying, "Got it now, asshole?"

When I would throw in a line that worked, he would say, "That's brilliant, man. I love that. Let's keep that in."

When one would not work, he would say, "Where did that come from?"

"I made that up."

"Well, fuckin' take that out! It sucks!"

You knew exactly where you stood with John Rich.

During a rehearsal for the first show—Lear loved having rehearsals—I threw in a word out of the blue.

JAMES

Well baby, I got 'til 5 o'clock to get us 72 dollars. I don't know but one way to get it.

FLORIDA

James, don't you dare go into that closet!

THELMA

What's he gonna do, mama?

FLORIDA

He's getting his pool cue.

J. J.

Dyn-o-mite!

It was not in the original script.

But no one on the staff reacted.

"Hold it," said Rich. "Stop!"

"What's wrong?" I asked, anticipating him telling me to "fuckin' take that out."

"I like that 'dyn-o-mite' thing," he said.

"What about it?"

"I think we got something here," he went on. "Here's what I want you to do." He demonstrated how to say the word, emphasis on the "O" and with a huge smile. When we ran the script again, he also put an iso (isolation) camera just on me, to focus on the word even more.

I asked him, "Are people going to go for this?"

He said, "It's gonna be great."

He was right. When I said "Dyn-o-mite!" at the taping, the studio audience howled with laughter.

For the second episode, which he codirected, Rich made "Dyn-o-mite!" the exclamation that ended the show. The audience loved it.

At first Esther did not mind, given the alternative. J. J. was a bit of a petty shoplifter in the early shows. He would have something in hand and be asked where he got it. He would answer with a sly smile, "I *found* it!" A stern Florida would say something to the effect of "I want that bought, not found." That was originally going to be J. J.'s catchphrase— "I *found* it!" But Esther did not want Florida's son to be a thief. She objected to the producers and writers, so that character point and catchphrase quickly disappeared from future scripts. I suppose for her, "Dyn-o-mite" was at least better than "I *found* it!"

Lear did not like it at all. He and Rich argued fiercely about that one word.

"You mean in the middle of an episode we're going to stop and have someone stand there and yell 'dyn-o-mite'?" said Lear. "It's a non sequitur. And it means absolutely nothing. It doesn't contribute to the story. It's asinine."

Rich answered, "It'll work."

"Say it with energy!" he told me. "A year from now, people are going to be yelling 'dyn-o-mite' out of cars, on the street, and wherever they see you."

I never said it on the third and fifth episodes, and the word is buried in the fourth episode. John fought to get it back in. There was such a rumble about that one word that, after I said it twice on the seventh episode—and by then Esther was adamantly against it—a writer's rule was instituted that J. J. could only say "dyn-o-mite" once per show.

I had no opinion on the subject. In fact, it may surprise some to know, I was more in agreement with Lear! I didn't know what the point of saying "dyn-o-mite" was either. Having a catchphrase, like Flip Wilson's "Here come da judge" or "the devil made me do it," never entered my mind. Little did I realize at the time how one word could change your life. "Dyn-o-mite" sure changed mine.

Rich was also responsible for me wearing my lucky blue hat on the show. I wore it at the readings and rehearsals, but when the time came to tape the first episode, I combed out my hair and put on the Afro Sheen.

"Hey, where's that hat?" Rich asked.

"In my dressing room. Why?"

"No, no, no. That hat is going to be you, baby. We need that hat for your character. I want you to wear that hat all the time. You put that hat on and make it happen!"

Esther complained about the hat.

"How come he's wearing a hat inside? What's the point?"

John answered, "It's for the character. He's wearing it." He wasn't concerned about hurting someone's feelings. He was there to help create a hit TV show. As far as I am concerned, Rich stepped up to the plate twice and hit a home run each time. That's an unbelievable batting average not only in baseball but also in comedy.

All of this happened within the first couple weeks in the life of *Good Times* in late 1973. When I told a crew member I was planning on going back to New York after the initial episodes, he said, "I think you're going to be here for a while. You might as well get used to LA." But New Yorkers never think they are going to live in LA. There was a classic Mort Sahl joke about a New Yorker who lived in LA for eight years and went into a liquor store to buy beer. The clerk asked, "Do you want a six-pack or a twelve-pack?" The customer said, "I'll just take two cans. I'll be going back to New York soon."

Good Times was a mid-season replacement, premiering at 8:30 p.m. on Friday, February 8, 1974. If the series failed to attract a sizable audience in thirteen episodes, we would be gone and I would be back in New York.

Days after the premiere aired William Hickey of the *Plain Dealer* newspaper in Cleveland wrote, "Jimmie Walker, who plays the teenage son, just might end up stealing the show. His portrayal of a loosey-goosey, light-fingered adolescent was priceless." Vernon Scott of UPI called me "that toothpick of a walking sight gag . . . maybe the funniest thing to happen to television in years."

I did not see any of that coming. I was as surprised as anyone that my character became the breakout star. J. J. was just funny and silly. But the audience decides who they will like and who they won't, what character they will be attracted to and what character they will choose to ignore. The TV public loved J. J. He was especially popular with younger kids, and that was a demographic the network wanted. The same thing happened the very same year on *Happy Days*: Ronnie Howard as Richie Cunningham was the star, but it was Henry Winkler as Fonzie who unexpectedly grabbed hold of American pop culture.

Because I wasn't given any guidance on how to play the character, I went with my own instincts. I based J. J. on my favorite character from one of my favorite sitcoms, Art Carney's Ed Norton in *The Honeymooners*. He too was tall and skinny and goofy—and wore a similar hat! When J. J., at six-foot-two and 130 pounds, flailed around with his thin arms and legs? That was a bastardization of Ed Norton.

Newsweek said of J. J.: "His beanpole body suggests a vitamin deficiency, his Silly Putty face flaps around a set of buck teeth that could have come from a joke store." *TV Guide* wrote, "He has the neck movement of an automatic sprinkler, and the bulb-eyed glare of an aggravated emu, all supported by a physique that resembles an inverted 6-foot tuning fork." Much of that could also have been written about Ed Norton. I even added the rhythm of how Norton spoke. At one point Manings and Lear said, "You have to blacken it up a little!" So I once again put on my ghettoese accent.

I was the person out there, and I certainly blended in my own unique flavor, but Carney's character was the foundation in the back of my mind. That is one reason I found it peculiar when my portrayal of J. J. was later demonized for "cooning it up" and being a racist, demeaning throwback to black comic actor Stepin Fetchit. Before me, Redd Foxx and Flip Wilson had been accused of the same for what they did on TV, and later Sherman Helmsley with *The Jeffersons* would too. Worse than being not funny enough or not black enough, we were assailed for being too funny and too black! But the fact is that J. J. was based on a white comic character, not a black one.

Good Times ended up as the seventeenth highest-rated series of the year and was renewed for a full complement of twenty-four episodes to begin that fall. "Dyn-o-mite!" swept the country. Everyone from Sammy Davis Jr. to opera star Beverly Sills repeated it on TV shows, and everywhere I walked the word echoed behind me.

I became the first young black sitcom star. Flip Wilson? He had a variety show. Bill Cosby? His first comedy series in the late '60s–early '70s s lasted only two seasons, he was in his thirties at the time, and he played a high school teacher. Redd Foxx? He was much too old.

The show was a critical hit too:

> "The only Black television show innovative enough to depart from the old Amos and Andy format (sorry about that Sanford and Son)." (Denise Mitchell, The Black American [New York], April 1974)

> "A noteworthy step forward in TV's treatment of black people . . . 'Good Times' is the first show to take black family life in the modern big city as its premise." (Lee Winfrey, Knight Newspapers, May 15, 1974)

Much of what has been written negatively about Good Times has been revisionist history. The truth is that blacks and whites, the public and the press welcomed the series with open arms, lauding it with high acclaim. So too was J. J. Esther and I even won Image Awards from the NAACP as Best Actress and Best Actor, respectively, in a TV series.

I made a triumphant return to the Improv in New York. Richard Lewis told writer Richard Zoglin in his book Comedy at the Edge: How Stand-up in the 1970s Changed America, "It was a night I'll always remember. . . . When Budd introduced him, the place went fuckin' nuts.

Before he opened his mouth . . . I remember thinking to myself, I'm never quitting. Until I hear a Budd Friedman say, 'Ladies and gentle-men, Richard Lewis,' and they're already applauding."

But for me the highlight was spotting a woman in the audience at the Improv who I had not seen in years but recognized immediately. She was with her husband. She remembered when we last spoke and so did I. Alice Trillin, the teacher at SEEK who said my comedy would never go anywhere, came up to me after the show. She said, "I think I was wrong about you." All I could do was smile.

Everything changed. Even producer Ernie DiMassa, who said I was "too black" for his middle American audience, finally booked me for a shot on the *Mike Douglas Show*. Not only did I go on many, many times after that, but Freddie and I, representing the new young comics on TV, also cohosted for a week.

My father tried to reach me too.

The last time I exchanged any serious words with him was about ten years earlier. I was about seventeen years old, working at Yankee Stadium, and for some reason he came to a game. While I walked through the stands carrying soft drinks to sell to the fans, he harangued me about how awful a person I was, how I was such a bad guy. He had gone to college, at Alabama A&M, and here I was working at a stadium and going nowhere in life. He told me I was a wise-ass who would never amount to anything.

Then he called my mother a "cunt"—that was the word he used. I cringe even now writing it. I consider that word one of the nastiest, most disrespectful that anyone can say referring to a woman—worse than "nigger."

"You know, I wish you could stand in my shoes for a minute," I told him.

"Why?"

I was a big Bob Dylan fan and I laid a Dylan line from "Positively 4th Street" on him: "Because then you'd know what a drag it is to see you."

Now, on the *Good Times* set, producer Manings called me into his office.

"This happens all the time when someone gets well known," he said. "People suddenly come out of the woodwork and want to get in touch with you. But we never know who these people really are. Anyway, someone has been calling us asking for you. He says he's your father and he says he wants to talk to you. We want to make sure we're not doing anything you don't want us to do. We don't know if he really is your father."

"He probably is," I said, "at least technically."

"Do you want us to get back to him or let you know the next time he calls?"

I did not have to think about my answer for more than a split second. I told Allan, "I want nothing to do with him."

He saw how strongly I felt and simply said, "Then we'll handle it."

I never again heard about him trying to contact me.

For the next season—our first full one—*Good Times* moved to Tuesday night at 8 p.m. (leading into M*A*S*H) and broke into the Top Ten, to number seven, with nearly eighteen million households—25 percent of the American television viewing public—tuning in each week. The show sometimes referred to as the "Black Waltons" or "Black Brady Bunch" ranked higher in the Nielsen ratings than *The Waltons* and *Maude*, Lear's favorite show of his own production. The cast was on the cover of *TV Guide*, and I was on the cover of *Ebony*, alongside Arthur Ashe, George Foreman, Johnny Mathis, Lou Rawls, and others for an article titled "The Unmarrieds: They Tell Why They Remain Single."

Given my parents' marriage, it should be no surprise that I have never been a fan of that institution. But though I played the field, I was never a Hollywood "player," never dated a starlet. Everyone has problems, but actresses have more of them. My girlfriends had regular jobs, such as a secretary. One of my main girls was the black and beautiful Samantha. I felt fortunate that she or any woman would go out with me. Yet even in an *Ebony* article that featured photos of the two of us together, I made it clear that we were not exclusive.

I suspect *Ebony* might have had a problem running photos of me with a white girlfriend, such as Diana, a singer/waitress at the New York Improv, a redhead with a big voice. She was the first woman I went out with who had a child. But she never whined about being a single mother. When I got a little juice because of the series, I brought her to LA, put together a band for her, and took her on the road as a singer—even brought her onto the *Mike Douglas Show*. She hung out with me and laughed at my jokes and was happy—for a year. There was never a break-up. We just saw less and less of each other. In my experience relationships never last forever.

Ray Peno, I mean, Jay Leno, dated a singer named Adele Blue for a long time. She was a girlfriend of another girlfriend of mine, another Barbara. This Barbara was almost six feet tall, a leggy, strawberry blonde from Kalamazoo, Michigan. She had come to LA wanting to do something with her life but didn't know what. We spent our first date in bed—for two days. She was sexy, feisty, and bitchy. Her midwest family could not believe we were together. Nor could they understand—this was the mid-'70s—why she would get a boob job.

We had the most intense physical relationship I have ever had with a woman. We were so volatile and passionate together that it reminded me of Lenny Bruce's relationship with his wife, Honey. We fought and fought and fought, and then we had the most incredible make-up sex. I was out of control with her. We had that crazy I-can't-quit-you love, where I would wake up alone at three in the morning at my place after an argument and go to her apartment to be with her. We were so nuts for each other that as hard as we tried, we just could not live together.

But at least this Barbara and I were together during the good times of *Good Times*. Adele stuck it out with Jay through years and years of struggle. Then they broke up just before he hit the big time. When he began to go out with Mavis, the spectacular, beautiful, and smart woman who became his wife, his career took off. I felt sorry for Adele that she never enjoyed at least some of the rewards of his success.

My success on *Good Times* backed up the network in convincing Lear to allow me to do my own thing. Of all the compromises he had to make in his long and illustrious career, I think that was the one that was the hardest for him. He bit his tongue and got on board the J. J. train.

But with the second season, "Dyn-o-mite!" was no longer a non sequitur. I was now Kid Dyn-o-mite! It became a nickname usually punctuating a rhyme: "About time you saw the light, to hire the great Kid Dyn-o-mite!"

The celebrity and merchandising machine went into action. There were J. J. buttons, t-shirts, posters, belts, socks, pajamas, trading cards, and a talking doll that wore a floppy hat, turtleneck sweater, and jeans—just like me—and it spoke nine phrases when you pulled the string. The J. J. Fan Club received a thousand letters every week.

I guess you know you are famous when people begin inventing stories about you, including that I was married. I had my "Paul McCartney is dead" moment too. Both issues forced me to write a letter to the members of my fan club:

> I am NOT married and have NOT been in any fatal motorcycle or automobile accident. I don't know where these rumors started but girls don't want to go out with me because they've heard I'm married—and people keep calling to find out if I'm still around—which I certainly am. . . . So if you hear either of these rumors, you can say you know they are NOT true—because J. J. told you so!

Another sign of fame is having a stalker. I was with Stacey, a beach-blonde, Anna Nicole Smith look-alike, aerobics instructor I was juggling, uh, I mean, dating, when a round black woman came up to me in the parking lot of the Store after a performance.

"We should be together," she said adamantly.

I brushed it off with "I don't think so."

She was angry. "Is this white bitch with you?" she said.

Stacey and I walked away. But every now and then while working at the Store, I would spot her standing outside. Nothing else happened though. Maybe she moved on to Sherman Helmsley.

Like Fonzie, J. J. was so cool, he was hot. That gave me the opportunity to break down a few barriers for blacks, such as TV commercials. For example, I did a spot for milk, dressed in a tuxedo and sitting in the back of a limo with a beautiful black woman on either side of me.

Some people may try to tell you that drinking milk isn't cool. I happen to like milk. . . . Let me tell you one thing, if you still don't think that drinking milk is cool, it hasn't cut into my action one bit, if you can dig that.

There had never been a black celebrity who came into people's homes every week who could have done that commercial before I did. J. J. truly was the first black male character on series TV who was overtly sexual, and he was able to be that only because he was funny. Breakthroughs often begin with a laugh.

When the opportunity was presented to record a comedy album, I went back to the Cellar Door like I said I would. I reminded Jack Boyle, the owner, that I had told him this would happen. He was happy for me— and glad he could put a few asses in the seats too. Yep, this guy he called a "nobody," merely an emcee or opening act, had become a somebody.

I was determined to impress upon the public that I was a stand-up comic first and J. J. second. I would not say "Dyn-o-mite!" on the album. I also wanted the title to be "Jimmie Walker—At Last."

"Are you fuckin' insane?" said Jerry Kushnick, my lawyer. "We're trying to sell records here, man! The title is *Dyn-o-mite*. Oh, and put that hat on for the cover photo!"

When the photographer for the cover posed me with a couple of sticks of fake dynamite in my hands, I balked.

"Do we have to do this?"

"If you want to sell albums, you do," he said. They ended up using a photo showing a lit fuse coming out of my finger.

But at the Cellar Door performance that was already recorded I never, of course, said "dyn-o-mite."

Art Kass, the head of Buddah Records—which had hits with Gladys Knight & the Pips, Bill Withers, Curtis Mayfield, and the Isley Brothers—noticed. He said, "We're going into a recording studio and you're going to lay down a real good 'Dyn-o-mite!'"

"Really?"

"Really," he said.

When you have a talking doll created in your image, keeping people from pulling your string is hard.

> *Dyn-o-mite! The Black Prince has arrived! . . . People always ask me, Brother Jim, how can you live in the ghetto with all those cock-roaches and everything like that? Well, I think cockroaches are the cleanest animals on earth. Every time you see them, they're in the bathtub!*

The album, which I dedicated to my mother, sold half a million copies. But I did not then and still never have said "Dyn-o-mite!" on stage during my stand-up.

The same week I was in Washington, DC, to record the album, I was invited to tour the White House. President Gerald Ford was not in at the time, but the house staff—which was almost completely black—made me feel at home. After all, the White House is our house too.

I also visited the Smithsonian—or should I say "attempted" to visit. The afternoon I was there hundreds of high school kids were also

there, as they generally are. They spotted me and went crazy, screaming, "J. J.! J. J.!" They ran after me, gathered around, and asked for autographs and for me to take photos with them. I did what I could, but
the situation got out of control and would not stop. There was always
someone wanting more. Finally, the security guards saw the chaos and
restored order.

I was uncomfortable about signing autographs anyway. Coming from
where I had come from, I did not feel I was better than anyone else. I
thought it was egotistical to think my signature was important, except
on a check! I always preferred a handshake. I still do. For me, shaking
hands is more real, more personal, more honest.

One day, early on in *Good Times*, I was doing the *Mike Douglas Show*
with Brenner and was taping at the Six Flags amusement park in New
Jersey. Half a dozen kids came up and asked for autographs. Brenner
took all of their pieces of paper and signed them. I told him, "I don't
do that," and moved away from them. Brenner gave me a nasty look
and finished his autograph session. When the kids left, he turned to
me. "Don't you ever fuckin' do that again when I'm with you." He was
very angry. "If you don't want to be bothered, just go back to where you
came from, where you were just another guy on the street. Then no one
will ask for your autograph." That was the only time Brenner ever had
a cross word with me.

Lear heard about what I was doing—or not doing—and ordered me
into his office.

"You need to sign," he said. "You're making people unhappy." We
may have argued a lot, but I always respected Lear. He was my Uncle
Norman.

I have signed autographs ever since.

> A white person asked me for an autograph.
> "Will you sign this for my friend?" she said.
> "Is your friend black?" I asked.

"Yes."
"Then I'll print."

Through the second season the black and white press continued to cheer *Good Times*. John J. O'Connor, the esteemed TV critic of the *New York Times*, was right on target:

> *Black viewers are being afforded material that provides immediate personal and psychic identification. . . . Whites are being given glimpses of black life that, however simplified, can't help but weaken artificial racial barriers. When an ordinary black family becomes a mass-public favorite, at least one change is no longer in the wind. It's here, right in front of our eyes. . . . The Evanses of "Good Times" are, in style and personality, considerably more than whites in blackface. It is their struggle for economic and social survival that provides the common denominator for a mass audience. The dividing line between "us" and "them" becomes less racial, more socioeconomic. . . . Never underestimate the power of being silly on television. (February 2, 1975)*

My job on *Good Times* was to get laughs. With the series dealing with so many very difficult subjects, J. J. was the comic relief, the color in the Evans family's otherwise drab existence.

In sitcoms someone has to take the pie in the face. If no one takes the pie, there is no comedy. If every character is earnest, there is nothing to laugh at. Sometimes that character is the star, sometimes it is a lesser character, but his or her role is a constant—take the pie. *I Love Lucy?* Lucy. *Mary Tyler Moore?* Ted. *Honeymooners?* Norton. *All in the Family?* Meathead. *Seinfeld?* George. *The Andy Griffith Show?* Barney. *Taxi?* Louie. *Cheers?* Cliff. *M*A*S*H?* Klinger. *Friends?* Joey. There are exceptions—such as the *Cosby Show* of the '80s. But just like with his stand-up, Cosby is in a class by himself.

On *Good Times*, J. J. took the pie. The writers did not have to elaborate. The script would read, "J. J. reacts," and I would do my thing.

I was Kid Dyn-o-mite! But for some, including members of the cast, I was taking too much of the pie.

Bad times were about to come to *Good Times*.

6

I Am Not J. J.

THE BIGWIGS AT THE MOVIE AND TV STUDIOS WERE NOT AWARE OF it, but there were many, many days during the run of *Good Times* when there was more comedy talent on the bottom floor of my three-story condo on Burton Way in Beverly Hills than anywhere else in Hollywood.

Sitting on the couch would be David Letterman next to Jay Leno next to Paul Mooney. Snacking on the food might be Robert Schimmel, Richard Jeni, Louie Anderson, and Elayne Boosler. Young Byron Allen would be trying to ignore the fact that his mother was in the kitchen waiting to drive him home. There were others whose names would never be recognizable to the public because they were not star performers, such as Wayne Kline, Marty Nadler, Jeff Stein, Jack Handey, Steve Oedekirk, and Larry Jacobson, but who would soon write for some of the most popular sitcoms and late-night talk shows in television history. All of them—all then unknowns—would gather at my home from one to five times a week because they were on my writing staff, commissioned to pen jokes for my stand-up act.

I was good enough as a stand-up to, well, stand up on my own—without J. J. Don't get me wrong. It was a combination of luck and being at the right place at the right time that brought me to J. J. and

Good Times. I'm grateful for that. But I was and would continue to be a stand-up comic.

Building that career was where I put all my energies. So I was always in need of jokes. Wherever there are stand-up comedians, there are comedy writers who give them many of their jokes. There have been and remain few comics who write anywhere close to all of their own material—no matter what the public perception might be (Cosby, once again, being one of those exceptions). Being funny and new as often as you need to be on stage is just too hard.

Everywhere a comic goes, people come up and say, "I've got a joke for you." They are almost always surprised when you do not seem that interested in hearing it. We are not trying to be rude, but we get a lot of jokes from a lot of people who make their living writing jokes. We hear jokes all day, every day. We do not need help with our jokes. We have help from the best comedy writers on the planet. They do this for a living.

To those who create it, comedy is not a joke. Comedy is serious.

In my early days a Phil Foster might give me a line for my debut on the *Paar* show or friends like Landesberg or Nadler might feed me jokes over coffee at 2 a.m. at the Camelot. Thanks to a decent steady paycheck from *Good Times* I could afford to pay a staff of hungry writers. Thanks to the show, I was offered more and better-paying stand-up gigs too. I was off the chitlin' circuit and into Mr. Kelly's in Chicago, the hungry i in San Francisco, the Copacabana in New York. Except for one year during the show's six seasons, I made more money from those gigs than from CBS. But the only way to keep up both the volume and the quality of the jokes I would lay on audiences was to have a staff of writers.

Success paid for them, but success also made them necessary. When no one knew who I was, much of my material came from observing everyday life. I could walk around in the general public and interact with people. But once I made a name for myself and was instantly recognizable, that was no longer possible. When you come into people's living rooms every week and then they see you in person, they can't believe you escaped from the TV! Instead of being able to listen in on conversations, I was the conversation. Instead of being the watcher, I was the watchee. I needed access to the eyes and ears of less visible comedians.

I knew Leno from our days in New York. He had moved to the West Coast and was establishing a beachhead at the Comedy Store. But no one was being paid there. He could pick up $150 a week working on jokes for me. He also told me about a friend of his, Gene Braunstein, a former classmate at Emerson College in Boston where their comedy team Gene and Jay played area coffeehouses. Leno asked if Gene could join our meetings and I said yes. Braunstein aka the Mighty Mister Geno quickly became my comedy coordinator.

I received my *Good Times* script on a Thursday or Friday. Mister Geno and I would get together on Saturday morning and run it for two or three hours—however long it took for me to memorize my lines. I wanted to have the script down pat so when I did my stand-up that night at the Store, I would not be distracted worrying about my "other job," the one at CBS.

During the week, as soon as I left the *Good Times* set in the afternoon, I jumped into my car and headed for a Chinese take-out place, where I would grab some food and phone Mister Geno. I would tell him I was on my way and then call one or more girlfriends to pick up pizzas, sandwiches, and sodas for everyone.

The writers arrived around five or six o'clock. At times there would be nearly two dozen of them in the room. The better writers were invited nearly every weekday, the lesser ones just once a week. The goal was for each of them to bring in twenty jokes. One by one they would pitch me their best ones. Most of the time it was every joke for itself. Sometimes I asked in advance for material on a particular subject, such as television commercials. Or I'd start a meeting with, "Did you see that on the news? We need to come up with stuff on that." Mitchell Walters, who was one of the Outlaws of Comedy with Sam Kinison, once said,

"Damn man, this place is packed. Pretty soon we'll be having meetings at Dodger Stadium. You'd hear over the loudspeaker: 'Anyone with material on the economy report to second base!'"

I had a guideline sheet I gave prospective writers:

AREAS TO AVOID:

ALL MATERIAL MUST BE AS NONETHNIC AS POSSIBLE

1. *NO religious jokes*
2. *NO ethnic humor (especially NO black humor)*
3. *NO abortion, Kotex, dildo, vibrator, prophylactic jokes, dick jokes*
4. *NO "GOOD TIMES" jokes*
5. *NO ghetto humor*
6. *NO bathroom humor*

Allan Stephan, another of Kinison's Outlaws, would pitch jokes that were too dirty or too rough. When he saw the guidelines, he said, "What jokes *does* this guy do?"

Along with telling writers what not to submit, the guideline sheet did list subjects I wanted jokes for: the economy, women's rights, family, parents, kids, doctors, lawyers, mechanics, dating, marriage, divorce, school, television shows and commercials, smoking, driving a car, diets and exercise, the post office, white-collar crime, and more.

We did not take a poll or a vote on each joke, but there would be a general reaction. If it was positive and I liked it too, I told Mister Geno to write down the joke in his notebook. If there was a lot of grunting and "That sucks!" or I said "No way," the joke was tossed and we moved on. But any critic had to be a little careful—their joke might be next on the firing line. Later, Mister Geno typed up a rundown of the finalists, and at the beginning of the next meeting he passed those sheets around. Often it would be Leno who would say, "Know what might make that work" and offer a fix on jokes that needed improvement.

That room was like the Roman Coliseum of Comedy, except everyone sat on leather couches and the only blood was from egos being stabbed. The writers were incredibly competitive. Their self-esteem was on the line and so too was money. Although I paid many of them on a weekly basis, others would get paid only if I bought a joke, usually for $25. They could be vicious with each other, much like when we hung out at the Camelot in New York or, now in LA, at the Jewish restaurant Canter's or Theodore's coffeehouse.

They would even go after me, the guy writing their checks! Jeff Stein, who partnered with Frank Dungan for what I referred to as Frank 'n' Stein the Monster Comedy Writing Team, would gripe to me when I turned down one of his jokes: "You don't like that joke because you're not funny! That's why you're not getting the laughs you think you should get."

You had to have a thick skin to absorb all the hits. It also helped to be vocal and forceful to push your jokes ahead, to fight for them to get noticed and appreciated. But slugging it out like that was not part of Letterman's self-effacing personality.

I first saw him at the Store not long after he drove out from Indianapolis in 1975 in his red truck and sporting a bushy reddish beard. I thought he had some good quirky ideas but also felt that he probably was not going to be a tremendous stand-up. He was too uncomfortable on stage in the stand-up format. Maybe, I thought, he could be a host of a talk show or game show. George Miller, who roomed with Dave and was another comic I had become friends with, vouched for him, saying, "I think this guy is funny." When I asked Dave to join our writers' meetings, he was very happy. Our sessions were becoming legendary, and he admired many of those in the room—none more than Leno. He was thrilled just to be around those guys.

His wife, Michelle, came with him to LA, but she eventually returned home. When he told me they had split, I said he should get a divorce rather than leave the relationship unresolved.

"You never know what could happen," I warned him as he sat in my townhouse. He looked at me innocently and asked, "What could happen?" I had my lawyer, Jerry, explain to him what he could lose if suddenly he hit in Hollywood. Jerry then helped Dave get his own lawyer and the resulting divorce was without hostility.

I put him on salary at $150 a week even though he thought he was ill equipped to write for a black comic. He has been quoted as saying, "[Jimmie] wanted me to write jokes with a black point of view. He was the first black person I had ever seen." That was an exaggeration. In truth he didn't have any problem coming up with "black jokes," as shown by these he brought to our meetings:

> *Birth control is one of the big problems in the ghetto. When I was a kid going out with girls, they would always say, "If you try to make love to me, are you going to use contraception?" I was never sure what that meant, so I'd say, "Hell, I'll use hypnotism if I have to."*
> (December 14, 1975)

> *You see where police broke up a homosexual slave ring? We had homosexuals back in the old plantation days too. You could always spot the gay slaves. They were the ones picking daisies.*
> (March 19, 1976)

> *I used to be real interested in camping. I'd find out when ya'll were away on a camping trip, then I'd come over and do a little shopping.*
> (April 12, 1976)

Among his nonethnic submissions was a doctor joke you could almost hear Rodney Dangerfield do:

You have to wait forever to see a doctor. Had the forty-eight-hour virus. Went to see my doctor. It cleared up in the waiting room. (February 8, 1976)

Unusual for Letterman would be a sex joke, such as this one:

The University of Washington conducted a study that proved girls with big chests get more rides when hitchhiking than flat-chested girls. Used to be all you needed was a thumb. Now you've got to have two handfuls. (February 8, 1976)

Occasionally he offered a joke that embodied that sharp wise-ass attitude of his, a joke that would probably kill on his show today:

I love professional golf. Only game in the world where a guy gets applause for his putts. (February 8, 1976)

Leno, his idol, rarely submitted any jokes. He would riff on the fly or comment about someone else's joke. He and Mitch were like jazz musicians, playing off the other instruments. Leno was the absolute best punch-up comic. Many times a joke would be close but not quite there. Something would be missing or needed to be tweaked for it to work. Jay was a master at that. He could save a joke like no one else.

However, Jeni and Schimmel were not enthusiastic about writing for me and did not contribute much at the meetings. But they needed the money. That was okay; I was doing well. If I could help them feel as though they were in show business and keep them from having to take a day job, then I was glad to do that. Sometimes, when they needed it, I would just give them $100. I considered it an investment in my career, one that might pay off later. Sometimes, such as when Schimmel needed money to help pay medical bills for the birth of a daughter, it was just the right thing to do.

Jeni was one of the best stand-ups comedy has ever had. Schimmel wasn't far behind, with a stunningly outrageous and explicit act. They thought, why are we writing for this guy? We're better than he is! Schimmel would tell me, "I'm writing jokes for J. J.? I'm not doing any fuckin' dyn-o-mite stuff!"

Louie Anderson was among my second wave of writers, but he was reluctant to come on board because he did not consider himself a joke writer. His style was closer to that of Cosby—more a storyteller. Mitzi Shore, who ran the Comedy Store, didn't think he was much of a stand-up at all and refused to put him in the line-up. "He's just a fat guy," she said. "I can't stand the fat stuff. All he does is the fat stuff and I can't stand the fat stuff."

I knew Louie was better than that, so I encouraged him to focus more on his stories about his large family and growing up in Minnesota. When he was ready, I forced Mitzi to watch his act again. The next week Louie became a regular. He would later pay it forward when he discovered Roseanne Barr when she opened for him in Denver. I then suggested to Mitzi that she team them up at the Comedy Store's new room at the Dunes in Las Vegas. Both became major stars.

I had a few women comedy writers on staff, though Boosler, my all-time favorite female stand-up and a friend from the New York Improv days, was the only one of note. Without question, the women had the dirtiest, funkiest jokes. When they told them, all the guys would cringe. One of Boosler's more mainstream lines was:

> Some guys expect you to scream "You're the best" while swearing you've never done this with anyone before.

Byron Allen was one of the black writers on my staff and the youngest of anyone. He was only sixteen years old. Wayne Kline had seen him perform at the Store, told him I was looking for people to write jokes, and invited him to a writers' session. He came with his mom! He pitched and pushed his jokes like everyone else—while his mom waited patiently in my kitchen.

> *Teachers always say if you cheat you only hurt yourself. I say, "That's okay, I can take the pain."* (Byron Allen, date unknown)

The best pure joke writers were not performers: Wayne Kline aka Wayne Wayne the Joke Train and Steve Crantz.

When Wayne entered the room, everyone thought, "Oh shit. We can't beat this guy." He was so fertile that if you said, "I need a couple of jokes on trees," he would ask, "The bark or the root?" Among his contributions at the meetings:

> *Black folks have a hard time getting credit. The first question they ask is, "Is this the first time you've been turned down for credit?"* (December 10, 1975)

> *I love to watch how men pick up women. Some guys are so uncool. You know how guys brag they never paid for it? I've seen guys out there look like they never got it free.* (March 26, 1976)

> *Used to be black folks couldn't get jobs. Now look in the paper. They got ads just for us. Wanted: bright industrious black college grad. Must have own shovel.* (April 14, 1976)

Steve Crantz was even more prolific, as if that were possible. I met him via fax. He was about twenty-four years old and living in Pittsburgh with his parents. He faxed me a few jokes and I used them. He also sold jokes to Joan Rivers and Rodney "I Get No Respect" Dangerfield. Rodney used this one from him:

> *Oh boy, everybody's got a family stone. I found out what my family stone was. My family stone was gravel.*

Crantz would send me fifty jokes—not a week . . . a day. No other writer would do that. He was amazing. Finally I asked him to come out to Hollywood to write for me and travel as my road manager. He was hesitant because he had never been away from home. But I had my lawyer, Jerry, call his dad, Dave, and assure him that Steve would have a place to live and be taken care of. When he arrived, I put Steve up in an apartment and gave him the use of a car.

The first time he came to a writers' session he fit right in. He was so funny, and he was funny all the time. His business card read: "Comedy Writer . . . I buried more people than Forest Lawn." He was a joke writer, not a sitcom or movie scriptwriter, not a performer. But he was so gregarious—talking all the time—that some people thought he was doing an act. He even looked offbeat—short and, though a young man, completely prematurely gray, and he was a chain smoker, two packs a day. He was totally out there, always "on."

Because he talked constantly, was always doing jokes, having Steve on the road was great because he took the pressure off me. I could just sic him on whoever was talking my ear off, and pretty soon they said, "Okay, I gotta go." But as much as Steve disliked living in LA—it was way too different from Pittsburgh for him—he hated being on the road even more. Two days here then move, one day there then move—that was not a lifestyle he enjoyed. Also, when he was away from LA, he was worried about everything—his apartment near Hollywood Boulevard, his car, anything, and everything.

Most of all, he deeply missed his family. After he was in LA a few months I took a call from his dad. He told me that Steve was afraid to tell me that he had moved back to Pittsburgh the previous day. Steve wanted me to know that he had left the keys to the car in the apartment and that the door was unlocked. Obviously, Crantz and LA were not a match. When I finally talked to Steve, he wondered if it would be okay if he sent me jokes once in a while. I said, "Of course."

Along with traditional comedy writers like Crantz, I wanted wild-man comics like Allan Stephan, Jeff Stein, and Mitch Walters at the meetings. I needed to hear that voice of craziness, people who would break the rules, even mine.

A couple of oddball Jeff Stein jokes (dates unknown):

I travel a lot . . . tried to save some money . . . took one of those no-frills airline flights. It was terrible—they made me row!

I meet some strange girls. I asked a girl out the other night and she asked if she could bring a friend. I said, "Sure." She brought her probation officer.

I needed to hear what was wrong for me, too outlandish for me, so I knew not to go there. Allowing that spectrum in a meeting was important because if I didn't, I would never know what was being done on the sharp edges of comedy, even if that was not a place I wanted to go. I also needed a voice of reason in the room, like Mister Geno or, later, Jimmy Brogan, who understood comedy and I could trust to say to a writer, "Love that but, really, no."

We worked at my house until about seven-thirty or eight at night. Then Mister Geno and I would roll over to the Store. On the way we decided which jokes to test out on stage. Mister Geno had a copy of them and would check them off as I tried them. If the audience liked the joke, he put a check mark next to it. If it flopped, he put an "X" next to it. I almost always taped my shows too. Later, we would go over the tape, analyze the audience responses, and work on changes. My rule has been that if a joke does not work three times, I take it out—no matter how much I personally like it. There are some comics who say, "To hell with the audience, what do they know?" But I believe you have to be true to yourself *and* you have to listen to your audience.

I thought I already had a good work ethic, taught to me by comics such as Brenner. But watching Lear control as many sitcoms as he was—as many as eight in one season—was inspirational. I learned from

him never to be satisfied with a performance, never "phone it in." Lear
told me, "Don't rest on your laurels. Don't just show up to pick up the
dough." To this day I tape the late-night talk shows every night to see
what the new comics are doing and what topics people are talking
about. I am not beyond learning something new.

The best jokes from my writers were collected into "chunks"
arranged by subject and were ready for any television appearance or
major gig. When I appeared on a TV show and did my stand-up, they
would tune in to see if any of their jokes made the cut. If none of them
did, they would not be happy. When they heard someone else's joke,
they would shout at the TV, "That's bullshit! My joke was better than
that!" Then they would come to a meeting and ask, "When are you
going to use my joke?" I'd say, "I'm getting to it, man."

A joke might experience so many changes in meetings or afterward
that in the end you could not decipher the original source. All I know
about the following joke was that it came out of a March 3, 1976 session
with me, Wayne, Jay, Byron, and Dave:

> You all into that astrology stuff? Some girls really believe that their
> lives are controlled by the planets. This fat girl told me the reason
> she ate so much was because her moon was in the house of Mer-
> cury. Looked more like it had been in the International House of
> Pancakes.

Maybe no one wanted to take credit for that one. But with such talent in that room, there were more hits than misses. Some of the un-
credited jokes that earned check marks:

> Kids always say they're seven and a half, eight and a half—always
> fighting for those halves. As you get older, you stop fighting for those
> halves, like you never hear adults say, "Yes, I'm forty-nine and a
> half."

The government just did a study. Found out the reason the unemployment rate is so high is because there are so many people out of work.

Went to the doctor. Had to get an X-ray. Just before the technician took the X-ray he ran behind the screen with me. Said he wanted to be in the picture too.

There's a new course they have in school now called Black Studies. But I always wondered what would happen if I flunked. Would I fade?

An article in Cosmopolitan *says that women can tell a man's sexual prowess by the kind of plants he grows. I'm taking no chances; I have a redwood growing in my bedroom.*

I was on the Johnny Carson show last week and I mentioned in passing that I had never gone out with an airline stewardess or Playboy Bunny before, and I do not believe the response I got. I got like two hundred letters from guys who said they've never been out with one either.

There is one place, however, where even the greatest jokes ever told do not stand a chance—on stage before a rock concert. No one was bigger during his heyday than rock star Peter Frampton, who hit in 1976 with "Baby, I Love Your Way," "Do You Feel Like We Do" and "Show Me the Way," when his folks invited me to open for three upcoming dates.

For the first one there were four thousand fans waiting for him at an outdoor amphitheater in New Jersey. The old line about rock fans at a concert is true: They had their drugs timed for the act they wanted to see—and I was not that act. All they knew was that I was the guy keeping them from seeing Frampton. The reaction was harsh. People were yelling, throwing things—pissed off. They kept screaming for Frampton. I finally yelled out, "Anybody have VD?" They all cheered. After a few minutes I walked off the stage feeling like I had been flushed down a toilet, driven through the sewer system, and dumped into the Hudson River.

The Frampton people still wanted me to do the next date! We flew charter to Vancouver, Canada. This time there were fifty thousand fans waiting at a football stadium. Again, nothing good happened for me. I told them I could not do the third date and flew back to New York.

Sometimes not even a staff of writers can help. Many years after *Good Times* I opened at the Hilton in Las Vegas for Gladys Knight, which I had done many, many times before. I went on stage for the first performance of an eight-night run and did my jokes. The audience was so quiet I could hear the air conditioner blowing. The next day I got an absolutely horrendous review. The writer was not wrong, because there were no laughs the night he was there. I was so unnerved that, before the weekend dates, I flew in some of my writers, including Mister Geno. They watched a show. Once again there were no laughs.

They were as confused as I was. "But these jokes work!" they said. They had no answer. Mister Geno and I resorted to picking up a few joke books and old comedy albums to adapt a few of their jokes. That helped a little, but I still ate it. I never knew why. The next shows I did elsewhere, with the original material, I killed again. Go figure.

I will never forget that week in Vegas, but I have let other bad nights slide. A cliché in comedy is that you never take the audience reaction at a Friday night late show to heart because it is always bad. No one has ever understood the reason. When Steve Martin received a Kennedy Center Honor a few years ago, a reporter said to him, "You haven't done stand-up in twenty-five years but you got a standing ovation tonight. Why don't you do stand-up again?" Martin reportedly answered, "Second show, Friday night."

For my writers who were interested in working on sitcoms, I brought to the meetings scripts from *Good Times*, *The Jeffersons*, and *Barney Miller*, the latter courtesy of Landesberg, who was starring as Detective

Dietrich. I urged them to rewrite the scripts as an exercise, to see if they could improve on the scripts that were being filmed. I also wanted to get them used to not only the sitcom form but also what the writers' room atmosphere was like on a series.

I must have done something right.

After Danny Arnold, the creative genius behind *Barney Miller*, had a heart attack . . . or two or three—he had an oxygen tent on the set so he could continue to work—ABC insisted he bring in more writing help. Landesberg suggested they take a look at the spec script Frank 'n' Stein had penned. By the following season Frank 'n' Stein were story editors. They later won an Emmy for the show and also created *Mr. Belvedere*.

> *People criticize TV commercials, claim they make us do things we wouldn't ordinarily do. It's true. After seeing a couple of commercials the other night, I got so fed up I turned off the TV and read a book.* (Frank Dungan, April 26, 1978)

Nadler met people from the Garry Marshall camp and almost immediately began writing for their smash hits *Happy Days* and *Laverne & Shirley*. He also wrote for *Chico and the Man* and *Perfect Strangers* (which originally was to costar Louie Anderson). Mister Geno would write most notably for *Who's the Boss?* The team of Rod Ash and Mark Curtiss would write for *Fridays*, *Shelley Duvall's Faerie Tale Theater*, and *Sledge Hammer!*

> *Everything is bad for you. I heard the government has just come up with another thing they say you shouldn't put into your body . . . bullets. The healthiest thing you can do nowadays is die!* (Ash & Curtiss, date unknown)

Wayne Kline wrote for *Fernwood Tonight* and *Laugh-In* before I got him on *Good Times*. He then worked at *In Living Color*. Most notably, he became a staff writer on talk shows—in the '80s on *Thicke of the Night* with Alan Thicke and the *Late Show with Joan Rivers*, then for Leno's *Tonight Show* from its debut in 1992 through 2009, when he moved over to the ill-fated *Jay Leno Show*. When Leno threw him overboard, he joined Letterman. Another writer, Larry Jacobson, would sometimes show up at my door at 11 o'clock at night with a page of jokes. He pushed and pushed and finally hit with *Married . . . with Children* before writing for Letterman and then switching to Leno.

The brilliant Paul Mooney wrote for *Good Times* and for me even as he was helping Richard Pryor craft his act in the mid-'70s. Years later he became the head writer for *In Living Color*, where he created Homey D. Clown, played by Damon Wayans. Steve Oedekirk also worked on *In Living Color*, where he connected with Jim Carrey and subsequently collaborated on the *Ace Ventura* films as well as *Bruce Almighty*. He also wrote *The Nutty Professor* for Eddie Murphy and *Patch Adams* for Robin Williams. Jack Handey wrote for Steve Martin and was responsible for "Deep Thoughts by Jack Handey" on *Saturday Night Live*. Allan Stephan would write and produce *Roseanne*. Alan Zweibel (*Saturday Night Live*) and the team of Jim Mulholland and Michael Barrie (the *Tonight Show with Johnny Carson*) probably still owe me some jokes!

Byron went from my writing staff to cohosting the TV series *Real People* for five years. He then went back to stand-up before creating his own syndicated late-night talk show, the *Byron Allen Show*. He sold that show station by station across the country. He would not give up. That series ran for another five years. Now he's a TV mogul, producing and hosting several shows, including *Comics Unleashed*, on which comedians chat about their lives.

Jumping to the head of the class, however, was Letterman, who was given his morning show in 1980. His director was Hal Gurnee, the same director I auditioned for when I made my national TV debut with Jack Paar. Letterman thought his morning show was great, but after weeks of low ratings, the network blew that baby out. He was devastated. Sitting on my couch, he went on and on about how hard he had worked and how he didn't know what he could do next.

"Don't worry," I said, "you'll get another shot." But the truth is that I thought he was done.

I felt the same thing about Steve Martin after I saw him open for singer Phoebe Snow at the Troubadour in LA around 1975. The crowd was filled with industry people—a tough audience. He wore a black suit, not a white one. He did his balloon animal bit. He played the banjo. He died a comic's lonely death.

I went backstage and told him, "Hey man, you have to let this stand-up thing go. You have a nice job writing for that Dick Van Dyke show (which costarred Andy Kaufman). The people in these audiences are the ones who might hire you for other writing gigs. If they keep seeing you do this act, they will never hire you again."

Steve said he had some gigs coming up with the Nitty Gritty Dirt Band and then he was going to New York to guest host a late-night show called *NBC's Saturday Night*. "Then I'll take a look and see what I should do," he said. On that late-night show (which was later renamed *Saturday Night Live*) he sang "King Tut," was one of the "two wild and crazy guys" with Dan Aykroyd, and became a sensation. That's right, people, I told Steve Martin to get off the stage!

I was wrong about him, and I am glad I was wrong about Letterman too.

Since *Good Times*, some people come to a stand-up gig to see Jimmie Walker and some come to see J. J., that kid who popped into their living room and was part of their family once a week when they were growing up. People approach me and say, "How come you ain't smilin'? Say 'dyn-o-mite!'" or "I love the show you did about . . . " But those who knew me prior to *Good Times* were surprised I was so loosey-goosey on the show. They knew me as fairly serious, someone who worked hard and was, basically, a loner. They knew that all I wanted to be was a stand-up comic, not a character on a sitcom.

I wanted people to see me as a comedian, not a cartoon character. Jerry Seinfeld overcame that difficulty perfectly by actually playing a stand-up comic on his TV series. The audience knew that was who he really was. For most of us, though, separating yourself from a successful character is problematic. Michael Richards, Kramer on *Seinfeld*, could not do it. Henry Winkler could not do it.

Leonard Nimoy tried to continue as a serious actor, but his fame as Spock on the cult TV sensation *Star Trek* overwhelmed him. Nearly a decade after he last played the Vulcan on television, he even wrote a book called *I Am Not Spock*.

I can relate.

I am not J. J. I just played him on TV.

What I did not know during the early days of *Good Times* was that J. J. would become a flashpoint for a controversy about race and that I would become the whipping boy.

7

The Whipping Boy

THE POWER THAT CAME WITH FAME DID GO TO MY HEAD—ONCE. Opening for Barry Manilow at the Circle Star Theatre in San Francisco at the height of his popularity, I was feeling pretty good about myself. I had come a long way and so had he—I knew Barry a little when he was the substitute piano player at the Improv in New York. When I arrived at the theater for a rehearsal, I saw a huge concert grand piano taking up the whole middle of the stage. This was a theater in the round. With the piano consuming so much space, I would have to work on the edges of the stage. I told the theater workers to move the piano to the side.

"Excuse us," one of them said, "but it's tuned and can't be moved. Could you work around it?"

"Absolutely not!" Then I went on a rant in front of the entire crew about how great an act I was and that I deserved my place on stage and if they didn't move that damn piano then I was going to walk!

Barry arrived and asked what was the problem. I told him in no uncertain terms. He was understanding but pointed out that if they moved the piano they would have to move it back to center stage after my performance, which would require tuning it again. There wasn't enough time to do that between acts. I did not care—I wanted the piano moved! Finally, the general manager of the theater came to us. I bitched to him too.

He nodded his head. "You're right, Mr. Walker."

I was feeling righteous indeed.

"You're right," he continued. "You should walk. Thank you for coming. You are released from your contract."

"But . . ."

He turned and left.

Everyone in the theater fell silent, including me. I slinked out feeling about six inches tall.

I won't sugarcoat what I did: I was wrong. As my mother would say, I showed out. The worst part was that I imagined everyone there thinking to themselves, "I used to like this guy." I wrote Barry a letter of apology, and to this day I am embarrassed about that incident. I never let anything like that ever happen again.

You are never as big a star as you think you are. Reality will knock you down a peg, sooner or later.

Sometimes when we meet, fans don't realize that they are talking to a real human being and not a TV character. Because I was in their homes every week for years, when people see me in person, they talk to me like a family member, like I know them and they know me. But neither is true. It seems so strange to me when people get so personal when we first meet.

Years after *Good Times* I was working out at a gym and a guy who made Arnold Schwarzenegger look like Don Knotts came up and said, "Mr. Walker, you changed my life."

I puffed up my chest a little, which took some effort.

"When I was a kid," he said, "everybody laughed that I was as skinny and ugly as J. J. on *Good Times*."

The air went out of me.

"I got so tired of that," he went on, "that I started going to the gym, working out. I entered bodybuilding contests. And I won the state championship. I went back to those people and showed them my first-place trophy! After that, they never said I was as ugly as you!"

Nice to hear it. Thanks. I guess.

During the run of the series I was a recognizable figure from TV, but I was a recognizable *black* figure from TV. I was reminded of that while dating Stacey. She loved having her long, blond hair blow in the wind as we rode in my convertible Mercedes. One day driving down Sunset Boulevard a cop pulled us over. I expected him to come to the driver's side and ask for my license. Instead, he went to the passenger side and asked Stacey, "Are you alright? We have a report of a woman being held against her will in a car on Sunset."

Yeah, right.

Stacey said, "No, I'm fine" and made a point of adding, "This is my boyfriend, Jimmie Walker." The cop recognized me, gave me a dirty look, and walked away without another word.

When I was invited to be a contestant on the *Tattletales* game show, I needed to have a woman with me so we could be one of its celebrity couples. I brought Stacey. The producers' faces flushed white—and I mean that in every way possible. They took me aside and said that, though they liked Stacey, they had affiliates in the South, and having her and me together would not be a good idea for the show.

"If you can bring a black girl," they said, "give us a call and we'll have you back."

I asked Jere Fields, a black actress I barely knew, to come on the show with me. We had no relationship whatsoever, but she pretended to be my wife. According to information on the Internet, I have supposedly been married to Jere ever since! This is probably news to her: I have not seen her in more than thirty years. Maybe that is the perfect marriage!

We never went as far as showing a serious interracial relationship on *Good Times*, only an innocent one with young Michael—not as threatening as an adult one. But real life was often reflected in the series. That was no accident. Lear regularly called me and other cast members into the writers' room to meet with them and the story editors to talk about our personal experiences as black men and women. Lear, in particular, wanted to absorb everything he could. Like my white friends at Yankee Stadium when I was a kid, he really wanted to know about us.

For me, these were almost like therapy sessions. A script about how black students were often promoted to higher grades without actually receiving the education necessary? Well, I could certainly talk about that. During the first couple seasons writers such as Roger Shulman and John Baskin, and Kim Weiskopf and Michael Baser for a couple of seasons after them, wanted to know not only what happened but also how I felt about what happened. They listened to what we said and tried to incorporate our thoughts into their scripts. They really cared—and it did not matter whether they were white or black.

Of course, there was not as much merriment in any ghetto, including my Melrose projects, as there was around the Evans household on *Good Times*. We were a sitcom, not a reality show. But there sure was a whole lot more reality than seen in any other TV series of any kind. I think there was more reality than most of today's reality shows!

Good Times explored topics never before explored on television. Our second episode had aspiring artist J. J. paint a portrait of a black Jesus. That episode, about whether to enter the painting in an art contest, would be as controversial today as it was then. (Black artist Ernie Barnes created many of J. J.'s paintings shown during the series, which helped make him and his distinctive style famous.)

Another episode that first season touched on the touchy subject of George Washington being a slave owner. Another slipped in the fact that high blood pressure was the number-one killer of black males. And then there was the one in which J. J. was passed on to his senior year despite failing grades. In that episode the family questioned the validity of standardized testing. An exam asked students to fill in the blank for "cup and _____." But instead of writing "cup and saucer," the inner-city kid wrote "cup and table" because at his poor home they did not have saucers to put between a cup and the table. Other subjects included James being too old for a government job program and the evils of a corrupt evangelist. For story ideas the writers only had to read the front page of the newspaper.

J. J. was always the good kid who should have gone bad but never did. In a two-parter the next season he was accused of holding up a liquor store on his eighteenth birthday, presumably for money to buy art supplies. The entire family held a vigil at the police station while they tried to raise the bail money. Florida was on the verge of an emotional breakdown. James was desperate. They almost turned to a loan shark. Then the real robber was caught and innocent J. J. was released. But he had already lost his job because his employer found out about the arrest.

In another two-parter the Satan's Knights recruited a reluctant J. J. into their gang. With J. J. on his way to a gang fight, James caught up with him to stop him. As the two tried to flee the fight, J. J. was shot. James wanted to hunt down the punk who shot his son, but Florida convinced him to let the system take its course after the boy was arrested. At the shooter's trial James showed compassion for the boy and his broken family.

Another plot that second season depicted a senior citizen with money troubles who was forced to resort to eating dog food. Other subjects: upper-class blacks ("Oreos"), teen pregnancy, and the highly charged issue of bussing.

The shows were thoughtful, which other people were in charge of, but also funny, which was in my wheelhouse. Through all of this, J. J. took the pie. He was goofy and outgoing, confident and street smart; he was never going to go to college, and he was sometimes lazy. He was like a lot of teenagers in any family, black or white. That J. J. existed did not mean that all young black men were J. J. any more than because there was an Arthur Fonzarelli on *Happy Days* that all young Italian Americans were punks in leather jackets. And not so by the way: Both

of them pretended to be more "street" than they really were. At heart
J. J. was genuine and well meaning.

Then, just before the premiere of the third season, all hell broke
loose. Esther said of J. J. in the September 1975 issue of *Ebony*: "He's
18 and he doesn't work. He can't read and write. He doesn't think. The
show didn't start out to be that. Michael's role of a bright, thinking
child has been subtly reduced. Little by little, with the help of the artist,
I suppose, because they couldn't do that to me—they have made him
more stupid and enlarged the role." Negative images, she continued,
"have been quietly slipped in on us through the character of the oldest
child. I resent the imagery that says to black kids that you can make it
by standing on the corner and saying 'Dyn-o-mite!'"

Talk about black-on-black crime! The media—both black and
white—jumped on the controversy. The show that the public and critics had praised for two years was now being trashed by its top-billed and
highly respected star. That was news, and the press took off with it.

I tried to stay out of the firestorm. I responded in the *Ebony* article
with "I don't think any TV show can put out an image to save people.
My advice is do not follow me. I don't want to be a follower or a
leader . . . just a doer." I deflected the subject as best I could when I told
TV Guide that "I'm no actor. I'm a comic who lucked into a good thing.
What the show has done for me, with all that exposure, is get me where
I'm goin' a lot quicker." I told anyone who would listen that kids needed
parental guidance and that sitting them in front of the TV with J. J. as
the babysitter did not qualify.

I never criticized Esther or John. You will not find one negative word
in print from me about either of them. I never had an argument or got
upset with them in person either. It was not in my personality to wallow
in my hurt feelings. It still isn't. I'm a realist. Life is what it is. I accept
what happens and then, hopefully, move forward. Bern Nadette, who
was so close with Esther that they were like mother and daughter, would
say, à la Rodney King, "Can't we just get along?" But I never thought,

"Oh gee, I wish we could be friends and hang out." I did not think that was that important or necessary. I just kept trying to be the funniest I could be on the show—which was my job.

Carl Rowan, a renowned black columnist for the *Washington Post*, had it right: "'Jr.' is a hilarious composite of all those enchanting, exasperating creatures groping along that treacherous path between adolescence and adulthood. If 'Jr.' is a little exaggerated for the sake of belly laughs, well, so was Jim Nabors' portrayal of 'Gomer Pyle.' That's entertainment, baby!"

I could not imagine that any comments I made to the press really mattered in the long run anyway. At the time I was quoted as saying, "I don't think anybody 20 years from now is going to remember what I said." I was a stand-up comic, and when this series was over, I would be on to the next case. So I stood there and took the hits. Lear would say in passing, "You're a good guy for taking all this."

I had no idea that the controversy would become part of television history or that decades later I would be signing memorabilia and t-shirts at *Good Times* events. I had no idea that the stigma would continue to today either. But the accusations of "cooning it up" fit the agenda of the politically correct and have been repeated over and over again. Although I sloughed it off in public, the fact is that Esther's criticism, and also that of John and others—some of it very pointed and personal—seriously damaged my appeal in the black community. I still suffer today from the controversy that they sparked and stoked.

I was wrong about my viewpoint not mattering to posterity. Because this book is my story, it is time for me to finally speak up.

Here are a few facts: J. J. did not smoke, drink, or do drugs. The only thing he was hooked on was Kool-Aid. He was not a criminal, hustler, gangbanger, or shady character. Yes, he did not work much during those first two seasons. He was in high school! Even then, he still had a goal in life: He wanted to be a painter and he worked at his art, boasting that he was "the Van Gogh of the ghetto." Yes, he used the word "jivin'," but he was not illiterate or stupid. He was a nice kid who never hurt anyone and who dearly loved his family. And only one person succeeded by saying "dyn-o-mite!"—me, not J. J.

So what was the problem? Because we were a *black* family, there was enormous pressure for every Evans to be better and for every situation to be cause for progress. For some, such as Esther, that Thelma and Michael were college material was not enough; J. J. had to be too. For her, J. J. could not be "just" funny. In the inflammatory *Ebony* article, she admitted as much, saying that she was "more dedicated to doing a show of worth than to doing a funny show."

Esther was right about one thing: The role of Michael was downsized as time went on. Feeding on the response of the viewers, the show's writers increasingly put the spotlight on J. J. That was unfortunate for the show and for Ralph Carter. Esther stood up for his character, but because Ralph was a kid, he couldn't do as much as the others to fight for stage time.

Making matters worse was that I was the outsider, the stand-up comic, the nonactor in a cast of veterans. During the first season the press was all about Esther and John. Beginning with the second season, however, I was the focus. All actors have egos, and theirs were bruised. At one point the producers stopped bringing all of my fan mail to the set so Esther and John wouldn't get jealous of the thousands of pieces that would pour in every week to me, not them.

Neither of them ever confronted me face to face about their concerns. We never had a discussion about the situation. That was not surprising, because in all the time I was on the show Esther and John rarely ever said a word to me off the set about anything. It sounds crazy and impossible, but that is the truth. They talked to the other cast members, but not to me.

During rehearsals John would talk "about" me rather than to me. He just didn't respect me and what I did as a comic. If I made a funny face, he would say to the director or the other actors, "Do we need to have actors mugging?" If I slipped in a joke in a sneak attack, he would say, "Do we really need that here?" I think he was trying to intimidate me, but I would not back off. He was the father figure on the set, but in reality I wasn't that much younger than he was. J. J. was a teenager, seventeen years old when the show premiered, but Jimmie Walker was twenty-seven. John is only eight years older than me.

I have always admired John as an actor. He has put together a tremendous body of work, including what he did on *Good Times*. His later performances in *Roots*, *Coming to America*, and *The West Wing* were terrific. In 1975, while we were both in *Good Times*, we were also cast in the comedy *Let's Do It Again*, starring Sidney Poitier and Bill Cosby. But, appropriately, we were never in a scene together.

This sequel to *Uptown Saturday Night* was about a pair of blue-collar workers who fix a boxing match by using hypnotism on an unlikely fighter to win a big bet. Given my skinny body type, I was on Poitier's radar for the role of boxer Bootney Farnsworth.

Poitier, who also directed the film, came to the Store to see me perform and afterward wanted to speak to me. But he ran into Landesberg instead.

"Is J. J. here?" he asked in that very soft voice of his.

Landesberg said, "His name is Jimmie, but I think he left."

"I'm doing a movie and I would like J. J. to come in to talk to us."

Landesberg phoned me. "I don't believe it, man, but Sidney Poitier was at the Store looking for J. J. and wants to put you in a movie."

I went to the office of the man, the black icon, who had starred in such great films as *In the Heat of the Night* and *Guess Who's Coming to Dinner* and was the first black to win the Best Actor Oscar, for *Lilies of the Field*.

"J. J., have you ever done movies?" he said.

"My name is Jimmie." Then I told him about my *Badge 373* experience.

"But no major part in a movie?"

"No, but I can do it."

"You don't even know what it is."

"That's okay. I can do anything." You have to have confidence!

Poitier put a director's optical viewfinder up to his eye and stared at me from every angle.

"J. J., let me see if you are mad."

I gave him my "angry."

"Oh, J. J., much too big. Take it down."

So I gave him a "less angry."

"Now let me see you happy."

I flashed him a big smile.

"Oh, J. J., much too big. Take it down."

I did.

"Oh no, less. The camera is not TV. This is cinema."

I smiled again, but less enthusiastically.

"Okay, I will direct you and then I will take it down even further."

I had only a few lines in the film. I spent most of my time boxing. But always Poitier would want my reaction "not so big. We don't want you to jump out of the screen." And he always called me J. J.

Poitier and Cosby would have made a good pairing for an *Odd Couple*. Poitier was so under control, so prepared, so soft spoken. Cosby, however, would hold court. He walked in talking about his comedy and about his life, and he never stopped. If Cosby is not talking, nobody is talking. One phrase you will never hear from Cosby is "So what do *you* think?"

Poitier and his crew would be almost ready for a shot and suddenly Cosby would say, "I got an idea. Hey Sid, why don't we change that so I come in from over here, you put this hat on and these glasses, and then that happens over there?"

A very calm Poitier would answer, "Bill, I already have the scene mapped. We have lighting. We have camera ready. A change would cause many problems."

"Come on, just try it once. Sid! Just once!"

"Alright. We will try it."

They would take another half-hour and make the changes. Then we would do the scene, and nine times out of ten that was the version of the scene that made the film. Cosby does pontificate. He does come down from the Mount with the tablets. But he has usually been right.

The film received good reviews and is still well thought of today. The rapper Notorious B.I.G. even took his alias, Biggie Smalls, from one of the characters. In an era of cheesy blaxploitation flicks, *Let's Do It Again* was a solid comedy.

I was busy on other projects too, from working with my own writing staff and performing at the Store to making my Las Vegas debut opening for Petula Clark at the Riviera and starring in a TV movie.

The Greatest Thing That Almost Happened was about a high school basketball player who learns he has leukemia before the state championship tournament. It was my first, and as it turned out, the only major dramatic role of my career. Talk about being fearless and plowing ahead. The man playing my father was James Earl Jones, probably best known at the time for *The Great White Hope*, for which he was nominated for an Oscar.

Landesberg commiserated with me about my insecurity about being able to hang in there with such an accomplished actor. "Did you know that when Laurence Olivier was going to do *Hamlet*, he felt he was not worthy?" he said dead serious. "I mean, how could he perform that role when the great Gabby Hayes had done it before? That's right. Gabby Hayes was once a great English actor before he left the theater to become Hopalong Cassidy's sidekick."

Steve created the whole bit on the spot. He was terrific with dialects and impressions, and he had Olivier in his refined English accent asking crusty cowboy Gabby, "Why do you want to leave the London theater and go to the United States? You are the best Hamlet ever!"

"I got to be seen!" replied Gabby in his Western drawl. "I got to be seen!"

"But my good man, you are going to play a cowboy."

"If I can play Hamlet," answered Gabby, "I can play Buckshot!"

Steve's bit helped me be a little less nervous when I went in for our first rehearsal.

But when James Earl Jones read his lines, he was completely monotone. No emotion at all. Boring. I was surprised. I thought this guy was supposed to be a great actor. A few rehearsals later he was doing the same thing. I told friends, "What's the big deal about this James Earl Jones?" What a letdown, I thought to myself.

So I was feeling confident about a scene with him on the first day of shooting. Until he opened his mouth. He was excited, completely into the scene, and he nailed it. He was James Earl Jones. I was stunned, wondering where all of this energy came from. Not being an actor, I did not know that he—and many actors—rehearsed at a lower energy level. Once we were actually shooting, he was amazing!

The Greatest Thing That Almost Happened—and even my performance—received very good reviews. I hear James Earl Jones continued with his career too.

I was also finally invited on to the *Tonight Show*, but Carson was not behind the desk. The guest host was none other than David Brenner, just like he said he would be years earlier. I saw him in the hallway of the studio and he said, "Hey, tonight we're going to do that cab story. See you out there." He broke out the cab joke he had concocted so long ago. I couldn't believe he even remembered it.

To the credit of everyone on *Good Times*, despite the jibes in the press, we were always professional at work. A reporter for *TV Guide* wrote that during our second season, at the end of the scene in the Satan's Knights episode in which J. J. was shot and laid on the sidewalk unconscious, James yelled, "Somebody call an ambulance!"

The director yelled, "Cut!"

Amos looked down at me and added, with feeling, "This'll kill us in the Nielsens if he dies!"

But our cast did not have a familial relationship. Amos later told reporters that "although we played a family on the show, the cast was not really like a family. We would punch in and punch out like any other job."

Norman would occasionally host dinner parties, but the entire cast never attended any of them. The Evans Family was a family of orphans. Looking back I think if we had the cast chemistry of a show like *The Jeffersons*, we could have run for a dozen years or more instead of the six that we did.

Of the original cast I got along very well with Ralph, though he was in school for much of the day. He was a cool kid. Bern Nadette was my only close friend, truly closer to me than my own sister. She helped me pick out gifts for girlfriends and hung out with me and my comedy buddies at Canter's and Theodore's. She went to the Comedy Store with us too.

"All you guys talk about is comedy! Comedy and jokes!" she rightly complained.

She was stunned at how visceral the conversations would be. George Miller would just rip people. "He doesn't have any jokes," he would say of another comic in that slow drawl of his. "That's not funny." Anything George said was funny, even the most biting cuts you ever heard. He said of comedy duos: "I love to see double acts break up. Then I can see them fail individually." A typical joke of his:

> I read this article that said your car reflects your personality. I don't have a car.

Bern Nadette tried to get into how comedians are with each other and came to a couple of writers' meetings. Finally, though, after I headed to the Store as usual to try the jokes out on stage, she said, "Stop! No more jokes!"

The attack piece in *Ebony* may have personally offended Lear more than me, because the article also slammed the show for not having enough black writers. No one outside of Norman Lear had done more to further the cause of blacks in the television industry, including behind the camera. Now, suddenly, according to some critics, Lear was running a plantation. After working so hard to make *Good Times* and other black shows happen, the backstabbing broke his heart. Beginning the day he came to the set with that article in hand, he never felt the same toward *Good Times*.

Beginning with that article I have rarely read anything about myself in print. Reading reviews is like an out-of-body experience, as if they are writing about another person. It is said that people believe 90 percent of what they read in a newspaper, but disagree with 90 percent of the 10 percent they think they know something about.

If someone writes something good in a review, they never get it exactly right, so it is not very useful. If it's a bad review, you get upset, which does you no good either. Besides, there is really no reason to read a bad review—because you can count on someone coming up to you and telling you all about it anyway!

"Did you see that review about you? Called you an Uncle Tom! Said you were, and I think the quote was, 'one of the worst things to ever happen to black people in the last thirty years.' I don't agree with that at all. Did you see that?"

"No, but I guess I don't have to now."

I suppose that is why I have never actually seen an episode of *Good Times*. I was there. I know what we did and what the show looked like. People told me all about every one of them—and still do. I know people enjoyed them—and still do—but I never had a reason to watch an episode.

Heading into our third season Amos and Rolle threatened to quit, so they were offered more money to stay. Esther quickly took it, but John hesitated. As he did, the writers came up with storylines about his character's possible departure. That's why John does not appear in two episodes of the third season. In one of them, Lou Gossett Jr. arrived as Florida's brother Wilbert. If John bolted, Uncle Wilbert was in the wings to take over as the man in the Evans household. John agreed to return at the last minute.

For season three I was bumped up in the billing hierarchy with a new credit: "and Jimmie Walker as J. J." on a single card. High school graduate J. J. now had a steady job (at first delivering chicken for the Chicken Shack and then for a rib joint) while attending art school at night. The storylines were as topical and incendiary as ever, including handguns in the home, slimy but smooth politicians, the high cost of medical care, adoption for an unwed mother, the disabled in society (a deaf friend), the numbers racket, lonely senior citizens, and community protests. Those were not even the most controversial.

In one episode J. J. and his girlfriend (played by Debbie Allen) decided to get married despite the objections of both sets of parents. They claimed to go to the prom but instead eloped. When she begins to get sick, J. J. discovers she is a heroin addict. When she loses her drugs, she runs away in search of another score.

In another the FBI came to the projects looking for Florida's nephew in connection with a bank robbery involving the Black Falcons. (Presumably, saying Black Panthers would have been too obvious.) Michael was incensed that the FBI was spending its time on a robbery when there were murder cases involving black civil rights leaders still unsolved. He confronted the FBI agents with "Who shot Medgar Evers?" recalling the activist killed in Mississippi in 1963. Michael and the FBI tangled in another episode after he had a pamphlet about dictator Fidel Castro mailed to the Evans home directly from Cuba.

But the episode that season that has endured the most strongly in pop culture is the one in which J. J. thought he had contracted a venereal disease.

THELMA
You got VD?

J. J.
You don't have to broadcast it on the Six O'clock News!

Ironically, that was among the first times VD was ever mentioned on national television.

J. J. worried that he may have given it to his girlfriend too. He scrambled to get himself cured before his parents found out. In the scene at the health clinic a young comic with a prominent chin and curly hair beneath his wool hat spoke his first lines on national television—Jay Leno. I had been pushing Lear to get Leno on the show for months. Every day I said to him, "How about Jay?" I became so annoying that when I passed him in a hallway, before I could open my mouth, he would say, "Yes, I know, I've got it, Jay Leno!"

Leno's character asked, "What are you here for?"

"I got a cold," lied an embarrassed J. J.

"Cold? That's funny," Leno replied, "everyone else is here for VD."

By any measure season three was as groundbreaking and positive in terms of the image and perception of blacks as the show's first two seasons. The public may not have realized it—and it may come as a shock to media critics today—but the writers and producers decided to cool it with the catchphrase too. For nine of the last ten episodes, J. J. never said "dyn-o-mite." And I didn't have a problem with that at all.

Our ratings did slip. We were the twenty-fourth highest-rated show of the year, with just under fifteen million households watching each week. But that had more to do with the competition than with what we were doing. We had beaten *Happy Days* head to head the previous season. Now Richie and Fonzie had built some momentum and were beating us.

By this point Amos was not happy about anything. Finally, Lear had enough of his complaining. Prior to taping the 1976–77 season—our fourth—he was fired: "I was informed by phone that I was considered a disruptive factor and that my option would not be picked up for that season or any other episodes," John recalled.

Such firings in Hollywood are rarely so public and blunt. When Mike Evans, who cocreated *Good Times*, left his role as Lionel on *The Jeffersons* after its first season, the story fed to the public was that he wanted to concentrate on his *Good Times* writing responsibilities. In truth, he didn't have any. What actually happened was that Evans demanded more money.

The first several episodes of *The Jeffersons* had been filmed; they would begin airing as a midseason replacement in January. We were all gathered at the Tandem Productions Christmas party in 1974, when Evans went up to Lear and asked for a raise or else a release from his contract. Lear turned to one of his executives, Alan Horn, and asked, "Would there be any problem with that?"

"No," said Horn.

"Okay," said Lear, "you're released."

That was not the answer Evans expected. Not only was he immediately replaced, but he was replaced by an actor with his same last name—Damon Evans. Mike would not be seen on *The Jeffersons* again for four years. Ouch.

When Amos was axed, he lashed out and did not mind getting personal. "The writers would prefer to put a chicken hat on J. J. and have him prance around saying 'DY-NO-MITE,'" he screamed to the press. "And that way they could waste a few minutes and not have to write meaningful dialogue." He charged that "the studio wants to boost 'Good Times' mediocre ratings by making Jimmie Walker—who plays my son J. J.—head of the family. What they are after is a powerful character to combat 'The Fonz.' And I'm not the one who can compete with that age group. . . . The character of J. J. will have to mature very quickly if he is going to become the family boss. Maybe he can pull it off. We'll see."

If the decision had been up to me, I would have preferred that John stay and the show remain more of an ensemble. Norton needed Kramden, Fonzie needed Richie, and J. J. needed James Senior. Nobody wanted me up front all the time, including me. Garry Marshall, the genius behind *Happy Days*, managed to get Ron Howard to take a backseat every now and then to Henry Winkler. But Amos was not willing to do the same with me.

Season four's opening episode began with my announcing myself as "Kid Dyn-o-mite!" My credit card now read, "And also starring Jimmie Walker as J. J." For the first time I was officially "starring."

In the storyline of the season's first show James had partnered in an auto mechanic's garage in his native Mississippi, where the Evans family planned to move into a new home. The episode ended with the news that he had been killed in an auto accident. Fans still recall the horrible revelation and Florida's reaction on the following episode: "Damn, damn, DAMN!" That was in a day when saying "damn" was not permissible on television. But this occasion warranted the expletive. That moment was one of the most memorable as well as one of the finest in Esther's laudable career.

With the family fatherless, J. J. became the man of the house. The show continued to tackle difficult subjects, including gangs, drugs, crime, politics, and even atheism, thanks to the introduction of a romantic interest for Florida who objected to "under God" in the Pledge of Allegiance. The Carl Dixon character, played by Moses Gunn, also brought up the subject of cancer when doctors found a spot on his lung.

In one episode that season a corrupt city alderman coerced J. J. into giving a speech on his behalf by threatening to cause the eviction of his family. J. J. took the mike but then mocked the politician. In another show, when J. J. lost his job, he became a numbers runner—the only time he did anything significantly illegal in the course of the series. After he bought expensive gifts for everybody, Florida uncovered the source of his funds. She demanded he quit and, when J. J. refused, she threw him out of the apartment. J. J. moved in with the hustlers and unhappily discovered they were also pimps and drug dealers. When the police raided the place, J. J. narrowly escaped arrest. In another episode a friend of J. J.'s lost his shot at becoming a sports star and became depressed. He locked himself in J. J.'s bathroom and overdosed on pills in a suicide attempt. J. J. saved his life.

This was all in a sitcom! There were episodes that were standard fare, the typical domestic situations that situation comedies always have had. But *Good Times* went as far out on the limb as any sitcom, even those from Lear.

As time went on, the scripts increasingly included aspects of the current lives of the actors, which is typical of TV series that are successful. For example, in season four, J. J. became a talent manager. He discovered first a female singer and, in another episode, a stand-up comic. For the latter he borrowed money from a loan shark to buy a gig at a nightclub. When the comic caught stage fright and bailed, J. J. could not pay back the loan. Thugs were ready to take their pound of his flesh. In the end the club owner paid the loan shark in return for J. J. mopping floors for a month. The name used for the management company on the show was Ebony Genius, which was what I laughingly called myself in my act and, not coincidentally, was the name of the management company I had in real life.

Running Ebony Genius was my lawyer, Jerry Kushnick, and a pit bull named Helen Gorman. During my first year on *Good Times* my ICM agent hardly paid any attention to me. One day his assistant, Helen, realized that I was a client. She told her boss: "There's a guy allegedly with us and you have never visited him on the set!"

He replied, "Hey, we're getting our commissions. So what?"

She asked if anyone was going to "cover" me—in other words, keep track of what I was doing and try to advance my career. Her boss, who barely knew what I did, said he was busy. Helen offered, "I'll cover him," which was very ambitious for someone merely an assistant. After talking to people who thought I was funny, thought I might have a future in show business, she even came to meet me on the set. She was the one who fought for my "starring" credit on the series, something I really didn't want or care about but that meant something in the business.

Meanwhile I had told Jerry about my idea for a management company that specialized in the comedy business, both writers and stand-ups. My theory was that if we could corral the best comedy talent—especially writers—we could become players in television. Naturally, I was thinking about the very talented guys on my staff who could use some management help. I asked Helen if she wanted to work with Jerry on that idea, and she jumped on it. She left ICM, Jerry moved to LA, and around 1975 we formed Ebony Genius Management, with me as president.

I believe I was the only black manager in Hollywood other than those who worked with music acts. The only other possibility would have been Monte Kay, who handled Flip Wilson. In his early years Kay supposedly was not averse to letting black artists think he was a fair-skinned black instead of what he really was—a white guy with a really deep tan.

Among our first clients were Letterman, Leno, Boosler, Frank 'n' Stein, Shirley Hemphill, and April Kelly. I suggested many others who I thought were talented. Helen's first question would always be "What's he going to do for us?" I would answer, "I don't know. But he's funny!"

Helen didn't think Dave or Jay were funny. To her Letterman was a dark, brooding figure. She could hardly understand why he was even trying to do comedy. As for Leno, to her Jay was a crazy guy who wore a stupid hat, a motorcycle jacket, a blue-jean shirt, and a big belt buckle. She especially despised when he would drive up to a Hollywood meeting on one of his big motorcycles. She would be nice to his face, but when he turned his back, the best she could say was "We'll keep him on the road and he'll be happy."

Whenever she wanted to drop Leno or Letterman, I wouldn't let her. When she felt trying to promote them was costing us too much

On my tricycle at eighteen months old, probably for the last time because I never learned to ride a bike!

Courtesy Jimmie Walker

A typical class photo. No inkling of a road comic in the making.

Courtesy Jimmie Walker

My sister Beverly and I during a stay in Alabama. This is about as close as we ever got, and she is obviously not happy about even that.

Courtesy Jimmie Walker

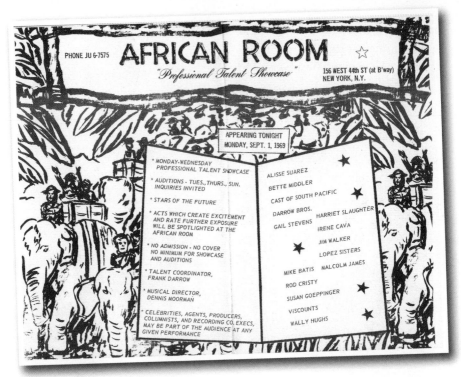

We were all unknowns at the time, as evidenced by the misspellings of the names of Bette Midler and a very young Irene Cara. *Courtesy Jimmie Walker*

Working the Apollo theater, wearing my safari jacket and one of my lucky turtleneck sweaters. I still have all of them, hoping they'll come back in style.

Courtesy Jimmie Walker

At the Improv in New York in the late '60s. Did I mention how much I loved turtleneck sweaters.

Courtesy Jimmie Walker

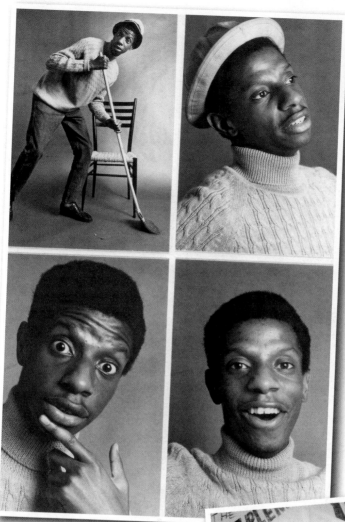

My first publicity photos, except for the one with the broom. That is a current photo of what I'm doing now.

Courtesy Jimmie Walker

As you can see, they spared no expense advertising my appearance at a local event in Harlem.

Courtesy Jimmie Walker

THE HARLEM YOUTH
FEDERATION
PRESENTS
A BENEFIT
DANCE
PLUS
ASKIA MUHAMMAD TOURÉ
*JIM WALKER "THE CONE POET"
SATURDAY APRIL 26 1969
EASTWIND
TIME 10 P.M. 23 EAST 125
WHO SHALL SURVIVE AMERICA?
FOR THE LEGAL
DEFENSE OF THE
HARLEM FIVE
HARLEMS DEFENSE
PO BOX 486
DONATION

Was it something I said
Courtesy Jimmie Walker

Sell, sell, sell!
Courtesy Jimmie Walker

My mother explaining to me why none of my jokes are funny.

Courtesy Jimmie Walker

OFFICIAL MEMBER
JIMMIE WALKER FAN CLUB
THIS IS TO CERTIFY THAT THE BEARER OF THIS CARD IS AN OFFICIAL MEMBER IN GOOD STANDING OF THE **JIMMIE WALKER FAN CLUB** AND AS SUCH, MEMBER IS ENTITLED TO ALL PRIVILEGES AND BENEFITS OF MEMBERSHIP.
CONGRATULATIONS YOU ARE NOW A JJ!

Carol Wilson
Carol Wilson, President
MEMBER'S SIGNATURE **JIMMIE WALKER-JJ FAN CLUB**

Courtesy Jimmie Walker

Dynamite magazine from Scholastic Press premiered in March 1974, the month after *Good Times*, but there was no connection between the two—until I was on the cover in April 1975.

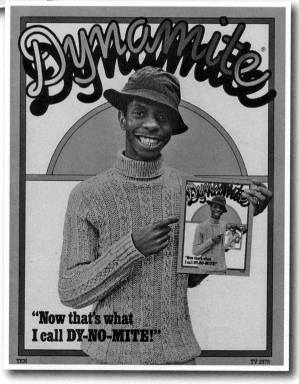

"Now that's what I call DY-NO-MITE!"

Mom and me on the *Mike Douglas Show*. What's with the handholding, Mike?

Courtesy Jimmie Walker

Look ma, on top of the world!

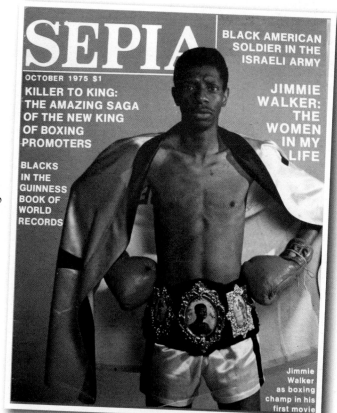

The Comedy Store Bombers, 1978. We were a very serious basketball team, as you can see by our center, Corky Hubbard, holding the basketballs. Standing (left to right): David Letterman, Tim Reid, Lue Deck, Big Roger, Darrow Igus, me, Johnny Witherspoon, Tom Dreesen. Kneeling: Jimmy Heck, Joe Restivo, Daryl and Dwayne Mooney (aka The Mooney Twins), Roger Behr, Jimmy O'Brien, Bobby Kelton. *Courtesy Jimmie Walker*

Friends and others, circa 1976. Seated (left to right): Elayne Boosler, Gene Braunstein, me, Adele Blue, Jay Leno, Michelle Letterman (Dave's wife). Standing: Helen Kushnick, Wayne Kline, Budd Friedman, David Letterman. *Courtesy Jimmie Walker*

One happy family on *Good Times* with the original cast. Top row: Me, Bern Nadette Stanis, Ja'Net DuBois. Bottom row: Ralph Carter, Esther Rolle, John Amos.

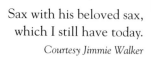

The only one who seems to be really happy is me!

Sax with his beloved sax, which I still have today.
Courtesy Jimmie Walker

money, she refused to pay the office expenses for making copies of their photos, résumés, and tapes as well as the postage for sending them to club owners, producers, and so on. I stepped in and paid for them out of my own pocket for two years. I did not want to give her any excuse to cut them loose—and I never told either of them.

I spent a lot of time and effort to get Leno work, and not just on *Good Times*. Merv Griffin liked having me on his show, so I told Paul Abeyta, his talent coordinator, that I would go on but only if for every time I was on, he would also give Leno a shot. And that's what he did. Sometimes Abeyta would call and say, "Yes, I know, a shot for Leno, but we need *you* for the show on Tuesday."

We started cooking, baby! Jay was on the road doing gigs nearly every week of the year; Frank 'n' Stein landed *Barney Miller*; April hit with *Mork & Mindy*.

No one came further than Shirley Hemphill. She arrived in LA from North Carolina with nothing. She was one of the rare black female stand-up comics. Nearly every night she showed up at the Store hoping to get on stage. We did not know that she was living in a single room on Skid Row in downtown Los Angeles and would walk the miles and miles to the Sunset Strip. When we found out, Johnny Witherspoon or I began to drive her home at night. I brought her to Ebony Genius and got her work on the road, an acting spot on *Good Times*, and finally the role of Shirley, the wisecracking waitress, on *What's Happening!!* Her proudest moment was when she was able to buy her own home.

In early 1977 Helen placed Letterman on *The Jacksons* variety show, where he received his first national exposure as a performer, and then on the *Starland Vocal Band Show* variety series that summer. We even produced a variety-show pilot called *Rising Star* that featured me, Letterman, Leno, his girlfriend, Adele, and a comedy troupe called the Village Idiots.

Boosler was getting some heat too. We had first met in New York at the Improv. Between comedy acts she would sing in a duo with Shelley Ackerman. But when they hung out with us comics at the Camelot, they were both very funny and could hold their own. I told them they could be a comedy team. They insisted they were singers.

But when she performed on her own, Elayne did throw in some jokes, much like Bette Midler had done. She was intelligent and had great stage presence as well as a huge set of balls. One of her early lines:

> *Hookers! How do they do it? How could any woman sleep with a man without having a dinner and a movie first?*

She was only twenty-three years old when I fought to get her onto the Ebony Genius roster. *New York* magazine did a major article on her the next year. "She can't miss," I told the writer. "Every time I talk to her on the phone she's killing me. Besides, there's no way that being the best-looking female stand-up of all-time is going to hurt her either." She already had her "identifier," the joke that audiences connect to a particular comic:

> *Sometimes I just don't feel wanted. Last night I went out with a guy who faked premature ejaculation.*

When she was doing stand-up regularly, Boosler was the best female comedian there was. But we never could break through to the big time with her. Elayne lacked vulnerability, and—forget political correctness—men want at least a little vulnerability in women, including comics. She was a bit too tough onstage and, maybe more importantly, in meetings with entertainment executives. She took no bullshit, no matter whose office she was in. I think a lot of the Jewish guys in the business felt emasculated by her, a Jewish woman, and backed away from collaborating to make her the star she deserved to be. Still, back then the headline of the *New York* magazine article was right on— "Funny Girl: New, Hot, Hip."

Life was good for everyone, except Jerry's wife, Lillian. I would drive to their house, and Helen would be there working. I didn't know where

Lillian was. When I left, sometimes after midnight, Helen would stay behind. I wanted to say, "Need a ride somewhere?" but it was not my place to interfere in their lives.

At 8 o'clock the next morning I would go to our office at 9000 Sunset Boulevard, and Jerry and Helen would already be there. Their relationship was something I knew was happening but did not want to know was happening. I felt for Lillian and their kids. But Jerry soon shacked up with Helen and divorced Lillian. Helen Gorman became Helen Kushnick, the name by which she would become infamous during the coming Late-Night War.

There was another name change too. I noticed that my company title had become vice president and then secretary. When I asked Helen about that, she said, "You know, we can't walk around as Ebony Genius. You're a comic. People don't look at you as a manager, a business guy. Let me and Jerry take it over."

"But we're doing well," I said, not at all happy about this palace coup.

"Jimmie, it's hard for us to sign new clients when they see us as Ebony Genius."

"Come on, people don't care what the name is or who's behind it as long as they're working."

Helen was the kind of person in Hollywood who you might not like but you wanted on your side. And if she was not on your side, you hoped she was not against you. She was a shrewd negotiator and would do anything—lie, cheat, or step on anyone—to get what she wanted. She kept pounding me about leaving the company and would not let up.

All I ever wanted from the management company was to make it possible for Letterman, Leno, and all my guys to work. I knew how miserable Helen would make my life until I gave in. I wanted peace, not constant war. Finally, I agreed to leave. I sold my share of the company for $10,000. That's right, people: I signed away the management fees, usually 15 percent, on everything Letterman, Leno, and all of the others did for only $10,000. That was not a smart move—not then and definitely not later—though no one at the time knew what Letterman or Leno would do in the future.

That future arrived sooner than I expected. Maybe Helen already knew, as I was conveniently exiting Ebony Genius, that NBC was thinking about giving Letterman a morning talk show. But though Letterman liked Jerry, he was not a fan of Helen. He knew that with me out of the company, he would have to deal directly with her—and he dreaded that. So when esteemed managers Jack Rollins and Charles Joffe—whose clients included the likes of Woody Allen, Billy Crystal, Robert Klein, and Joan Rivers—approached Dave, he listened. They were among the best managers anyone could have, and they could take Letterman to the top, which is what they told him.

"I'm really thinking about moving to Rollins and Joffe," Letterman said to me.

"Look, Dave, I said when you signed with us that if you wanted to go someplace else, you could go someplace else. We will never do anything to stand in your way."

"I'm glad I have your blessing."

But when Helen found out about his decision, she threatened Rollins and Joffe. Unless they paid up, she was not going to let Letterman free of his contract.

I got in her face. "I promised Dave we were not going to stand in the way!"

"You are no longer part of the company," she shot back. She was right. Gone was Ebony Genius; they were now General Management. "We'll do what we want," she said. "Fuck you!"

Rollins and Joffe paid them for Dave's contract, perhaps $25,000. Whatever the figure, that was a good deal for Rollins and Joffe. But the money was not the point. I keep my word, and Helen had broken it for me. She was unscrupulous, a quality that Leno would better understand at a later time.

Jerry remained my lawyer, which turned out to be fortunate for my mother.

After almost twenty years of marriage Mr. Boyce passed away from cancer. Almost immediately my mother tried to contact my father again. When she told me, I was furious: "I'm telling you right now, if you ever talk to *him* again, I'll never talk to *you*."

She tracked him down anyway. He was living in a nice apartment in Brooklyn, off the river. He had not changed at all: He was over sixty years old and had two girlfriends. And now my mother became his third girlfriend. She would go all the way to Brooklyn from the Bronx to clean his apartment so other women could join him there at night.

This was beyond my comprehension. I had been giving her money for this or that and I wanted to buy her a house, but I told Jerry to stop all that. I did not want my father to get his hands on any of the money I made and gave to her. He said he would do that.

I found out later that he lied and kept my money flowing to her. He even arranged to buy her a house with my money. He meant well. He said, "She's your mother! Come on, she's your mom!" But I did not want her to be with my father. Yet I could not stop her. All I could do was refuse to talk to her, which I did for three years.

In its fourth season *Good Times* had held its own in the ratings, still Top Thirty, still nearly fifteen million households, even with yet another day change, to Wednesdays. In the second to last show of the season J. J. said "Dyn-o-mite!" for the final time. In another of the last episodes that season Esther said "dyn-o-mite!" for the first time.

Perhaps that was too much for her to swallow.

She had lobbied from the very inception of the show that this black family would not be a single-parent household, that there would be two strong family figures, male and female. And J. J. was not the male role model she had in mind. The introduction of Dixon, the owner of a small appliance repair shop, did not fill the void either. Under the pretense of illness Esther left the show the summer after season four.

When season five began, viewers were told that Florida and Carl were married and living in Arizona. They were not to be seen. Ja'Net was now top billed and Johnny Brown, who played building superintendent

Nathan Bookman in earlier episodes, came on board as a regular cast member. I was excited to have Johnny around because he too was a stand-up comic, so he naturally became my best friend on the show.

Another new member of the cast was Janet Jackson, who played Penny Gordon, a victim of child abuse who followed J. J. home one day because she had a crush on him. No episodes of the series were more serious than these involving child abuse. Penny was from a single-parent home, and her mentally stressed mother, played by Chip Fields (who had not landed the part of Thelma years before), burned her with an iron and broke her arm. Neighbor Willona, now the surrogate mother for the Evans Family, adopted her.

Janet was only about nine years old, but she was a great little actress. She was a stage veteran even at that age, having been in The Jacksons and also on the *Sonny & Cher Show*, where she played a tiny Mae West character, a bit she repeated on *Good Times*.

Coincidentally, around the same time I was linked in a weird way to her brother Michael. Director Sidney Lumet saw me at the Store and wanted me to play the Scarecrow in *The Wiz*, the film adaptation of the Broadway musical that was an all-black version of *The Wizard of Oz*. I guess he figured I sure looked like a scarecrow. There was no audition, but the filmmakers did ask if I could dance. I said no, I could not dance at all, which is the truth, despite J. J.'s antics. That didn't seem to bother them. They said they would work around my disability and they put an offer on the table. Diana Ross was set to star as Dorothy and my old friend Richard Pryor was the Wizard. I also knew Nipsey Russell was cast as the Tin Man because he called to encourage me to sign the contract.

But *Good Times* could not free me for the several weeks I needed to be away to shoot what became the most expensive movie musical produced to that time. Replacing me as the Scarecrow was a guy who really could dance, Michael Jackson. That's right, people: Michael Jackson was the second choice! I wasn't terribly disappointed about losing the role, though, especially after the film became one of the biggest bombs in movie history.

Many years later I was playing the Palace Station in Vegas and was into my Michael Jackson chunk, which was killing. I have always done jokes about the Jacksons. An old one:

Things are so tight, the Jackson 5 had to lay off two brothers.

Now Michael was the focus:

Is it my imagination or is Michael Jackson getting whiter by the minute? Really, I remember the old days when he was black.

I looked into the front of the audience to my left and saw an older man getting up and rumbling around.

Now he has this little Debby Boone nose. He can't even breathe through that thing anymore. It's embarrassing what's going on, it's embarrassing for all black people.

Though the audience was laughing, I heard the foulest language coming from the old man in front.

"You motherfucker! How dare you! You're a piece of shit!"

Sometimes people don't like the act, but this was way out of line. I looked a little closer at him—and I recognized Joe Jackson, father of Michael, Janet, Jermaine, Tito, Jackie, Marlon, and Randy.

He waved his cane menacingly at me and limped onto the stage, screaming, "How dare you attack my son! He has more talent in his right pinkie than you have in your whole body!" The audience, however, could not hear what he was saying.

I was so surprised that I did something a stand-up is not supposed to do with an audience member—I touched him. I went to him, grabbed his hand and turned him around to face the audience.

"I was just talking about the King of Pop," I announced. "The man who produced the King of Pop, ladies and gentlemen, Mr. Joe Jackson!"

The crowd, of course, applauded like crazy. A big smile swept across Jackson's face, and he happily waved to the audience. As he walked off the stage he said, "Don't you ever fuckin' say anything about my son again!"

Back on *Good Times*, J. J. grew up in season five. Working full time as an artist at an ad agency, he truly took on the father role. From vetting Thelma's new boyfriend and disciplining Michael, who the police caught with Penny joyriding in a stolen car, to having an affair with a married woman that caused him to develop an ulcer—J. J. matured. Gone too was the blue hat.

That season also had the strangest episode in the entire run of the series, when J. J. dreamed about being white and thus getting a promotion. The blue hat returned for only that episode to help identify J. J.'s alter ego, played by a white actor. The episode was so noteworthy that the *Wayans Bros.* show parodied it nearly twenty years later, with Bern Nadette, Johnny, and Ja'Net making guest appearances. Shawn Wayans played J. J. and Marlon Wayans played Michael.

In their sketch they turned the idea upside down, with Shawn upset over the Affirmative Action aspect of a computer firm hiring him only because he was black. He then dozed off as he watched a *Good Times* marathon and dreamed he was in the sitcom as J. J., who was in a similar situation and seeking advice from Willona, Thelma, Michael, and Bookman. When he woke up, Shawn said, "That's it, that's what I'm going to do!" A sitcom had given him the solution to his dilemma. Doesn't it always?

Our ratings for the season plummeted as we barely cracked the Top Forty. With John and now Esther gone too, there was no family on *Good Times*—and the audience changed the channel.

Lear phoned Esther on the set of *I Know Why the Caged Bird Sings*, a TV movie in which she was starring, and asked her to come back. He sent her two dozen roses, promised her a raise, and assured her that the character of J. J. would be modified and that Carl Dixon would be wiped from existence. She never approved of the Dixon character, believing

Florida would not have moved on so quickly after James's death and that the devoutly Christian woman would never fall for atheist Carl.

Esther returned for the 1978–79 season back on top of the credits—and her crusade against J. J. continued. She explained to a reporter for a black newspaper, "I go to schools in underprivileged areas and the first thing the children say to me is, 'Where's J. J.?' I tell them, 'I hope he's in the library learning to read. Don't emulate J. J., copy Jimmie Walker.' Jimmie Walker is a hardworking young man." She added, "Jimmie and I don't have a great relationship, because we are two different people. I can work well with him, but I can work well with the Devil."

Thanks. I guess.

Again she lambasted the show for not having more black writers: "You can't tell me what it's like to be black unless you are black. . . . We've usually had a fringe black writer on the show but one without too much to say."

Again, a few facts: During our first three seasons creator Eric Monte wrote the pilot (he also wrote the popular film *Cooley High*, which became the basis for the TV series *What's Happening!!*) and Bob Peete, who wrote several scripts, became a story editor and production consultant. He would later write and produce for *What's Happening Now!* and *Amen*. Thad Mumford (*The Cosby Show*) wrote for us and so too did Paul Mooney and Levi Taylor.

Another fact: Black viewers did not notice the color of the writer. Of all TV series—dramas and comedies, black or white—blacks rated *Good Times* among their top three favorites throughout its run. Obviously, the writers did not have to be black for the black audience to love *Good Times*.

Nevertheless, Lear scoured the country, turning over every rock at every black college, in an effort to find good comedy writers who were black. Nothing would have made him happier than to have a staff of black comedy writers. Me too, not only because it would help *Good Times* but also because I could bring them to Ebony Genius, which was still going at the time. An issue of *Black Stars* magazine from April 1976 quoted me saying, "I've been looking every place, man, but I just haven't been able to find any good craftsmen in the field. If I can find some they got a job, it's that simple." I gave my office address and begged for anyone interested to get in touch with me. Lear too had an open-door policy, one not available to white writers. But sitcom writing is specialized and difficult, and neither Lear nor I would accept mediocrity just because someone was black.

That is why when we discovered Michael Moye, it was an extraordinary event. Right out of college, his spec script was so good that we shot it almost exactly like he wrote it. That almost never happens with even a veteran writer. He penned several episodes during our last couple of seasons before writing extensively for *The Jeffersons*, developing *Silver Spoons* and, most notably, creating *Married . . . with Children*. In fact, the original idea for *Married . . . with Children* from Moye and his partner Ron Leavitt was that the series would be the anti–*Cosby Show* in philosophy and feature an all-black cast. That would have been even more revolutionary than *Good Times*—a black sitcom with characters you did not have to like.

Though we had shows that final season about alcoholism, the lack of medical care for the poor, and interracial dating, the series became far less edgy than it had been earlier. Ratings continued to slip, until we were barely in the Top Fifty. The show was pulled off the schedule in January 1979. Beginning in May several more shows aired, and a final wrap-up episode was broadcast on August 1.

Titled "The End of the Rainbow," the happy ending conclusion found Michael heading off to college, Thelma's athlete husband Keith signing with the Chicago Bears, and Thelma announcing her pregnancy and asking Florida to live with them in their new condo to help with the baby. Willona was also moving and, as it so often conveniently turns out in sitcoms, to the same Bakersfield Street complex in an affluent Chicago suburb as Thelma and Keith. The Evans Family was finally leaving the ghetto.

J. J.? He proudly strutted around in his superhero outfit as Dyn-O-Man and revealed that he had sold his Dyn-O-Woman comic strip. He had succeeded, fulfilling his dream of becoming an artist.

Good Times aired between a rock and a hard place. If we had been a white show, we would never have lasted six seasons. Being a black show is what made us unique and special. Blacks could relate to us, and whites were curious about us. However, being a black show that tried to be socially relevant cut short our run. We had to be more than a sitcom; we had to be important. The characters in our show always had to rise up, always had to be better than other people. We were not allowed to just be a sitcom, and J. J. was not allowed to just be the guy who takes the pie. No other sitcom had ever been saddled with those expectations, not even *All in the Family* or any of Lear's other comedies. The Evans Family had no choice but to overcome.

In the end Lear was proud of the show. "The white audience had an opportunity to have a black family in their homes every week," he later said. "They were there because they were funny; they were there because they were facing problems that white families were facing; they were there because on some subliminal level, if no other way, people realized that what hurt me in my white family hurts them too . . . The oneness of the black experience and the white experience, I think if it [the series] mattered at all, that's the way it mattered the most."

On *Good Times* J. J. made people laugh, but it was Norman Lear who made them think.

Good Times was unlike anything on television then and still today, whether a comedy or not. I think the show would be too edgy for network TV today. In the mid-'90s, several years after he was the king of sitcoms, Lear tried another spin-off of *All in the Family*. For *704 Hauser*, a black family moved into the Bunkers' old house in Queens. The father was played by—guess who—John Amos. The son was black but with the twist that he was not liberal; he was an arch conservative, holding views not unlike my own in real life. He also dated a white Jewish woman, again reflecting some of my own life. I wonder if Amos realized that this time he was playing a father figure not to J. J. but to a character much more like Jimmie Walker!

I talked to Lear when he was writing the pilot episode at his summer home in Vermont. He said he wanted the show to be gritty and urban and funny—like *Good Times*. I told him, "Well, there is no better place to be inspired to write a gritty, urban show about blacks than Vermont." Only five episodes aired in 1994. America no longer wanted socially relevant sitcoms.

In 2006, at the Fourth Annual TV Land Awards, *Good Times* received the Impact Award for being "a show that offered both entertainment and enlightenment, always striving for both humor and humanity, with comedy that reflected reality."

I guess J. J. wasn't such a "negative stereotype" after all.

8

Freddie, Richard, Andy, Mitzi, and Budd

THE COMEDY BUSINESS HAD MOVED FROM NEW YORK TO LOS ANGELES. For stand-up comics success on a series had become the fastest road to fame and fortune. I wasn't the only comedian from our crew in New York to have a sitcom in LA—just the first: Freddie arrived too, cast in *Chico and the Man* after a spectacular shot on the *Tonight Show*.

Freddie and I both made our network television debuts on *Jack Paar Tonite*, and both of our sitcoms debuted in 1974: *Good Times* in February and *Chico and the Man* in the fall. In the TV world I was the young black and he was the young Hispanic. But we had different views of success. The hotter he became, the more out of control he became. Sex, drugs, and alcohol dominated his life, and many of the people around him fed his ego and his demons. Some people gave Freddie drugs, and TV producers gave him a new blue Corvette. Today we call them enablers.

Freddie always called me a "goody two-shoes." I didn't drink or use drugs and I wasn't a partying kind of guy. But we were still friends. He lived a few blocks from the Store, along with more than a dozen other comics, in an apartment building that came to be known as Fort Bursky, because it was managed by the parents of comic Alan Bursky. Bursky had, at age eighteen, been the youngest comic ever to appear on the *Tonight Show*. But he didn't have enough shots ready, and so his career never lived up to its beginning. Freddie would call and say, "Let's go over to Hollywood Boulevard." Along with Bursky, we would stand in front of the teen magazine section of a giant newspaper stand. Freddie was on the cover of dozens of those magazines. He stood there hoping people would recognize him.

The next year *Welcome Back Kotter*, which starred Gabe Kaplan, another regular from the Improv, hit the air. The actor who played the breakout character Vinnie Barbarino was a young John Travolta, and suddenly he was on the cover of those same teen magazines. Freddie was incensed. He bought a high-powered crossbow and went with some friends to Travolta's apartment. I doubt if he meant to kill Travolta, but he sure wanted to scare the hell out of him.

He knocked on the door but no one answered. Thank God. Freddie fired a few arrows into the door and left. Hey John, now you know where those arrows came from!

Unlike Freddie, I preferred my privacy. When I went home to New York for the premiere of *Let's Do It Again*, I wasn't able to walk around the streets at all. I had to hole up in my hotel room. I did not like that. I remembered the story about the restaurant busboy who became a star. When he was a busboy, he had to eat in the kitchen. Then he finally made it—and he still could not eat in the dining room because he caused too much excitement as people came up to ask for autographs and pictures. So again he had to eat in the kitchen.

Freddie did not know that fame does not make you happy. But there he was: famous *and* unhappy—he was always telling people how unhappy he was. He did not know how to deal with that, at least not alone. He would phone me at three in the morning and say, "Hey man, I'm really depressed. Could you come over?"

"Freddie, it's three a.m.!"

"I understand. No problem."

He sounded so desperate and pathetic and alone, so I would rush right over. I'd find his apartment filled with people, and he'd say, "Hey, I just wanted to see if you would come." He was in constant need of attention.

In 1975 we were both in Vegas, with Freddie headlining at Caesar's Palace and me opening at the Riviera. He seemed very happy, which was very unusual. He said he was getting married.

"But Freddie, you're nailing every chick in town! How are you going to be married?"

He had met a cocktail waitress at the casino. "She thinks I'm great. She loves me. She understands me." That's what he wanted and needed to hear.

"Freddie, it's never going to work," I warned.

"Fuck you! You're a pussy! You don't know me!"

So he and Kathy Cochran married.

When I was back in LA, I saw Freddie—with another woman.

"Freddie, what about this marriage thing?"

"Man," he said, "I just couldn't resist."

Even though I saw him with other women—even during the time he was so happy because Kathy was pregnant . . . and with a boy—I never saw him and Kathy together. After Freddie Jr. was born, that was all he talked about. He loved his child so much.

Then one day, a week after he performed at President Jimmy Carter's inaugural ball, he met me at a club and he was as down as I had ever seen him. Kathy was divorcing him, on the grounds that his drug dependency threatened her safety and that of their child. He told me he loved her. He could not believe she would leave him.

"Really, Freddie? How about she's leaving you because you're still dating!" He gave me an evil look.

The next day I received a call saying that Freddie had shot himself and was in serious condition. He died January 29, 1977. He was twenty-two years old.

Some say Freddie committed suicide. They told police that he made a series of phone calls to friends and family saying that "life isn't worth living." But Freddie was always doing that. Many times he would play Russian roulette in front of people who did not know his gun was unloaded. It scared the hell out of them. That's what he wanted—for them to be concerned about him. That final night, even after his worried business manager showed up at his hotel room in Westwood, Freddie continued to make those calls. The manager dialed Freddie's psychologist, who told him that the comedian was acting out, that he was in no danger.

After he phoned his mother and Kathy, Freddie reportedly pulled a .357 Magnum from under his sofa. The manager intervened and the gun went off. Freddie shot himself in the head.

I was flying to Union City, New Jersey, to play the Latin Quarter when I heard the news. Within minutes Brenner, Gabe Kaplan, Landesberg, singer Tony Orlando—who was a very close friend of his—and I, along with still others, called each other. At first we were told he might pull through, then that he might have brain damage. When I arrived at the airport, I was told he was dead.

I went on stage that night and said, "You may have already seen this on the news. Freddie Prinze has passed away. He was a friend of mine. I will always miss his funk and his swagger."

Like his mother and many others I believe Freddie did not commit suicide. I believe he was simply looking for sympathy, was playing at shooting himself, and accidentally, tragically, did. In fact, the original suicide verdict was later officially changed to "accidental shooting."

Suicides, say the experts, rarely pull the trigger with others watching. Freddie wanted attention—nothing more and nothing less. There was nothing any of us could have done to forever fill that need in his life. However, I cannot help but think that Freddie would still be alive today if Brenner had been around to give him guidance. Brenner was older, had more worldly experience than us, and his intellect and advice meant a lot as we grew up both on stage and off. He was our mentor, our House Dad. But he was a Philly/New York kind of guy. He hated LA. When we went west, he stayed behind.

Freddie was chronically unhappy, but that did not make him much different from any other comic. I always say that there is no such thing as a happy comedian. Off stage, we are always bitchin' and complainin' about somethin'—money, clubs, billing, whatever. There are a few who are content, but for the vast majority there is always something to make us dissatisfied. The only place we are happy is on stage trying to make people laugh.

When I get on stage, that is my heroin fix. I'm on top of the world. Leaving the stage, there is still a little bit of a high as people come up to say they liked me. But as soon as I walk outside into the night, that feeling disappears. I come down as fast as a junkie. The approval of strangers had filled a hole that now returns. The next day there are agents who will not pick up my calls, club owners who will not answer my e-mails. There is rejection, again and again—until the next time I get back on stage and hear the laughter of strangers. I am thankful for my heroin, those minutes I get on stage.

Life, however, happens off stage.

I met Lilly when she was a twenty-year-old student at Santa Monica College. With long black hair and often not wearing makeup, she looked like singer Rita Coolidge. Extremely bright, shy, and quiet, she had been estranged from her family and living with friends for a few years. She didn't watch much TV and wasn't starstruck by Hollywood. Instead, she spent most of her time reading and studying. Unlike with my second Barbara, we never argued, never got loud or crazy. We had such a smooth relationship that one day I realized we were living together and wondered how that happened.

I am not easy to live with, but Lilly made everything easy for me and for us. She would never interfere or bother me when I was working. When she needed to study, she would go into the spare bedroom. Sometimes she traveled with me when I went on the road. And she laughed at my jokes! What more could a comic want? But still I fooled around with other women. Lilly knew but never called me on it. Women are my one vice. That is one reason why I could never marry. Unlike Freddie, I know I could not be faithful. Yes, I am a dog, but at least I am an honest dog.

After a weekend alone on the road I came home to find Lilly more quiet than usual. She said nothing was wrong, but I knew something was. I finally coaxed it out of her: She was pregnant. She said she was happy about that. But I was not. I never wanted to have kids. When I was with wild-child Barbara, her desire to have children was a stumbling block in our relationship. I never thought I would be a good father. I never had the role model that would show me how to be one.

Lilly was understandably upset about my reaction. She said I would not have to take care of the child, that she would do everything. But like marriage, I felt that if you made a commitment, then you should stick to it. If I was going to be a father, then I was going to be a father. It would have to be "us," not "her." And I was not capable of "us." A couple of days later she had an abortion.

The drive home from the doctor was somber and silent. We never talked about the abortion again. She fell into her regular routine and was as nice and easy as ever with me. But when she went into the spare bedroom to study at night, I could hear her softly crying. Increasingly, she spent more and more time in that room.

I was on the road as much as ever. One night I met a woman at a club and we went to a hotel room. After the abortion this was the first time I had slept with another woman. A neon sign flashed over the bed board proclaiming the obvious: I am not good enough for Lilly. I recognized that I was too selfish to be able to be a bigger part of her life. When I returned home, I told her I would get her an apartment of her own. She never said a word, which said a lot—in her heart she had already moved on. We found an apartment she liked and she moved in. I took care of her for more than a year after that.

Lilly would have been a great mother. I know she was the best woman I have ever been with. I wish I had known that at the time.

At least I didn't have a drug problem to go with my relationship problem. Just like Freddie, Richard Pryor had a drug problem and a woman problem. His second marriage (he was married seven times to five different women) was to Shelly Bonis, a blonde Cher look-alike from Beverly Hills, and they had a daughter, Rain. I remember once going to Richard's house in Northridge to babysit her, and there was a carafe of cocaine on the coffee table. Richard pointed to it proudly and said, "Walker, I have your whole year's salary on that table!"

Pryor was hardly the only one indulging back then. Danny Aiello and I went to see Richard at a Madison Square Garden concert produced by Sid Bernstein and headlining Sly and the Family Stone. Compared to Sly, Richard was a weekend warrior. As we stood backstage Sly announced that he would not go on until he was given a brick of cocaine. The wheels were quickly set in motion. But the delivery would take a while.

Singer Kathe Green went on. Then Richard went on—and was booed off the stage as comics always are when opening for a rock act. The coke still had not arrived. They sent out Rare Earth, Motown's token white act, and told them to stretch their time. By the end of their set Sly had scored his coke. He was now also very stoned. He walked on wearing a fur coat and a fur hat, and he then proceeded to fall off the stage.

I had no desire to imitate Sly or Richard or Sam Kinison, who was in the worst shape of anyone I ever saw when he performed at the Riviera in Vegas one New Year's Eve. Surrounded by his Outlaws of Comedy, including Carl LaBove, Jimmy Shubert, and Allan Stephan, Sam sat in a chair in his dressing room. It was pitch-black except for one small light, but I could see a small pile of cocaine on the table next to him.

"Hey, Sam, how are you?"

"Jimmie Walker?"

"Yeah, man. I just came to see the show."

He mumbled something incomprehensible and then tumbled off his stool. Carl picked him up and placed him back on the stool.

A Riviera exec who was there was worried. "Are we going to be able to get him on stage?" he asked. Carl took him to a corner of the room where they had an animated conversation.

"Oh yeah! Everything's good," I heard Carl say as they came back to us.

"You have to go on now," Carl told Sam.

Sam slurred, "Yeah, yeah, yeah."

Two of the Outlaws grabbed Sam under his arms and carried him to the edge of the stage.

"Ladies and gentlemen, welcome the new year with Sam Kinison!" The crowd went wild.

The Outlaws gently pushed him onto the stage. I was amazed that Sam regained a little of his senses. But he was so wasted. He tried to do his material, but he was physically unable. He forgot his bits. He staggered around. He fell down. I have never seen anything like that on stage before or since. Afterward some fans asked for their money back; the Riviera turned them down, saying, "but he was on stage."

I suppose the strangest thing is that Sam did not die from drugs but rather a car accident a couple years later. If you had seen him that night at the Riviera, you would have thought he would not be on this earth another twenty-four hours.

Being drugged held no joy for me. All I needed to avoid temptation was think of my uncles, Cornelius and Herbert, and how alcohol destroyed them. My view was not a secret; I had a reputation in town for not partaking, though I never preached about it. Freddie and Richard would say, "You're a pussy!"

In turn I had called Pryor "the wildman" since our New York days, when he wore a tie-dyed shirt and big Afro and was a staple at the Café Wha? and the Village Vanguard. One year a local publication named him the Best Comic in the Village, and the next year I was the winner. We became friends after he was kicked out of his apartment. I asked him why he got kicked out.

"I haven't paid the rent for two months," he said matter of factly. "I'm going to need a place to stay."

I was working at WMCA, so I had a little change. I gave him $175 to get a room in some fleabag hotel for a month. We were friends thereafter, but he remained "the wildman." He only got wilder when, after his success with Gene Wilder in movies such as *Silver Streak*, Columbia Pictures gave him $40 million for a five-year deal. That could buy a lot of coke!

Once, while he was working on new material, he performed at the Comedy Store hours a night for two weeks straight. He was coked up and getting frazzled. At one of those shows a guy yelled up to the stage, "Hey, Richard, my girlfriend fucked your wife the other night!" Pryor jumped into the audience and pounded the guy.

Maybe the drugs gave him courage, because he was not always so brave. Back in New York he had hooked up with a pretty little white girl, a waitress named Susan. I made it a double date by taking out her girlfriend. We went to Small's Paradise, a Harlem club owned by Wilt Chamberlain (Malcolm X was a waiter there in the 1940s). It seemed like there were a thousand black people in the club—and our two white chicks. We were at the bar when two black women came over and spat, "Are you with these white bitches?"

Richard looked at me—an admitted coward—looked at the seething black women, and said, "No!" We both walked away from the bar, leaving our dates to fend for themselves.

Another time a bunch of us went to Chinatown after a show at the Improv, including Pryor and a white comic named Bob Altman, who went by the name Uncle Dirty and wrote for Richard. Dirty was always bragging about something—how much money he made, how he was the hottest comic, something. We were having dinner at a Chinese restaurant, and Dirty boasted about his twentieth-degree black belt and that he was a martial arts champion.

For whatever reason Richard decided he was not going to pay the check. He told the waiter that he found a cockroach in his food and instructed us to get up and walk out with him. As we approached the door a dozen Chinese waiters, cooks, and others formed a wall to block us from leaving.

"You know that martial arts stuff you were talking about?" Richard said to Dirty. "You're going to need it now!"

Of course, we knew Dirty was full of shit and we couldn't fight our way out of a takeout bag. We went for our wallets.

Legend has it that when he was playing a Vegas date, a casino owner tried to convince Richard to tame his act a little. Richard snapped. He rushed into the casino itself, ripped off his shirt, jumped onto a card table, and yelled, "Blackjack!" Even if that did not happen, no one would have been surprised if it had. Anything was possible around Richard.

One day in June in 1980 I got a call around midnight. It was my agent.

"Did you hear about Richard Pryor?" he asked.

"What? Drug overdose?"

"Close," he said. "He was freebasing coke while drinking 151-proof rum. The alcohol ignited and he caught on fire!"

"So why are you calling me?"

"He was supposed to do a new movie with Mel Brooks, *The History of the World, Part I*. Since he won't be available, I got you a meeting with Mel this morning."

"Geez," I said, "Richard's still smoldering!"

That's Hollywood. I went to the meeting, but Gregory Hines ended up with the part.

The drugs and the madness ensured that Richard was rarely in any physical or mental condition to put together an act. He could never have done it on his own. There was brilliance that came out of him, but Richard would never have remembered any of it. He had the characters, like the wino, who gave Richard pathos—funny but also sympathetic. He also had the energy and he did the performance. But it was Paul Mooney who helped radicalize him, collaborated with him, wrote down his bits, arranged his act, and put it all together for him. Mooney also got Richard's ass on stage. And then to get Richard to do a performance again and again—that was a yeoman's job. Without Mooney there would not have been a Richard Pryor, and he does not get near enough credit for that. Every black comic who has followed in Pryor's footsteps, from Kevin Hart to Dave Chappelle, owes Mooney a debt of gratitude.

No one, however, could have reined in Andy Kaufman—because there was no Andy Kaufman; he was always someone else.

I was at the Improv in New York when he first appeared as Tony Clifton. As one comic finished up, Budd went on stage to bring on the next act.

"Oh," he said, supposedly interrupting his introduction. "I think I see a young man in the audience who used to work here as a singer and now he has his own room in Vegas. One of the brightest talents in show biz today, ladies and gentlemen, Mr. Tony Clifton!"

Andy sat in the audience sporting a cheesy suit, black toupee, mustache, and sunglasses. The audience didn't know who Tony Clifton was, but they politely applauded.

"I wonder," Budd said, "if it's possible for Tony to come up and sing a song. Maybe if we give him a round of applause, he'll come up."

Again, some applause.

Clifton said, "Nah, nah."

Budd fired them up. "Ladies and gentlemen, a little more applause, let's get him up here!"

Onto the stage trotted Clifton. He looked around for a minute and said, "This place is a fuckin' dump! How much does it cost to get in here?"

Someone yelled, "Seven bucks."

"Really? You paid seven bucks to come to this fuckin' dive? I don't know why I'm up here. This is shit."

From the back of the club a woman's voice was heard. "Hey Mr. Clifton, where are you working in Vegas?" It was one of the waitresses, maybe Bette, Liz, Shelley, or Elayne.

"Excuse me, who the fuck are you?" answered the ticked-off Clifton.

"You said you had your own room in Vegas," she said. "We might come out there and see you."

"Are you here with your boyfriend?" Clifton asked.

"Yeah."

"He's paying for your drinks too?"

"Yeah."

"That's what I mean. These fuckin' broads, man. They come to the fuckin' show, they don't pay a fuckin' dime, they have to spread their legs later so they can come to this show, and when I'm on stage they have to take up *my* time."

Sometimes a guy in the crowd would get upset at his abuse of the woman: "Hey! Take it easy, man!"

The woman would chime in with "I just wanted to know where you were. You don't have to be an asshole."

The audience would agree and applaud for her.

Clifton pushed further. "Excuse me, fuckin' lady, if you think you're tough enough to knock me off this stage, bring your ass up here and do it."

The "customer" would strut angrily onto the stage. As she did, the fire exit door next to the stage was opened from the outside. Andy had taught the waitresses how to take him by an arm and flip him so he flew through the door and out of the club. The move was the beginning of his wrestler character a few years later. Then the door would slam shut.

The audience, not really sure whether what they had witnessed was real or an act, would applaud wildly in either case. At first, I too thought Tony Clifton was funny, and his Elvis too. But Andy just went on too long. It is said that jokes have three beats—badda, bing, punch line. Andy's humor was five beats. It just kept going and going. I watched him and thought, "Are we there yet?" I was not surprised that Kaufman said he went to a Pryor concert and never laughed once. That's because Richard had actual jokes.

He stayed in character off stage too. When people saw Andy at the bar after his act, they would say, "Hey Andy, that was great." He would blow them off because he was still Tony Clifton, and Tony Clifton was a prick. If he had played Foreign Man onstage and another comic said, "Andy, I liked that bit," he would talk like Foreign Man and ask, "Who this Andy?" He was the same with everyone, including the hordes of women who flocked around him.

Boosler, who dated him for years before everyone moved to LA, thought he was great. There are others who also thought he was brilliant. To them I said, "Next time, you need to bring enough drugs for everybody."

For Richard, Freddie, Andy, and all of us who had come to the West Coast, our first stop was at the Store. Formerly the legendary Ciro's nightclub, in 1972 the place was reopened as the Comedy Store, featuring a ninety-nine-seat theater, by comic Sammy Shore, who had opened for Elvis Presley the previous few years in Vegas. For Sammy the club was a playground for him and his comic pals, from Buddy Hackett and Redd Foxx to Rudy DeLuca and Flip Wilson. The next year, when Sammy had to return to Vegas for an extended solo gig, he left the club in the hands of his wife, Mitzi. By the time he returned a month later she had not only transformed the Store; she had begun to transform comedy itself.

She painted the inside black, put in a two-drink minimum for the now two shows nightly, created a Monday open-mic night, and established lineups and time slots for every comic. Mitzi was the first to have a schedule, right up there on the wall—no waiting around. Instead of comics hanging out until the owner said, "You're on," there was a plan. You had some idea when you might take the stage. In New York, like at the Improv, you could show up at 9 p.m. and not get on until 1 a.m. Now at the Store, comics had to call in on Monday to find out when or if you were booked for the rest of the week. When comics met at

Canter's or Theodore's, the first words out of their mouths were, "Did you get your times?"

Your slot was for twenty minutes, and when you saw a red light flash, that meant it was time to wrap it up and for you to get off the stage. When Pryor or Robin Williams came by, they took the number of slots needed for one to three hours. But everyone was fine with that because it was written into the schedule. It did not always go smoothly, but at least there was an idea of order.

Not unexpectedly given the drastic changes, divorce proceedings between Sammy and Mitzi followed. In exchange for lower monthly alimony payments, Mitzi was given the business and custody of their son, Pauly.

Only months later Budd Friedman arrived to open an Improv in the Fairfax District on Melrose Avenue. By some cosmic comedy coincidence, he too had gotten a divorce from his wife, Silver, and she too had won his comedy club in the settlement. Seeing the comedy tide switching coasts, he decided to open a new Improv in LA. It is amazing how many laughs have since come out of two divorces.

By this time I was a fixture at the Store. But I had my roots with the New York Improv and with Budd, as did many stand-ups. So when Budd needed money to get the club going and offered me stock in the company for $2,000, I bought in, more as a grateful friend than a businessman. I never expected to see a dime of it returned. Freddie, Harvey Korman, and others also invested. Then when Budd needed help to launch the club, I, Freddie, and many others who had played the Improv in New York and now had a little juice performed there to get him on his feet.

Mitzi was pissed.

"You can't play the Improv," she said in that grating, whiny voice of hers. "It doesn't work that way. You're a Comedy Store guy. What about loyalty? How could you even think of playing there?"

In New York everybody played everywhere, several clubs a night. No problem. But she saw the Improv as the competition and, therefore, the enemy.

I ignored her and continued to roll into the Improv on any given night after playing the Store. What was great about the Improv was that the building had a foyer that doubled as a hangout room for the comics. At the Store you could only gather in the busy waitress area or outside in the parking lot.

"How dare you go there!" Mitzi screamed at me. "You go down there again and you're banned from the Store!"

I went to Budd. "Fuck that!" he said. "You belong with me! You started at my place and this is where you should be!"

"Come on, Budd! I'm just a comic trying to get a laugh somewhere." The same tug-of-war was going on with other comics. Just like a child in a divorce, I should never have been put in the position of having to make a choice between parents. Mitzi and Budd wanted custody—only this time it was custody of certain comics!

Mitzi was a pioneer and I loved Mitzi, but she was also crazy to work for.

Jackson Perdue was doing well at the Store. One week he called in for his schedule and was told there were no spots for him. The next week he called again, and again there were no spots for him. He called Mitzi.

"Why am I not scheduled?"

"You're not aqua enough," she said.

"What?"

"I saw you on stage and you had a nice aqua shirt on and you were fabulous," she explained. "The next night I saw you in a yellow shirt and you didn't look so good. From now on I want you in aqua every time I see you." He changed shirts and was back on the schedule.

That was the sort of thing she would do that drove comics insane. She never did that to me. I guess she liked my wardrobe.

We were forced to choose which parent we would spend most, if not all, of our time with. Pryor, Letterman, George Miller, Tom Dreesen, Landesberg (who was living with Mitzi), and others chose the Store. Freddie, Leno, Richard Lewis, Andy Kaufman, and others chose the Improv.

The Store was where I had been performing on a nightly basis. The Store had my name on the marquee, attracting the tourist crowd on Sunset Boulevard thanks to *Good Times*. I decided to stay with the Store. In this divorce settlement Mitzi won custody of Jimmie Walker.

Budd went ape-shit. He labeled me "the most ungrateful comic I've ever known." I felt personally very hurt. A lot of comics hated Budd—comics rarely like club owners—but I never had anything bad to say about him. Years later a check came in the mail that repaid my $2,000 investment by at least twenty times, and other major payments followed. My stake in the Improv had paid off handsomely. But Budd never understood that the real issue was between him and Mitzi.

Oh, by the way, none of us were paid—at either venue—to perform. The only difference between someone starring on a TV series and Joe Unknown was that I could ask to perform certain days and at certain times—say, Wednesday, Thursday, Friday, and Saturday at 10:15 p.m. Otherwise I was just like any other stand-up.

Whether in LA or New York, comics at the showcase clubs performed for free for the chance to work out material on stage and the exposure in front of talent coordinators, casting directors, movie and TV executives, and so on. Never mind that the clubs charged admission and sold drinks. Comics were allowed no more than one guest admission unless it was your parents. If it was your birthday, you might be given two free soft drinks or food. That was all—even after Mitzi expanded the Store in 1976 to add a 450-seat Main Room to the smaller Original Room and opened a second Comedy Store in Westwood near UCLA.

With the Main Room her idea was to pay the major acts that came to play there. But she could not attract anyone. So she bundled Letterman, Leno, Robin Williams, myself, and others into "best of" packages that would play the Main Room, two shows a night on weekends. Just like when we would "workshop" at the Original Room, she did not feel compelled to pay any of us.

One Sunday morning in early 1979, after doing two shows in the Main Room the previous night, a group of us went to Theodore's. But Bob Shaw, one of the comics from the Original Room who sat with us, did not order any food.

"You want anything?" someone asked.

"No, I'm fine."

He wasn't fine. He was hungry and he was broke. Despite some of us performing two sold-out shows where paying customers were shelling out $10 to $20 a head and buying expensive drinks, none of the performers had received anything. No one on stage, whether the Main Room or Original Room, should have left the Store that night hungry or broke. A lot of us were doing just fine, thank you, but there were too many comics who were working and yet still struggling, including sleeping in their cars. It didn't seem right.

Everyone was upset about Shaw's plight, especially Boosler, Leno, Gallagher, and Mooney. Mooney, the rabble-rouser that he was, went in to talk to Mitzi about the situation.

"Look, the comics think we should have a little share of what's coming in. What do you think might be fair, for us and for you?"

"What are you thinking?"

"I don't know. Maybe like $5 a show. To cover food and maybe some gas."

Mitzi exploded. "You motherfuckin' ungrateful bastards!"

Mooney was stunned.

"We're the biggest, most important goddamn comedy club in the country," she continued, furious and defiant. "You're lucky to be on my fuckin' stage. If you don't want to be on my stage, fuck you! Because I'm not going to pay you fuckin' guys a fuckin' dime!"

Even Mooney, who took no shit from anyone, was so taken aback that he did not know what to say in response.

After relaying to us her reaction, he gave us his understated punch line: "I don't think she's going to go for it."

"Maybe we should stand up to her," someone suggested.

But Mitzi carried a big stick. Many comics were afraid to say any-thing more because those who protested might suddenly find them-selves relegated to going on at one in the morning, if they got on at all, or be sent into exile at the Comedy Store in Westwood. The Westwood Store held nowhere near the importance in entertainment circles as the flagship on Sunset.

I was lucky enough to be making a living. I could withstand the po-tential threats and pressure, and so could a few others. Strategy sessions were held, including at my townhouse, and a group was formed called Comedians for Compensation. Larger meetings, often chaotic, took place at a union hall.

If Mitzi had simply said, "Hey, I'll think about it" or "I'll give you a few bucks a show," the whole controversy would have ended right there. But instead, she dug in her heels. There was no reasoning with her. She posted a notice in the waitress area, where we would congregate before going on stage, threatening that anyone moving forward with the idea of a "comedy strike" should expect to never again perform at the Store.

But by March the only option left was to strike. Yet everyone knew that if major comics crossed the picket line, the comics' organization would be unable to put any pressure on the Store or the Improv, which also refused to pay the comics. Dreesen told Bill Knoedelseder for his book *I'm Dying Up Here: Heartbreak and High Times in Stand-up Com-edy's Golden Era* that he drove to my home first to get my support. I re-call the emissaries being Gallagher and Leno. In any case, my position was clear: I loved Mitzi and did not want to hurt her, but I believed every comic should be paid something. In a way, the fact that they were not getting paid at the clubs helped bring talented writers who needed money, such as Leno, to my staff. But what was right was right. I told Gallagher and Leno that I would not join the picket line but neither would I cross it. Robin Williams then said the same thing, and Mooney brought Pryor on board. The marquee comics were a united front.

Faced with that solidarity, Mitzi offered to pay the performers in the Main Room half of the cover charges. But that did not help those in the Original Room, those who needed financial help the most. So Comedians for Compensation turned her down.

The time for talk was over. The strike was on—and it would be at the Improv as well as the Store. A mysterious fire at the Improv changed those plans. The bar, restaurant, and restrooms were saved, but the performance space went up in smoke. Police ruled it arson, and there were accusations about who was responsible, but no one was ever charged. Comedians showed up to help Budd salvage the venue and built a stage at one end of the restaurant. The Improv was back in operation two days later.

Feeling that a strike at that vulnerable moment would destroy him financially, Budd reached out to the comics. If they did not picket the Improv, he promised to adhere to whatever agreement Mitzi came to and to pay retroactively the commensurate amount. No specific numbers were offered, but the gesture was an olive branch, so the comics agreed to the deal. Leno, Boosler, Seinfeld, and others once again performed at the Improv.

Pickets walked the sidewalk in front of the Store. Among the signs were "The Yuk Stops Here," "No Bucks? No Yuks!" and "I Said I Wanna Be a Star Not I Wanna Starve." The press conferences were probably the most entertaining in the history of the labor movement. As time wore on, the press and the public sided more and more with the comics. Less secure comics gradually became braver and began speaking out. For us, Gallagher, Leno, Boosler, and Mooney were our leaders. Dreesen, who was respected by both sides and was a secure working comic, became the spokesman.

The Comedy Store Bombers, the basketball team we had formed for benefit affairs, played a charity game at the Forum, the then-home of the Los Angeles Lakers, during the first week of the strike. It was the last game that Letterman, Dreesen, Tim Reid, I, and others would play

together as the Bombers. We never again could put on the uniforms
Mitzi bought for us.

I went to the "union" meetings to keep informed. I also visited Mitzi,
sometimes with a comic named Danny Mora, who was in Mitzi's camp,
to see if there was a way to end the strike.

"Come on, Mitzi," I kept saying. "Maybe you should look at giving
the guys a few bucks for a show."

But she was hell-bent on not giving up anything.

"Fuck you!" she said. "Get the fuck out of here!"

The strike went on for months. I thought we would never win. But
I was busy. With *Good Times* no longer taping, I had gigs in Vegas and
on the road. When I was in town, I did game shows like *Hollywood
Squares* and *Match Game*. Through it all, I was concerned that when
the comics did return—and they would eventually—there would be re-
taliation from Mitzi.

One day, according to Knoedelseder, comic Biff Maynard, a Mitzi
supporter, swerved his car into the Store's parking lot where Leno and
other strikers were standing: "There was a loud thump, and Leno went
down." Leno faked that he had been hit. But his theatrics ratcheted up
the tension and seriousness surrounding the strike. Mitzi immediately
heard about the "accident." She called in Dreesen and told him she
wanted to settle the dispute. By the next morning there was an agreement—comics playing the Main Room would receive 50 percent of the
door; those in the Original Room and at Westwood would get $25 a set.

The picketing stopped and the comics went back to work. But the
strike had destroyed relationships. Some comics, like Dreesen and
Boosler, said they would never again play the Store. Others never forgave the comics who crossed the picket line.

And Mitzi broke her promise not to retaliate. Leno, who was a guy
worthy of going on at 10:30, was getting time slots at 1 a.m., until he
finally left. Letterman, Skip Stephenson, Allan Stephan, and Sam Kinison were sent to the minor leagues, to Westwood.

Showing just how strong a figure Mitzi was to our era of stand-up comics was a conversation I had with Letterman during a break on his show more than a dozen years after the strike.

"How do you think it's going?" he asked me.

"I think we're doing okay," I answered, assuming he was talking about our on-air banter at his desk.

"No, I mean the show. How do you think I'm doing?"

"Dave, you're doing fine."

"I have a feeling the network wants to get rid of me."

"Really?" Like I said, there is no happy comedian.

"I just wanted to know what you thought," he said. Then he added, "Mitzi called. Do you know why she would be calling me?"

By this time Dave had headlined his own talk show for many years. He had Emmys, was well respected, was pulling in millions of dollars a year, and could do almost anything he wanted in show business. But still he was worried about talking to Mitzi.

I told him I had no idea why Mitzi would call him.

"God, I don't know what she wants," he said nervously. "I have to call her back, right?"

"You're David Letterman!" I said, trying to drown out his insecurity. "You don't have to do anything Mitzi wants anymore!"

He thought for a second. "Yeah," he said. "I guess you're right."

If Mitzi could wield such power with a Letterman, imagine her influence over lesser comics, such as Steve Lubetkin. I had seen him perform in New York and thought he was a decent talent. Others hyped him much more, hailing him as the next hot comic. That hard-to-match reputation preceded him to LA, and everyone looked forward to seeing what all the fuss was about. He was immediately given good spots in the lineup at the Store. But his performances were a letdown. I do not know what happened, but when he arrived on the West Coast, he lost his funny. After bombing hard, he was given less advantageous spots, early in the evening, like 8 p.m., or very late, like 1 a.m. Soon he did not justify even those. Within months he was out of the rotation completely. In desperation, he teamed with his girlfriend, Susan Evans, to form a duo, Lubetkin and Evans, and was sent to Westwood. After that failed he returned to the solo spotlight at various venues, but not at the Sunset Store.

Feeling increasingly dependent on Mitzi for his career, Lubetkin was reluctant to go on strike. But one night he did take to the picket line. Mitzi saw him and completely severed her relationship with him. That threw Lubetkin into an emotional tailspin, and he turned on Mitzi. The strike became his obsession. On the picket line outside the Store, he was like a rabid dog. Standing on the sidewalk, he went on and on about how much he hated Mitzi. When the strike ended, knowing that retribution was coming his way, he felt hopeless and helpless.

Late in the afternoon of June 1, 1979, the thirty-year-old went to the roof of the Sunset Hyatt, next door to the Store, and leaped off. Many believe he was so mad at Mitzi that his intent was to go through the roof of the Store, crash into her office, and crush Mitzi sitting at her desk. Instead, he fell into a dumpster in the Store's parking lot. The suicide note in his pocket said, among other things, "I used to work at the Comedy Store. Maybe this will help to bring about fairness."

But Lubetkin's death, though dramatic, had no effect on the settlement or the work situation of the comics. Mitchell Walters, who opposed the strike, said of Lubetkin, "He bombed to the very end."

Yeah, I know: That was an ugly thing to say. But it gets ugly among comics. That's how we are. People laughed at us when we were kids. Then we had them laughing with us. Then we had everybody laughing at each other. For most people it hurts too much to say funny things about themselves. But we comedians always laugh at ourselves. Because if we don't laugh, we're going to cry.

Early in my New York Improv days Brenner invited me one night to his apartment. I went to the doorman and he rang Brenner for permission to let me up.

The doorman put down the phone and said, "You can go up." I headed for the elevator. "No, no, you have to use the delivery elevator."

"I'm not delivering anything. He's a friend of mine."

"I just spoke to him. He said for you to use the delivery elevator."

When I reached Brenner's apartment, I was furious. He opened the door, and there he was with Landesberg, laughing their asses off. It gets ugly among comics. That's how we are.

The strike set a precedent for showcase comedy clubs around the country: Comedians should be paid. My generation of comics made that happen. There are young stand-ups today who don't even know such a time existed when you did not get paid and you paid for everything you ate or drank.

Perhaps the only good to come from the strike other than the welfare of comics was that the picketing of the Store allowed the Improv to get on its feet and inspired the Laugh Factory to open. Jamie Masada was just sixteen years old when he started the Laugh Factory right down the street from the Store.

His first performer was Richard Pryor. The story goes that when Masada tried to pay him, Richard handed him a $100 bill instead. He wrote on it, "You need this for your rent, boy."

9

A Black Sheep among Black People

NORMAN LEAR AND I WOULD HAVE LONG CONVERSATIONS ABOUT politics and social issues—and we disagreed about everything. He really got upset when I said the NAACP, though useful during the struggle against segregation, had become ineffective and should dissolve. "I can't believe where you're from!" he said. Because I was a black from the South Bronx, apparently it was inconceivable that I would believe such a thing. Meanwhile here he was—white, Jewish, and from New York— and a charter member of the NAACP!

As Groucho Marx once said, "I don't want to belong to any club that would have me as a member." I don't like marching in lock step with everyone else, even if they are black like me. Blacks are supposed to think a particular way about society and vote for particular people in an election. If you do not, we are told, then you are not really black. I disagree. My view is that everyone—black, white, or whatever— should have their own mind and speak that mind. What I call myself politically is "correct." Whoever I vote for is the "correct" one!

You see the movie American Graffiti, *about the '50s? They told me I couldn't be in it though because there were no black people in the '50s. All the black people holding out waiting for the '60s, saying, "Damn, when the '60s coming? That's when the riots gonna be, ain't it?"*

When I worked at WMCA, there was a mosaic of voices, from extreme liberal to extreme right wing, from Alex Bennett to Bob Grant. I heard it all.

Grant pioneered confrontation talk radio. He might open his show with "I'm coming into work today, I'm in a cab and you think an American would be driving the cab, because they're American cars, but he's not. I go to get a bagel and who's making them? Some guy from Puerto Rico. The waitress comes over, she can't speak English. What is wrong with this country? Are there no Americans left in America? Today on *The Bob Grant Show*, Americans only! If you are an American, call me. I do not want to hear from anyone from foreign countries. Alright, first call. This is Bob Grant."

Of course, it would be someone with an accent.

"Who put this guy on? Get off my show!"

I was the engineer behind the board.

"These black people. I've had enough," Grant would rant on. "Civil rights, Affirmative Action—this is garbage! We're all Americans! You think I'm a racist? I have a black engineer!"

When someone called and said, "I'll never listen to you again," he fired back with "I didn't want you to listen to me in the first place! Get off my show!"

I was a little stunned in the beginning. I had been blackenized with the Last Poets. I heard all of the Panthers firsthand. Now, in the hallways of WMCA, I saw Kathleen Cleaver leaving the *Alex Bennett Show* as Bob Grant was walking in. I truly heard both sides of a story. When someone said something that made sense to me, I thought, "That's a good point." It did not matter to me if they were black or white, liberal or conservative.

I learned about other cultures too.

Every Saturday night I engineered for a show hosted by Malachy McCourt, an actor and writer born in Brooklyn but raised in Ireland. He would bring on fantastic Irish musicians such as the Clancy Brothers and Tommy Makem as well as tremendous storytellers like his younger brother Frank (who would later write his *Angela's Ashes* memoir) and actor Richard Harris. They opened the show at 8 p.m. by singing Irish songs, fueled by the bottles and bottles of Irish whiskey they brought into the studio. Listeners called in and joined them, singing along on the phone. It was crazy and funny and I loved it.

They also talked about Irish history and culture. When they hit Irish politics—especially the troubles in Northern Ireland—the show turned very serious, so the serious drinking commenced. They would get so drunk that often there would be dead air. By the end of the show, at midnight, they were passed out and sleeping on the floor. I would shut down the studio, and as scheduled, the station would air tapes of other shows. The engineer who came in at five in the morning would find the Irish guys, wake them up, and hustle them out.

Being behind the board opened my horizons. When you are in the ghetto, you know nothing beyond the ghetto. Whether it was other cultures, such as Jewish or Irish, or other viewpoints, I was exposed to more of the world than most of us from the projects had been. Diversity should not just be about color but also about ideas, including different political ideas.

I always liked politics, even in junior high and high school. Various Kennedys, including Bobby, would come to the South Bronx to speak, and I was interested in what they had to say. I just wished they would not always use the gym for their speeches because that meant my buddies and I could not play basketball there that day. However, they did give us free T-shirts with some campaign slogan on it in exchange for us sitting in the audience. I admired the effort of the Kennedys to come to the ghetto. No one else in their position did. I think they really cared.

I was politically aware enough as a teenager to be impressed by Lyndon Johnson when he became president after John F. Kennedy's assassination. Here was a traditional Southern Democrat who was on the side of black people, pushing integration and the War on Poverty. I took advantage of those government benefits too. When I was on the receiving end of poverty programs, Affirmative Action and minorities-only efforts like SEEK (which still exists today), I was all for them. They did help many people, including me. But Affirmative Action and the rest outlived their time.

I believe in compassion not condescension, equality not entitlement. Affirmative Action put us into the category of second-class citizens. Standards had to be lowered so we could move forward. We were stigmatized as being less capable than whites, that we had not earned our opportunity. Those programs were needed once, but like being in first grade, you can't stay there forever. You have to move on.

There was an awful lot of waste and abuse in government poverty programs. At the time I did not mind. We could go bowling! Black pro bowler Bobby Williams came to the hood to give us pointers, and we went bowling at local alleys for free. Arthur Ashe did the same for tennis lessons.

I ran into Ashe years later at the Fontainebleau Hotel in Miami Beach. He was there with his little niece and nephew. "Give them an autograph!" he demanded. It was one of the few times in my life that someone did not ask politely. I imagine he was thinking, "You owe me for the tennis lessons, man!"

We did not need bowling or tennis lessons, at least not paid for by the government (i.e., taxpayers). What most kids needed then—and still do now—was education.

I wish I had been held back a grade or two in junior high. That's right, people! Pushing me and my buddies through school to the next grade, without the most basic of reading and writing skills, hurt most of us later on in our lives. Some of us overcame, but most did not. Too many black leaders play the race card and say don't hold back black kids because it makes them *feel* inferior. Well, if they can't read and write, then they *are* inferior. It is not about race; it is about education. Holding them back in school may be the only way for them to get ahead in life.

There were exceptions in the ghetto, kids who were self-motivated and blessed with brains and went on to achieve. Sonia Sotomayor was born of Puerto Rican parents and raised in the projects of the South Bronx by a single mother. Her inspiration to become a lawyer? The *Perry Mason* TV series! From the age of ten she knew exactly what she wanted to do with her life. When I was in the Melrose projects, thinking that someone from my neighborhood would graduate from Princeton and then Yale Law School and then become a Justice on the US Supreme Court was pure fantasy. Hers is an amazing success story because it began in the same poor ghetto I came from.

But most of the rest of us had no interest in school. If we had standardized testing that meant something—you pass or you aren't promoted to the next grade—we would have been forced to pay a little more attention and maybe learn what we needed to learn. Putting a kid in a class he isn't ready for does more harm than good. The teachers cannot spend the time bringing him up to the level of everyone else when there are so many other kids who need attention and show more promise. When the kid is ignored, he loses whatever desire he may have had for education. He gives up. Those were the kids at the Melrose projects who sat on park benches all day doing nothing.

I know this because I was one of those kids. But then I simply got lucky. Early enough in my life I found that one thing I absolutely loved to do, that something that gave me joy and could create for me a life and a living. I found comedy. But the exceptions do not justify the system.

Remember that saxophone my mom bought me and kept getting out of the pawn shop? Playing that sax was the first thing I did as an entertainer. Twenty-plus years later I picked it up again—in Las Vegas—and it finally led me to college.

Right after *Good Times* ended I moved to Vegas, back in 1980 when the town had less than 175,000 people and all of the classic casino hotels, such as the Dunes, Aladdin, and Stardust, were still standing. I kept an apartment in LA, but Vegas became my base of operations as I played various casinos, flew around the country doing stand-up, and starred in a couple TV series that followed *Good Times*.

Living in Las Vegas is not as glamorous as people think. It is more like living in Iowa but with Times Square within driving distance. The biggest difference between Los Angeles and Vegas is that in LA you are surrounded by people involved in the entertainment business in some way or other, whether they are performers or writers or grips or hair stylists or whatever. If they are not, then they want to be. Their lives are completely immersed in Hollywood. You can never get away from the business.

In LA everybody is a star or thinks they will be one or is sure they should have been one. That may be Angelina Jolie eating at Denny's, but her waitress knows she could have been just as big a star if she had had the same breaks. The valet parking my car could care less about Jimmie Walker. He is positive that he's funnier than I am.

In Vegas or anywhere outside of LA people treat you as something special because they recognize you. There is a lot of "Oh wow, it's you!" Okay, but I already know it's me.

Moving to Vegas put some distance between me and Hollywood and also gave me an opportunity to do other things in life. Like playing music. I took out the same sax I had when I was a kid, which I had kept all through the years, and started practicing.

I was still terrible.

Nevertheless, I enrolled in the Music Department at the University of Nevada, Las Vegas (UNLV) as an auditing student. I was a thirty-something on my first day at college.

I even asked if I could be a member of the pep band. Amazingly, they said yes. The band was filled with eighteen- to twenty-two-year-olds who had already been playing ten years or more. They were really good—better than the All-City band in New York that was out of my league when I was a teenager. Just among the other sax players were Cleto Escobedo III, whose Cleto and the Cletones became the band for *Jimmy Kimmel Live*, and Paul Taylor, who would later have hit jazz albums.

The instructor gave us music sheets and expected me to play like Cleto and Paul. Uh, sorry. Fortunately, the teachers and students in the music department were understanding and willing to give me the private lessons I could not afford as a kid. But I never got much better. I was what they called a "manpower player": I didn't have to be good—I just had to make a lot of noise! But playing that sax—my old sax—was so much fun.

We were often on the road four days a week, playing for the crowds at football and basketball games and special events. At the time UNLV was a basketball powerhouse, with future NBA stars like Larry Johnson, Stacey Augmon, and Armon Gilliam. Arenas were filled with upwards of twenty thousand fans. We traveled just like the team—even had our own bus. We checked into hotels at one or two in the morning and practiced in banquet rooms during the day. We went all over the country, from North Carolina to Chicago, Maryland to New York and Houston. It reminded me of my days traveling with the Motortown Revue—and still there was that one person on the bus able to sleep through all of the noise.

I kept my "day job" back in Hollywood and went to work for a producer who was very different from Norman Lear. Aaron Spelling had already produced the hit TV series *Starsky and Hutch*, *Charlie's Angels*, *The Love Boat*, and *Fantasy Island* (I had starred in episodes of both of the latter), and he would later be responsible for *Beverly Hills, 90210* and *Melrose Place*. What Lear was to half-hour comedies, Spelling was to one-hour dramas. As soon as *Good Times* was canceled he cast me as a former car thief trying to stay straight in a police drama series called *B.A.D. Cats* (B.A.D. as in Burglary Auto Detail).

After all of the heat surrounding *Good Times*, *B.A.D. Cats* was a welcome change of pace. Spelling was simply into the game of network television—having hits, making money, and moving his chips around. Unlike Lear, he was not trying to deliver a message. They had very different styles too. Where Lear acted like the local head of the Parent Teacher Association, Spelling acted like the president of the United States.

When he was about to visit the set, a runner informed us, "ETA on Aaron. He's coming by to talk to you in nine minutes." Later: "ETA on Aaron. Here in two minutes." Then two security men showed up. Then E. Duke Vincent, Spelling's right-hand man, with his Palm Springs tan and gold chains around his neck, walked onto the set. Finally, at exactly his appointed time, came Spelling.

"Hey, I love the show. The network thinks it's great. Keep doing what you're doing. Gotta go." Then he exited with his entourage.

B.A.D. Cats was an easy gig—two hours a day, three days a week. But the series only lasted six episodes on ABC. Today the show is remembered only for being an early role for a young actress named Michelle Pfeiffer, who played a policewoman nicknamed—believe it or not—Sunshine. Michelle was about twenty years old and always so excited. At lunch she would say, "This is great! I'm going to be in all the magazines! I'm going to buy a house in Malibu!" Turned out she did become a star, but not thanks to *B.A.D. Cats*.

A couple years later Spelling decided to give sitcoms a try and pulled me in for ABC's *At Ease*, which was about a couple of conniving guys in the army. We had so much fun on that series. Unfortunately, the show was not funny at all. We were gone after three months.

Bustin' Loose, however, had a chance. Based on the Richard Pryor film, I starred along with Vonetta McGee in the all-black cast of the syndicated sitcom. I was not keen on doing another "black show" and the pressure that goes with it: Is it relevant? Is it black enough? But I had them hire Allan Manings from *Good Times* as a producer, whose experience I thought would help. I played Sonny Barnes, a former con artist working through five years of a community service sentence under the supervision of a social worker raising four orphans. I hoped *Bustin' Loose* might go on for a few years. But after one season we were off the air.

All along I was also doing game shows, which gave me tremendous exposure and helped promote my club gigs across the country. Shows like *Hollywood Squares* proved that I could ad-lib. I know they gave funny answers to some of the stars—Paul Lynde, Rose Marie, and maybe one or two more—but not to the others, not to me. Those shows also kept me in touch with friends from my days at the Improv in New York, such as Stiller and Meara, who were frequent guests and brought their kids, Amy and Ben, along. Amy wanted to be an actress and Ben wanted to direct films. He had a Super-8 camera constantly in his hand, shooting something or other.

"Ben, take it easy," I told him. "You're only eleven years old!"

He always chatted with me and Nipsey Russell, and he especially loved to hear Nipsey's little raps:

> *I am a bachelor, and I will not marry*
> *Until the right girl comes along.*
> *But while I'm waiting, I don't mind dating*
> *Girls that I know are wrong.*

Next thing I knew, little Ben was a regular on *Saturday Night Live*. After that, he was starring in movies like *There's Something About Mary* and *Meet the Parents*, and also directing, like he always wanted. A few years ago, when *Parade* magazine asked him for his comedy inspirations, he named Robert Klein, George Carlin, and me. I was flattered and surprised. I had no idea he had been paying attention.

Ben grew up in the '70s, watching the Golden Age of stand-up. But it was in the '80s when stand-up truly exploded onto TV screens. All

you needed for a TV series was a brick wall, twenty comics, and an audience. Producers taped everything, chopped it up—sometimes joke by
joke, not even comic by comic—and, magically, they had a series of
half-hour gangbangs, uh, I mean shows. They were everywhere, network, syndicated, and cable, on Showtime, HBO and Ha! (the predecessor to Comedy Central), from *An Evening at the Improv* and *Comedy
on the Road* to *Comic Strip: Live.* I thought the phenomenon was great,
and I was on many of those shows—multiple times too. What could be
bad about comics getting more exposure?

Turned out there was a lot wrong. The good comics were on too
much—familiarity breeds contempt. The bad comics were on too
much—not being funny breeds contempt. Comedy clubs across the
country suffered as well. People would not pay to see stand-ups when
they could see them perform for free in the comfort of their own home.
So by the end of the '80s, clubs were going under.

What was a road comic supposed to do then? I returned to my first
arena of professional show business—radio. Some twenty years after my
only on-air gig in Norfolk, Virginia, I would once again have my own
show. But it was politics, not comedy, that put me behind the mic.

I had written guest columns for the *Los Angeles Times* op-ed section
explaining my thoughts on national and world events. Readers noticed
them and so too did various radio talk show hosts, mainly conservative
ones, who invited me on their shows as a guest. Though I don't call
myself a conservative—we don't agree on everything—obviously I am
not a liberal. I was officially a Libertarian for a brief time, but they never
win anything. I say I am a Logicist. I believe in logic and common sense.

On the air with folks like Rush Limbaugh, I talked about my belief
in smaller government, personal responsibility, free-enterprise capital-
ism, and America in general. My opinions on race, not typical from a
black man, really stirred the pot, everywhere from TV's *Politically Incorrect with Bill Maher* to Bill O'Reilly and Sean Hannity on both radio
and TV. I said that instead of our obsession with racism, blacks should
focus on economic development. I said that the War on Poverty did

little for the poor precisely because the bloated federal government was in charge. I slammed Jesse Jackson, Al Sharpton, and every other black leader who picked up a protest sign at the drop of a hat if it would get them on TV. Like me, many conservatives also emphasized the need for education and were tough on crime. I wasn't afraid to say, even though I was a black man, that I agreed with them.

I taped the radio shows and sent them to people in the talk industry. Andrew Ashwood, probably the most insane man to ever program talk radio, contacted me. Most programmers are clean-cut, suit-and-tie, corporate types. Ashwood was different: He wore tie-dyed T-shirts; had a beard and long blond hair; smoked pipes, cigars, and cigarettes; drank in the studio; and was overweight and out of shape. He liked what he heard on my tapes and arranged a three-week try-out at WLS in Chicago, where I was partnered with someone else they were testing out, Roe Conn.

Our show was down and dirty, bashing, banging, talk radio. I trumpeted my support for the death penalty, especially for audiences who don't laugh at my jokes. But I went further: I said I was all for bringing back public hangings. Every Sunday, in the park, bring the kids. Now that would be deterrence. Forget scared straight—that's scared stiff.

But the station kept Conn, who became a fixture on Chicago radio, and released me. That did not deter Ashwood.

"Hey, man, heard the tape from LS," he said. "Loved the liveliness. Fuckin' great! You didn't get hired, but fuck it, man—you were great!"

Later Ashwood was programming WOAI in San Antonio, Texas. He launched "The Great American Talk-off," in which well-known people from across the country competed for the station's early afternoon talk show slot. Fred Goldman, father of murder victim Ron Goldman in the O. J. case, was one of them. So was I. I didn't win, but Ashwood thought highly enough of what I had done to make demo tapes of my performance and send them out to other programmers.

He pounded on Neil Nelkin, the program director at KKAR in Omaha, Nebraska, to hire me, and I was given a one-year contract. I moved to Omaha and was put in the same lineup with Limbaugh, O'Reilly, Dr. Laura, and Hannity.

The slogan for my show was "Give me an hour and I'll give you the power." Omaha is middle America, and I consider myself a mainstream American.

America is not perfect. We have made some bad decisions in the past and will continue to make some bad decisions. Nor is America the land of opportunity for everyone. I know a lot of people who have worked hard and been honest but have not succeeded—people who busted their asses and ended up homeless. They are like comics I saw at the Store who tried for years and never got on that stage. On the other hand, there are people who have achieved fame and fortune and never worked a day to deserve them. That's life, and life is not always fair.

But I believe in America. This is a great country. Because we are free. I did not always appreciate that. You do not learn patriotism living in the projects. Once I got out into the world, met people who were different from me and worked with them, I grew to appreciate how you can make choices about your life. The choices do not always work out, but in America you have the freedom to choose—and you have the freedom to speak about your choice.

* * *

I pledge allegiance . . .

Michael Newdow of Elk Grove, California has periodically sued to have the Pledge of Allegiance banned from being recited in public schools because the phrase "under God" offends atheists.

The great thing about the freedoms Americans have is that Newdow has the right to leave this country anytime . . . unlike in Cuba. He also has the right to speak his mind . . . unlike in China. Okay, so he is offended by "under God." But I bet doctor/lawyer Newdow won't burn any of his American money because the phrase "In God We Trust" is printed on every bill.

I'm offended too, like when a pretty woman doesn't give me the time of day. I'm offended when I get my tax bill. I'm offended by the prices at Starbucks. I'm offended by boy bands. But I get over it!

"I pledge allegiance to the flag of the United States of America and to the republic for which it stands, one nation under God, indivisible, with liberty and justice for all."

If anyone is offended by that, then don't say it. But you have no right to stop anyone else from saying it either. If "under God" ever becomes illegal, then call me an outlaw!

* * *

I strongly believe in the Constitution and the Bill of Rights—but as living documents. I am not a strict constructionist. I know this may come as a shock to some of my conservative friends, but the world has changed since the eighteenth century. Once upon a time blacks were declared to be three-fifths of a human being and women could not vote. America changes. We must deal with new realities.

Family values, for example, have changed. Comedians love politicians who trot out that photo of their smiling, happy family. We love speeches about family values—and they come from the mouths of liberals, conservatives, and everyone in between. Let's get real, people. Marriage does not work for most people in the modern age. Marriage is a great concept, just like there should be no racial hatred and there should be no poor people. But most marriages end in failure, called divorce. The traditional family is no longer Ozzie and Harriet. Today, a mother and two kids is more traditional.

Marriage does not even work for gay people! For me, marriage is be-tween a man and a woman, as it has been for, oh, all of human history. But gay marriage is here and is not going away. Gays have a rallying cry of "We're here! We're queer! Get used to it!" Even though I oppose gay marriage and, instead, support civil unions, they are right. So let's not waste our time—the time of our government—trying to turn back the clock. Divorce will do for gay marriages what it has done for straight marriages—create millions more single-parent households.

I feel the same way about the new reality of illegal immigration. Illegal immigrants, mainly Latinos, are here and will continue to come here—and there is less and less we can do about it every day. There are already too many who have made it through. They have overwhelmed the system. The toothpaste is out of the tube and cannot be put back in. We acknowledge that we have failed every time we declare an amnesty.

At this point I say children should receive amnesty but not the adults who came in illegally. At least with children, they can be Amer-icanized, including learning English. I love going to a fast-food restau-rant and listening to three generations of Hispanic women at a table. The grandmother speaks to her grown-up daughter in Spanish. The daughter talks back in Spanish but then turns to her child and speaks English. I think we should all learn other languages, especially Spanish, but we live in America, and English is the language that has bound us together in the past and will in the future.

If nothing else, insisting on English being spoken is a statement that illegal immigrants ought to adapt to our country, not the other way around. Unlike the legal immigrants who arrived here in the early twentieth century, today's illegal immigrants feel it is a right and not a privilege to be in America. Yes, the Statue of Liberty is inscribed with "Give me your tired, your poor / Your huddled masses yearning to breathe free." But nowhere does that refer to *illegal* immigrants. Yet now that they have gained political power and can vote politicians in or out of office, they are not going back.

The new number-one minority is Hispanics. Blacks had been the country's largest minority since the 1600s. Now we can't even hold that job!

Recently I learned about my own heritage. Most blacks in America are not raised knowing much about the generations who came before them. Many are afraid of what they suspect they will find—slavery.

I knew nothing about my father's relatives. I knew only a little about my mother's Perryman family further back than her generation—her and her sisters, such as Inez and Birdie Mae, and her brothers, among them Cornelius and Herbert. Fortunately, Cornelius Perryman has never been a common name for a black man born in Alabama. With my mother Lorena conveniently named for her mother and Cornelius for her father, my coauthor, Sal Manna, was able to trace that side of my family back nearly two hundred years.

I learned that my great-grandfather George was married in Dallas County, Alabama, in 1875 to my great-grandmother Ella. His parents, my great-great-grandparents, were a farmer also named George and a woman named Eliza. They had been born in South Carolina—he in 1818, she in 1822.

Because census documents prior to 1870 list only the sexes and ages of slaves, not their names, we do not know the whereabouts of great-great-grandfather George before that year. Upon emancipation, though, a majority of slaves took the surname of their previous owner, and a slave owner with a large plantation near where George lived was named Jeptha Vining Perryman. Perhaps he had been George's master.

In any case, by 1870 George had been emancipated and was living with Eliza and their children, including great-grandfather George, in Lowndes County, the county in Alabama that a century later was referred to as "Bloody Lowndes" for the civil rights struggle there. In 1965, more than a hundred years after blacks were freed, most of the residents of Lowndes County were black—but not one of them was registered to vote.

I am proud to say that my family has been in this country at least since 1818. We came in chains. We were immigrants of a sort, but we arrived on these shores legally. We survived. We persisted. We are here today. Let us not wallow in the past. You can keep the forty acres and a mule. The idea of reparations, compensating the descendants of slaves for the forced labor of their ancestors, is an idea whose time will never come. Instead, we should celebrate our freedom and our achievements.

We will always be a minority, and politically, I will always be a minority within that minority because I treat each issue on its own, not according to party.

I believe in Planned Parenthood, for example. A lot of parents today do not want sex education taught in the schools. They need to open their eyes. Your daughter is not fat. She is due in September! Just in time for back-to-school baby clothes!

I also believe that when the Declaration of Independence says that we, as Americans, have the unalienable rights of life, liberty, and the pursuit of happiness, health care is included. Without the availability of health care, there is no life, no liberty, no pursuit of happiness.

One of the few stories my mother told me about her growing up involved Aunt Vivian. She had two sons, Harold and Lloyd, and Lloyd suffered from asthma. She would take them and ride the bus—the black bus—some seventy miles from Selma to Birmingham to visit the white doctor who treated blacks for free one afternoon a week. He was inundated with patients and often did not finish until after the last black bus had left to return to Selma. If she missed that bus, Aunt Vivian, who worked as a maid, slept in the bus station with her kids until the next morning's first bus home. She did that every other week for many, many months.

One day she came home and told Aunt Inez, "I'm just so tired."

"You're being lazy," said tough Aunt Inez.

Vivian lay down, closed her eyes, and went to sleep. She never woke up. My mother did not know the cause of death, except to say that "she just wore out."

Stories about the difficulty in obtaining health care are still heard today. I am sick and tired of hearing about people who do not go for medical help because of the cost, about people with insurance who are turned down for treatment, about people who do not fill their prescriptions or are removed from hospital beds because they do not have the money. We have some of the best medical technology in the world, but most people in the United States cannot afford it. The price of medical care today has grown too high. One of the leading causes of bankruptcies is medical costs. Even if you have done everything right—insurance, savings accounts, and so on—a serious illness can decimate everything you have accumulated in a lifetime.

The health care system that exists today does not work. We are losing money, lives, and hope. Every American has preexisting conditions—it is called life. Universal health care will cost everyone, but there is nothing more essential to us as individuals and to our society than our physical well-being. America is the last holdout against universal health care in the civilized world, and that needs to change.

* * *

Some of our wounds in the health care system are self-inflicted:

America, we are junkies, drug addicts, and I'm not just talking about crack, coke, or heroin. No, I mean the prescription kind— Oxycontin, Vicodin, Zoloft. The majority of people in drug rehabilitation aren't there for heroin or cocaine but for some kind of prescription addiction. And what's worse is that Americans think this is normal.

We need drugs to stay awake, to go to sleep, for pain, to be happy, to slow down, to speed up, to fight depression. Who knows when it started, but it is now out of control. The phrase "natural high" doesn't apply to Americans. Add in alcohol, and the United States is the number-one drug-addicted nation in the world. Students,

teachers, actors, athletes, talk show hosts, housewives, business ex-
ecutives, young and old are doing some kind of prescription mind-
altering drug. People on these drugs function daily in our society
and would never think of themselves as addicts.

It's all in the family too. Kids take them from their parents' medicine
cabinets and use their parents' doctors to get prescription drugs.
Multibillion-dollar drug companies and doctors are the pushers. Ad-
dicts know they can get drugs from their doctors anytime as long as
they check in once or twice a year. And if one doctor won't give
them the drugs they want, they'll just go to another doctor. Accord-
ing to water pollution experts, people in America should be warned
that our water supplies have traces of many prescription drugs.

I would love to say I or someone else has a great idea about how to
stop this abuse. I don't. But the first step toward recovery is recog-
nizing that you have a problem. America has a problem.

* * *

I voted for Ronald Reagan as president. I did not vote for Barack
Obama for president. I'm sure announcing either of those statements
will guarantee that I never get invited to an NAACP Image Awards
retrospective. Unlike the vast majority of black Americans, I have
never been a registered Democrat. That, in and of itself, puts me on a
blacklist in the black community.

That Obama had the same skin color as me was not important in
determining who would get my vote. I did not agree with his political
philosophy. Ideas matter, not political parties. I loved Reagan as our
president *and* I loved Bill Clinton as our president. Republican Reagan
appointed more blacks, women, and minorities to government positions
than anyone before him. Democrat Clinton, who was the blackest president we have had yet—Obama included—ended the welfare system.

Speaking of Clinton: Here is some more common sense from a Logicist. People in positions of power have a greater opportunity to cheat in their marriages than other people do. This has been happening since, oh, the beginning of time, and it will continue to happen as long as there is power and sex. Clinton happened to get caught. Times have changed. More politicians will get caught more often in the future.

> *I was in Washington, DC, and Marion Barry meets me at the airport, gives me the kilo to the city. . . . This Marion Barry thing is a black-and-white issue. You know what I'm talking about? You take Jimmy Swaggart and Marion Barry. . . . When Jimmy Swaggart gets caught, he just admits it, just comes on TV: "Yes, it was me. I'm sorry. Please forgive me. My wife, my kids, please forgive me!" Marion Barry, who was caught in a hotel room on film—alcohol dripping from the lips, palming a girl's breast, cocaine coming out of the nose—says, "It's not me! I'm innocent! Frame up!"*

* * *

I got off on a good foot in Omaha. A thorn in my side, however, was a local black activist, the sort of guy who if you ran over a chocolate doughnut, he would scream, "Hey, that's a black doughnut! You hate black people!" He was Omaha's Al Sharpton. When I came out against honoring Martin Luther King Jr. with a national holiday, he came down hard. I felt there should be a day of remembrance, just not a day that shut down the entire government. He wanted to shut me down—and launched a campaign to do exactly that.

I believe most Americans are common-sense folks and appreciate hearing the truth even when it is harsh. But those are not the ones who call talk radio. Eventually the ratings for my show fell off. After about fourteen months I was let go. A year later I was back on the air at KMJ-AM in Fresno, filling in for Ray Appleton on his local talk show alongside the syndicated shows, once again, of Limbaugh, Hannity, Glenn Beck, and so on. I continue to substitute host there to this day.

Getting fired is one thing, but getting axed for expressing your opinion, especially if it's a joke, is more insidious. I was once fired from a cruise ship gig that I had been doing for four years because someone did not like a political joke I made in front of the usual crowd of fifteen hundred people.

> *George Bush went to Canada and an official there called him a*
> *"moron." Bush said, "That's not true. I'm a Presbyterian."*

Now that seems pretty harmless and silly to me. But someone in the audience complained to the cruise ship line that I had made the president look stupid. I was responsible for making the president look stupid? Really? Because I upset one person, I lost my job. Some people just can't take a joke.

Gabe Kaplan had a routine in the early '70s in which he would impersonate Howard Cosell at the Crucifixion of Christ announcing the action as if it were a sporting event. Christ was a running back and the cross was the football: "Here's a little guy carrying his cross down the street." As Christ was raised up onto the cross, Kaplan as Cosell said, "Up goes Jesus, up goes Jesus!"

I was at the bar at Catch a Rising Star after his performance. Two big guys came up to me.

"Is Gabe Kaplan here?"

I waved Gabe over, thinking they were going to say, "Hey, we liked the show—just wanted to tell you."

Gabe put out his hand to shake theirs. One of the guys grabbed him by the throat.

"You think it's funny, Howard Cosell at the Crucifixion?"

Gabe looked scared and mumbled something.

"Don't you EVER make fun of Jesus again! That is blasphemy, you fuckin' son of a bitch! That is the Bible!"

He slammed Gabe against the wall.

"I don't ever want to hear you do that again, you goddamn mother-fucker!"

From what I have been told, Gabe never did that bit again.

Comedians, beginning with the first court jesters, have always poked fun at the powers that be, no matter who they were. But in this politically correct world we live in, people can get crucified for a joke—especially white people. Blacks are often given a pass, but not whites. They can't speak out or register their thoughts about race nor can they have an open dialog without being considered racist. I feel sorry for them.

When football player Junior Seau was asked how to stop San Diego Charger star running back LaDanian Tomlinson, he said, "You give him watermelon and load him up with fried chicken and tell him to keep eating." Seau, who is a minority himself, was wearing a Tomlinson jersey at the time. He later said Tomlinson, a former teammate, was one of his best friends and that there was no issue. Tomlinson agreed and said he didn't know what all the fuss was about.

Fuzzy Zoeller, a white pro golfer, was once asked what he thought Tiger Woods might serve at the Masters dinner the year after he won. Zoeller replied, "Tell him not to serve fried chicken . . . or collard greens or whatever the hell they serve." Zoeller was called a racist, had to apologize to Tiger, and lost Kmart as a sponsor.

Gambler Jimmy the Greek was having dinner at a Washington, DC, restaurant when he told a reporter that blacks were better athletes because their slave owners bred them to be stronger. He was fired from his network TV job.

Senator Trent Lott said the country would have been better off if segregationist Strom Thurmond had been elected president in 1948. He was stripped of his leadership role, lost a number of other privileges, and had to make a public apology.

Limbaugh had people bailing out on him faster than a ham at a bar mitzvah when he said on ESPN that black Philadelphia Eagles quarterback Donovan McNabb was overrated because people wanted to see a black quarterback succeed. Limbaugh was fired from the sports network.

And then there was Don Imus, the Granddaddy of Shock Jocks, who jokingly called the Rutgers women's basketball team "nappy-headed hos." That was nothing more—and actually a lot less—than black women are called in rap songs. But when a white man said it, all hell broke loose.

Today, when it comes to talking about race, "White people, don't go there."

Because we are not allowed to offend someone, we are forced to say or do things we do not believe. We become liars; we become hypocrites. Political correctness, so embraced by liberals, masks the truth. Rather than coming to terms with an issue, talking it out, and dealing with the reality, we pretend it does not exist.

Make no mistake about it: There is racism on all sides. That is not a good thing, but it is a real thing. If blacks were in the majority, we would be the worst racists. Check out how a white is treated at a rap concert versus how a black is treated at a Larry the Cable Guy concert. The white guy would be harassed; no one would touch the black guy. That is the new double standard.

* * *

America, we've lost our funny. We have lost the ability to laugh at ourselves and at others, both people we know and people we don't know. We are afraid to laugh for fear of the PC police, who will call us racist, sexist, homophobic, whatever. Classic sitcoms like The Honeymooners *("to the moon, Alice" . . . spousal abuse),* I Love Lucy *("Lucy, you got some splainin' to do" . . . anti-Latino) and* All in the Family *(almost everything) would not even get on cable TV in this climate.*

The Rat Pack—Sammy Davis Jr., Frank Sinatra, Peter Lawford,
Dean Martin, Joey Bishop—made fun of each other's cultural dif-
ferences. But they and entertainers like Will Rogers, Jack Benny,
W. C. Fields, Mae West, and others would be PC'd out of business
today. On a series of popular national TV commercials, cavemen
point out the absurdity of our PC culture.

America needs to go into Comedy Rehab to get its funny back.

* * *

People—black and white—laughed at this joke from my album in 1975.
We should be able to laugh at it today:

A delivery boy knocks on my door and says, "Excuse me, boy, is
the master of the house home?" I said, "Now hold on, man. I am
the master, the king, the high exalted ruler, and I'm tired of people
coming to my house saying black people can't do this, black people
can't move here, black people can't do that. There are black
people in every conceivable area of the American mainstream of
life. There are black scientists, there are black lawyers, there are
black store owners, there are black doctors, there are black den-
tists, there are black people in every possible area of life. It's people
like you that keep perpetuating these racial stereotypes that keep
messing everything up, man. Now I want you to leave my wa-
termelons here and get out!"

The races don't have to hold hands and sing "Kumbaya" together,
but it would be nice to see them respect each other enough to be honest
and open. For example, we have heard about white guilt over slavery
and the treatment of blacks. But there is also black guilt that is almost
never talked about, a feeling that I have experienced.

When I delivered groceries for the Grand Union market, I wheeled
large carts down the street to very well-to-do, two-story, townhouse

residences on the Upper East Side. Of course, I used the delivery entrance in back. One day I was carrying a box of peaches and eating one on my way up the stairs inside the home. I heard someone on the steps behind me and cupped the peach in my hand so they would not see it.

I turned around—and saw a little white girl, maybe eight years old.

"I see the peach in your hand," she said. "You don't have to steal it. If you want it, you could just ask."

That I still remember her, with her two braided pigtails, is evidence enough of how embarrassed I felt. If she were black, I would not have had the same feeling of guilt.

Maybe that explains what I did decades later in a record store in Chicago. Three black kids came in, grabbed a stack of CDs, and ran out. There were white people in the store and there were black people in the store. What hurt me the most was the look of the black people. They were embarrassed. Those black kids reflected on us—all of us. I went to the white girl who was the clerk at the cash register.

"How much did they steal?"

"Looks like about a dozen CDs."

"I'll pay for them."

She said, "You don't have to do that."

"I want to."

Customers came over and told me I should not feel I needed to pay for them. The clerk didn't know what to do. I saw the manager and called him to us.

"I'm demanding to pay for what they stole," I said. I gave him maybe $120, money I really did not want to spend for CDs I did not buy.

But what those kids did made us look bad. They made all black people look like what white racists expect us all to look like. I felt guilty for them. I needed to do something that said, "We are not all like that."

There have been many times when I have been walking down a street at night, with a white woman by herself either in front of me or behind me, and I have crossed the street to the other side. Why? Because

I saw that she was nervous—if not scared—of a black man. She had every right to feel that way. Our reputation precedes us.

I went to a tough high school. When the referee would shoot off a gun to start a track meet, the track team would shoot back.

There is an old joke about two guys arguing and one says, "Don't you know who I am?!" The other guy says, "Well, if you don't know who you are then I can't help you." I know who I am. There isn't a black man in America who has not been profiled, followed, or wrongly accused by police, myself included. That is a fact of being black.

According to the Census Bureau, one out of every four black men in America is in jail. I take no chances. When I get in a car, I make sure I have no more than two other black guys with me.

In 1997 I was in Kansas City promoting my upcoming shows at Stanford & Sons comedy club. Along with another black comic, I went to a TV station at around 5:30 in the morning for an interview. It was winter, so we wore hoodies and big coats. We were buzzed into the building and made our way through the hallways by ourselves.

"Hey boys, what are you doing here?" We turned around and saw a white guy, presumably a security guard.

"Get out of here!" he shouted. He looked like he was going to take off to get help.

"We're on the show," I told him.

He walked up closer and recognized me. "Oh, Jimmie Walker! Sorry, come on in."

This sort of thing happens all the time to black people. I know that if I go into a department store, a security guard will probably watch me, maybe follow me. I'm used to it. I understand it. We are paying for the sins of our fathers and brothers. There have been times when I have

gone to a clerk at one of those stores to show my credit cards and iden-
tification so they could go on with their other business.

But this time was different. The contrast between his first reaction
and when he saw that it was me was so strong that I needed to speak up
about how blacks who are not "stars" are sometimes treated. During the
TV interview, when the host asked what I thought of the racial climate
in Kansas City, I said I had always liked KC but that there was prejudice
everywhere, even at Channel 4. Then I described what happened.

The incident made the front pages of the local papers. The NAACP
called. The *Hard Copy* entertainment news show called. For two days
I felt like Jesse Jackson.

The belief among whites that black men are dangerous is based on
the perception and truth that lots of blacks commit lots of crimes. Because of that belief, white people cross the street when they see a group
of black men coming toward them, and those of us who are law-abiding
citizens are under constant scrutiny.

> *Crime is bad all over. Guy trying to steal my tires got run over by*
> *the guy trying to steal my car.*

The root of the problem is not white perception but rather crime
by blacks, the majority of which is black on black. We need to make
ourselves better people, our community a better community. We need
to respect ourselves and others, create a society in which education is
a priority, and strive to be and do the best we can in the short time we
have on this blue planet. I did not agree with much of what the Panthers said back when I was opening their rallies, but I do agree with
this: We have to improve ourselves, because nobody else is going to do
it for us. We need to be the solution, not the victim.

Jesse Jackson was crying at the inauguration of Barack Obama because he realized his days of being able to blame whitey for everything
were over. With Obama's election, America officially entered an era of
Colorless Politics. The list of major black government leaders grows

every year—Deval Patrick, governor of Massachusetts; Harold Ford, former Congressman from Tennessee; Adrian Fenty, former mayor of Washington, DC; Cory Booker, mayor of Newark, New Jersey; Keith Ellison, Congressman from Minnesota; Kevin Johnson, mayor of Sacramento, and on and on. Whereas in the past, being black meant you could *not* get elected, this new generation is just black enough *to* get elected. They are not leaders of the black community; they are blacks who are leaders. That is progress.

> *I have a PhD in Whitenology. . . . I understand how to handle y'all now. See those two white folks chained up outside? They belong to me!* (Jimmie Walker, 1975)

> *A black president, people! New rules: All white people report to the cotton fields for reorientation!* (Jimmie Walker, 2009)

I don't mind being a black sheep among black people. If you express your opinion and everyone likes you, you are probably not saying anything.

10

The Late-Night War

"CONGRATULATIONS ON YOUR FRIEND LENO," LEAR SAID. "I KNOW how hard you fought for him in his career. This must make you very proud."

It took all I had to not scream out in pain. I thanked him, hung up the phone, and lay down on my bed close to tears. A few minutes later Paul Abeyta, who had been the talent coordinator for the *Merv Griffin Show* called.

"Congratulations, you son of a bitch! Your boy got in there! Wow, the *Tonight Show*. Man, after going to the mat for him all those years, this must be a great day for you."

It was 1992, and Jay Leno had been announced as the permanent host of the *Tonight Show*, replacing Johnny Carson.

Performing on the *Tonight Show* was the ultimate breakthrough for a stand-up comedian. And if after your shot Johnny gave you the "okay" sign with his fingers, that was the seal of approval for your entire career. Even better, if he then waved you over to sit on the guest couch, like he did with Freddie Prinze, you had gone to comedy heaven.

Though I was on the *Tonight Show* many times, I was never on with Johnny as the host. Carson liked certain comedians and comedy styles or attitudes and not others. For instance, he was not a fan of Boosler, who was on with him once and then was relegated to appearing only with guest hosts. Steve Martin was on with Johnny at first, but after a bad shot he was banished to guest host nights for awhile before returning. Johnny was middle America, and his taste in humor reflected that. Comedians who were too edgy, too strange, too controversial were not among his favorites. He was not a fan of Jimmie Walker. I was always on the B-list, which was used when a guest host—such as Brenner or Joan Rivers early on and then Letterman and Leno later—subbed for him.

Carson was not a fan of Leno either. Back then, Leno, with his long hair and sarcastic East Coast vibe, had some peculiar bits. He was what some called a rock 'n' roll comic. Johnny was not a fan of rock 'n' roll either. Leno did his first couple shots with Johnny, but they did not go well. Johnny preferred fellow midwesterner Letterman. So Dave became a guest host after only three appearances as a stand-up. Letterman, who greatly admired and respected Leno, had to fight for Leno to return as a performer, even asking Carson personally for the favor. But after four shots, ending with an appearance with a guest host, Leno was gone—for eight years. He has since said he was just not ready. The fact is that he was one of the best stand-ups around and he bombed, and when he could not get on the *Tonight Show* again, he was seriously pissed off.

Leno had remained with the management company now in the hands of Jerry and Helen Kushnick. Though Dave left, the two comics stayed friends. When Letterman scored his *Late Night* talk show on NBC in 1982, he booked Leno almost immediately. He had Leno perform about once a month, doing his Elvis impersonation or his "What's My Beef?" bit. Those appearances raised his stock considerably by keeping him in front of America on a regular basis. Without those shots Jay would never have survived long enough to later win the *Tonight Show*.

At the time Carson was hosting the *Tonight Show* four nights a week, with a guest host taking over the duties on Mondays. After rotating guest hosts for years, the show named Joan Rivers as the permanent guest host in 1983. But when she landed her own show on FOX in direct competition with the *Tonight Show*, an angry Carson fired her and she never appeared with him again. In 1987 NBC cut deals for Leno and Garry Shandling to rotate the Monday hosting chores. But when Shandling's self-named cable comedy series began to consume more of his time, Leno was left as the exclusive guest host.

Soon after, Arsenio Hall took over FOX's late-night slot from Rivers. His syndicated *Arsenio Hall Show* debuted in 1989. The first black late-night talk-show host, Arsenio brought a different flavor to TV. He was urban and hip. But perhaps the most obvious cultural difference between him and Carson involved the music acts that would perform on their shows. Carson preferred big-band greats such as Buddy Rich, Joe Williams, Pete Fountain, and Tony Bennett. Arsenio would bring on cutting-edge stars such as Madonna, Prince, and Rick James as well as fresh contemporary country artists like Garth Brooks. Boosted by Arsenio's "cool music" factor, his ratings rose, nearly challenging Carson's. But no one dared tell Johnny that his musical tastes were dated. Only when Leno guest hosted on Mondays could NBC book the new generation of music artists for the show.

Suddenly the *Tonight Show* was drawing a younger, if not larger, audience on Mondays than on nights with Carson behind the desk. Advertisers, affiliates, and the network noticed. Leno, who at one point was likely to forever be a road comic, was now a player.

The saying goes that life is easy, comedy is hard. When it comes to having a life in comedy, sometimes that is near impossible. That was why the comics who started out together in New York would try to help each other when any of us enjoyed some success. We knew how difficult it was to survive and succeed. So we shared our good fortune when we had the chance. That was why what Leno then did to Steve Crantz was unforgivable.

After the homesick Crantz had returned to Pittsburgh, we didn't talk much for the next couple years. He lived near his parents and took a job as a pharmaceutical salesman and even as a photographer for the

Allegheny County police department's crime lab. But he was still writing jokes, still telling jokes. Whenever we did talk on the phone, he obviously still wanted to be a comedy writer.

Some ten years after he left we both agreed he should take another shot at Hollywood. Again, I paid his way to LA and got him an apartment and a car. He immediately fell into the rhythm of our work just like when he was first in LA. He was incredibly fast and sharp. When I needed to work on an upcoming shot for a late-night show, Mister Geno and I would go over my jokes in the days before the appearance. Then, maybe an hour and a half before the shot, Crantz and I would get together. If something had just hit the news, he would have a joke about it within minutes.

I was about to go on Letterman's show in February 1988 just after sports commentator Jimmy the Greek was canned for his comments about black athletes. Crantz came up with the joke I used when I sat in the chair next to Dave's desk:

> A lot of people are very upset with Jimmy the Greek. It didn't bother me. I didn't care. But the network wants to get rid of Jimmy the Greek because of all this. So they want to hire a black oddsmaker . . . they're hiring Zeke the Zimbabwean.

The line killed. From that moment on I called Crantz "the Greek."

But not everything was the same as it was the first time he was in LA. I could no longer afford a staff and employed the Greek only as a freelancer. He needed to sell jokes elsewhere too and had me reach out to the guys from the old staff to see about getting him work. Everyone else in that original writers' group was doing very well; nearly everyone was on the writing staff of a show. The Greek, who had not stuck it out in Hollywood with them, was now in his midthirties and coming back as the new guy in town. He expected them to say, "Hey, Steve, where ya' been? Great to see you." But they barely remembered him. He was a sensitive guy, and that hurt. He did submit jokes for Leno's Monday monologue though. Jay paid fifty bucks for every joke that made it on the air.

The Greek suffered some brutal disappointments. When he thought a big break was within reach—staff gigs for *The Second Half*, a sitcom starring John Mendoza, or *Live from the Laugh Factory* for impresario Jamie Masada, who loved the Greek—for some quirky reason it would disappear.

Jerry Kushnick, who was also a fan of the Greek, eventually asked Leno to put him on staff. Crantz had certainly helped bail out Leno a decade earlier when Helen and I were trying to nail down Leno's first TV special in 1979 for Showtime. It had been a battle to get that project going. Showtime was backing away. But I kept pushing.

"Why are you fighting for Leno?" Helen asked me. "Save your own ass. Do what you want. Forget about Leno!"

"He's my friend!"

When Showtime gave the go-ahead at the last minute, I put Crantz and Wayne Kline, Wayne Wayne the Joke Train, on the job right away writing the material. We needed comedy writers who were good and fast, and they were the best at that combination. Steve and Wayne pulled the special together in a week.

So now with NBC giving Leno a little extra money for his Monday gig, Jerry, his manager, figured Jay could pay back the Greek by putting him on staff at the *Tonight Show* at the minimum salary, about $1,750 a week.

But Leno wasn't keen on the idea. He thought the Greek was too "jokey," too much like a Bob Hope type of writer. Also, because he chattered all the time, some people could only take the Greek in small doses. Leno was one of those people.

I called Ray Peno and said, "Come on, bring the Greek in!"

Helen had her usual reaction, asking, "Why do we need the Greek? What is he going to do for us?"

As usual, I said, "He's funny!"

Jerry kept pressuring Leno and finally got the Greek the gig. Leno was not thrilled, but he did it for Jerry and me. Steve was so incredibly happy. Being a full-time comedy writer was all he ever wanted to do with his life, and now he was doing it, in Hollywood, for the *Tonight Show*.

Every day the Greek and I went over the jokes he wanted to send to Leno for Monday. Jay needed about fourteen jokes a week from a staff of about eight writers, including the prolific Wayne Kline. Each of them might submit ten a week. The Greek would tell me thirty a day! Then he would send Jay twenty pages—not twenty jokes, twenty pages—every week. The sheer volume overwhelmed Leno. He complained that Steve was clogging his fax machine and told the Greek to slow down.

While we were on the phone together, the Greek and I would watch the *Tonight Show* on Mondays, waiting to hear Leno do one of his jokes. But Jay never told any of his jokes. Week after week and never one of Steve's jokes. The Greek became frustrated and then angry, getting to the point of hating Leno. Jay must have noticed, because he came to Jerry and me and said he wanted Steve off his staff. But we convinced him to keep the Greek—even though he still did not use any of his jokes.

When Jerry got cancer and passed away in 1989, Leno told Helen and me that he was going to let Steve go. I begged him over and over not to do it. I knew what being fired would do to the Greek. That job was his life. He had worked really hard, and he was damn good. But my only ally, Jerry, was gone. The fact that I could not stop Jay from firing the Greek pained me terribly.

The Greek phoned me at about 8 o'clock that night. He was beside himself, crying crazy tears. We talked until three in the morning. During the next few days I saw him depressed for the first time. No longer his chattering self, he became withdrawn and moody. I said I would pay him something every week, but there was no way I could cover what a staff salary might be. Leno threw him a bone by agreeing to let him once again submit as a freelancer at fifty bucks a joke, just like everyone else. I suggested to the Greek that he lower the volume of his submissions to Leno so as not to piss him off any more.

What did he do? Instead of writing thirty jokes a day, he wrote sixty jokes a day, often working from the moment the *Tonight Show* went off the air to 4:30 in the morning. He continued to fax Leno twenty pages a week. I paid him for some of his jokes too, using them in my act. But not Leno, until one day the Greek thought Leno did use one of his jokes.

During Operation Desert Storm, the Greek came up with "They're putting up a no-fly zone in Iraq. Too bad we can't have one of those at Denny's." He faxed the joke to Leno and to me.

Jokes are like the blood flowing through a comic's body. They are part of you, and without them you are no longer a comedian. That is why stealing jokes is a very serious offense, though many comedians, including famous ones such as Steve Martin and Robin Williams, have at one time or other been accused of that crime. In general most well-known stand-ups brush it off if a comic lower on the ladder "adapts" a joke, like when I was starting out and borrowed from Godfrey Cambridge and Dick Gregory. No harm, no foul. But if it is a comic around the same level as you—and especially if the same audiences are hearing both of you—then it becomes an issue. Once word travels through the comedy grapevine that a comic stole a joke, that stigma can follow you the rest of your career.

The situation becomes even more heinous when an entire routine is identified with you and someone else infringes on the territory you have staked out as yours. I was at the Improv in New York one night when John Byner, who did impressions such as his great one of George Jessel, did his Ed Sullivan during his act. While Byner was on stage, Will Jordan happened to come into the club. Jordan's stock in trade was *his* Ed Sullivan impression. He was the one who established "really big shoe" (meaning "show") as the quintessential Sullivan impersonator catchphrase.

Jordan was livid watching Byner. When Byner came off stage, Jordan confronted him.

"Hey, you're doing my Sullivan!"

"What are you talking about?" Byner said. "We all do Sullivan."

Jordan yelled, "The shoulders, man, the shoulders! *I* do the shoulders! No one did that before me! You stole my Sullivan shoulders! The walk, the spin around, the shoulders, they are all mine!"

As their argument heated up, enter David Frye. Though Frye became famous for his impressions of Richard Nixon and other political figures, he too did a stellar Sullivan.

Frye interrupted Jordan. "Wait a minute, *I* had the shoulders! *I* did the no-neck bit!"

Jordan came back. "But I was first! Nobody did the shoulders but me!"

The three of them almost came to blows.

The reality is that many comics will sometimes come up with the same idea at about the same time. That does not mean one person stole the joke from another person.

Leno did the Denny's no-fly zone joke on his show and it killed. The Greek thought that not only was he going to get $50 but Leno would then call him up to say, "You know, I made a mistake. You're back in the house."

But the Greek did not get a call or a check. He asked me to contact Leno. Jay said that someone on his staff had written the joke. I have no doubt that was true because within ten minutes of the Greek faxing me that joke, three other writers had faxed me essentially the same joke. But the Greek had gotten his hopes up and now he was crushed. From that day forward he grew more distant from everyone in LA, including me. He stopped talking to some people completely, and when he did talk, he would explode angrily about Leno.

Within two weeks he moved back to Pittsburgh, back to his parents' house. I couldn't reach him on the phone, but I spoke with his dad. He told me the Greek was very down, not his usual happy self. Eventually, he became the cohost of a Pittsburgh radio morning show, billing himself as Steve the Jokeman. But he had already been to the mountaintop, so anything else was a comedown.

Three years later his smoking habit finally caught up with him, and the Greek was diagnosed with lung cancer. He moved out of his parents' house and into an apartment. He told them not to call him. He said he would call once a week and if he did not, that probably meant he was dead. He no longer cared to live or for anyone to care whether he did or not.

A week went by without a call home. The police busted down the door to his apartment and found him dead.

The Greek was a great funny guy who could not catch a break. I only wish more people had the chance to really know him. Though a Lubetkin who jumps off a building to his death is memorialized, there are so many more talented people—like the Greek—who come to Hollywood but then leave as if they were never there at all.

The Greek's obituary in the *Pittsburgh Post-Gazette* quoted, of all people, Leno. "He was what you would call a good old-fashioned joke writer," Leno said. "He was like a joke machine. He could bang out a bunch of them. If you said, 'I need jokes on Clinton hurting his knee,' he could give you two pages. Some guys write topical or cerebral—he could've written jokes for Bob Hope."

I was very unhappy reading that quote. At best it was hypocritical. Make no mistake about it—Leno could hire and fire whomever he wanted; he did not kill Steve Crantz. But he sure as hell didn't show any heart. As one comedian has said to me privately: "Jay Leno will show up at your funeral, but he'll be the reason you died."

The Crantz episode was not an isolated situation either. Bob Shaw, Leno's old partner from his Boston days and the comic whose poverty helped instigate the Great Comedy Strike, was another funny guy who never received his just due. At one point he fell ill and needed a couple of shots to qualify for the performing union's insurance plan. Boosler called Leno and asked him to book Shaw for the two shots. Why not? Shaw was his friend! Leno passed. Boosler went ballistic and never forgave Jay. Fortunately, Shaw eventually became a writer on *Seinfeld*. He also cowrote *A Bug's Life*.

Only when Leno began guest hosting the *Tonight Show* on Mondays did Helen express any genuine confidence in him—because he became her chance to land the biggest prize in television. But for Leno to take over the *Tonight Show* she would have to push Carson off his throne: No one knew when Johnny wanted to step down. Besides, everyone expected Letterman, his favorite, to be his successor someday. After all, he was doing his own successful show right after Carson, and Johnny clearly had anointed him.

Helen had a plan. I know that because she told me what she had in mind. I tried to dissuade her, saying it would be "suicide" for Leno to stab Carson in the back. When I brought up Letterman's widely accepted right of succession, she said, "Fuck Letterman! We'll kill his show!" There was nothing anyone could do to stop her.

Her scheme included doing a complete makeover on Leno. She had him cut his hair and she put him in suits. No longer would he drive to the studio on his motorcycle. When Jay was on the road, he would visit the NBC affiliates and make friends. When he was in LA, he would glad-hand the press and praise Johnny. She also stopped him from doing the Letterman show in New York, which did not sit well with Dave. When I appeared on Letterman's show, producer Bob Morton begged me to call Jay and ask him to do the show again. But nothing I said would help.

That Letterman appearance was the legendary show with guest Shirley MacLaine. Dave wanted to have fun talking about her past lives. She did not and said "maybe Cher was right, maybe you are an asshole." Dave was so shocked that even he struggled to joke his way out of the awkward situation. When the segment ended, Shirley refused to shake his hand. After the commercial break, I came on.

My first line was "I was so happy Shirley MacLaine was here. I talked to her and we found out that in one of her previous lives I was one of her slaves!" It killed. Dave laughed, easing the tension, thank you very much.

Meanwhile, behind the scenes Helen was at work trying to oust Johnny. Among her tactics was to ask certain hipper guests to perform only on the *Tonight Show* when Jay was hosting. If they crossed her, she threatened that they would never appear on the show again. She also planted stories in the entertainment trade magazines about Carson being out of date, about NBC wanting him to retire sooner rather than later, and about Leno being the network's desired successor. Then she arranged for a February 1991 story in the *New York Post* that laid all of that out for the public for the first time. Carson was made to look feeble and impotent, and he was embarrassed. Finally, in May, Carson announced that he would retire the following year.

Leno—not Letterman—took over the *Tonight Show*. Author Bill Knoedelseder said it best: "Given the opportunity, most—if not all—of them [his fellow comics] would have done what Leno did, but they probably would have felt worse about doing it. Nobody blamed Jay, but everyone understood why Dave felt betrayed."

Helen became the executive producer of the *Tonight Show with Jay Leno*. As part of the deal the Kushnicks sold to NBC their management company, which largely consisted of clients I had brought in many years earlier—dominated now by Leno, who I had fought to keep her from dropping. The price tag was $7 million. When I finally revealed to Leno how Helen had forced me from my own company years earlier, he refused to believe it, felt I was slandering her. He told Helen what I had said, and she banned me from the *Tonight Show*.

I wasn't the only one. Helen made it known that if any guest appeared on Letterman's show or anywhere else when she wanted them, they would not be welcome on the *Tonight Show with Jay Leno*. Helen vowed to bury both Letterman and Arsenio, who foolishly boasted that he would "kick Jay's ass" in the ratings. She launched a Hollywood reign of terror. Agents and managers were downright frightened, but they kept the prohibition quiet.

Then country singer Travis Tritt was booked to do Arsenio. The *Tonight Show* also wanted Tritt—and on a date before his Arsenio appearance. Tritt's manager, Kenny Kragen, tried to accommodate Helen, but in the end he had committed Tritt to Arsenio first and felt he had to stand by his word. Helen went berserk, saying she would never speak with Kragen again and slammed the phone down. According to author Bill Carter in *The Late Shift*, Helen's office then called Kragen back within half an hour and canceled an upcoming appearance by another of his clients, Trisha Yearwood.

To most power brokers in Hollywood Helen wielded a big stick. If you crossed her, you could be dead in the water. As a matter of fact, that is what she would yell: "You are dead!" But Kragen, the man behind the "We Are the World" and Hands Across America antihunger benefits, had enormous credibility and respect throughout Hollywood. He also had guts and integrity. Helen had not figured on Kragen deciding that enough was enough. He went public in the *Los Angeles Times* about what was going on. The floodgates opened with revelations about Helen's vindictive style running the *Tonight Show*. The backlash against her was fierce.

NBC, who was not happy with her anyway, began to move to force her out. On Howard Stern's radio show, Helen charged that she was being picked on because she was a woman and threatened to sue the network for sexual discrimination. Apparently she felt she held the trump card—Leno. If she was purged, she would take Leno with her.

She did not realize what those of us in comedy circles already knew—Leno would do whatever was good for Leno. Helen was fired. Jay kept his job.

Soon after, Helen was diagnosed with breast cancer and had to have a mastectomy. To show how despised she was, a "joke" made the rounds among comedians: "She's alright, she still has her dick." Like I said before, comedians can be tough.

With Helen no longer in charge, Leno agreed to have me on his *Tonight Show*. But he still spoke with her, and her antipathy toward me made him refuse to work with me on my shot, like he had done many times before when I appeared on Carson or Letterman. This time I would have to go over my shot not with him but with Jimmy Brogan, who had become his right-hand man and comedy coordinator. I had helped Brogan get the gig as one of the regular emcees at the Comedy Store when he was on my staff. Now he was doing for Leno what Mister Geno and then Brogan himself had done for me back in the day.

"You can't do the Jeffrey Dahmer line," Brogan said after looking over the jokes I had planned. Dahmer was a notorious serial killer who, at the time, was incarcerated for several gruesome cannibalistic murders. Also at that time another convicted murderer was about to be executed, again sparking a debate about capital punishment, and I had an oh-so-topical joke that connected the two killers.

"Why can't I do the joke?" I asked Brogan.

"Jay doesn't like Jeffrey Dahmer jokes."

"What are you talking about?" I said. "Jay does Dahmer jokes all the time!"

Later that day it was showtime. I went into my shot. The audience was laughing, the band was laughing. I was rolling at breakneck speed. The spot came for the Dahmer joke and I did it:

All this talk about capital punishment, about whether the electric chair is humane, about lethal injections being humane. I have an idea that'll make everybody happy: If you want to get rid of a murderer, you rub barbecue sauce on him and put him in a cell with Jeffrey Dahmer.

Excuse the expression, but the joke killed.

I looked out the corner of my eye at Leno at his desk. He was not laughing. He was not happy.

I finished my shot and walked to the couch. Leno did not shake my hand. He said, "Jimmie Walker. We'll be right back." During the commercial break he told me, "You had to do the Dahmer joke."

"Didn't it kill?"

"That's not the point."

When we came back on the air, we did a couple more jokes and then we were finished. Jay was still not over it, saying, "The point is I asked you not to do the line and you did the line."

My point was that funny mattered. Even Branford Marsalis, then the bandleader, came to my dressing room and said my shot was the funniest he had heard on the show to date.

Here's the kicker: A couple weeks later Leno was quoted in a national magazine with a joke about Dahmer. It was my joke! I was shocked. When I called him to talk about it, his staff referred me to Brogan. I have not been on the *Tonight Show* since. When I have seen him in passing, Ray Peno says, "Brother Walker," and imitates a bit in my act where I go, "Well, well, well." That's all.

Stand-up comics are a brotherhood. We have seen each other bomb, seen each other helpless on stage, seen each other at our worst. So when we have a chance, we give each other a hand. What I am most proud of in my entire career is not what I have done but that I helped out "my guys"—Letterman, Leno, Frank 'n' Stein, Louie Anderson, and all the others.

Once upon a time all of my guys wondered if they were good enough, if they had a chance to make it in this business. An actor can get by without being dramatic. If a comedian isn't funny, then he's not a comedian. They were funny, but a lot of folks come to Hollywood with talent and never succeed. I have seen many great comics who never made it. There was no rhyme or reason or logic why they didn't— except luck did not come their way. Maybe my guys would have hit the big time without me being around. But it makes me happy to think that when they needed a hand, I was there for them.

I have continued to do that with my opening acts, becoming for them what David Brenner was for me. Dustin Ybarra, a Hispanic kid from Texas, was seventeen when he opened for me in Dallas a few years ago. He was very talented, but he was raw. Sure, he was big in Dallas and all his friends and fans laughed at his jokes, but he had to get among other comics, compete with them, grow that thick skin, make himself better. I took him under my wing and helped him move to New York and get an agent. As the song goes: If you can make it in New York, you can make it anywhere.

The world is going to end in 2012. That's what they say. I'm kind of hoping that it does. Cause I've got this couch from Rent-a-Center. No payments until 2012. That's a free couch right there! The guy said, "You know you've got to pay in 2012." I said, "Bro, we're all going to pay in 2012!" (Dustin Ybarra)

I'm glad I don't go to school now. Bullies are so mean. Now they kick your ass and put it on YouTube. You go home and your parents already know you got your ass kicked. You walk in like, "Mom . . ." She goes, "I know, sweetie, 'Fat Kid Cries' got forty-two thousand hits. Your ass-whomping went viral. Congratulations!" (Dustin Ybarra)

He took my advice, and, with material like that, before long he was getting spots around town. A couple of MTV pilots followed, then *Live at Gotham*, and now he is in major films.

Jay has had the opportunity to help those who had helped him as well as encourage and develop a new generation of comics. He was made the keeper of the franchise, the *Tonight Show* of Jerry Lester, Steve Allen, Jack Paar, and Johnny Carson. Along with Letterman, Merv Griffin, Mike Douglas, and others, they helped launch and support the careers of so many comedians. That the same cannot be said for Leno is a shame. He abandoned the stand-up comic. That is not just my indictment; that is the widespread belief in the comedy community.

An exasperated Boosler once asked me about Leno: "What does he think? That the one with the most toys wins?"

"Yes, Elayne," I said. "He does."

No one begrudged Leno his success. What was expected, however, was that he would help other comics, whether behind the scenes with the Greek or on his stage for Bob Shaw or some unknown stand-up needing his first shot. When he closed out his first *Tonight Show* run in 2009, he said that sixty-eight children had been born to his staff since 1992. Too bad he couldn't also say he had brought a new major stand-up comic into the world during that time. Instead, in now some twenty years of hosting his own show, he has not broken a single significant stand-up act, which is amazing given the reach of the *Tonight Show*. The only comedy career he has launched has been that of Ross Mathews, who is more of a personality than a stand-up.

However, Chelsea Handler and her *Chelsea Lately* show has been a tremendous platform for comics—Whitney Cummings, Natasha Leggero, Jo Koy, Josh Wolf, Heather McDonald, Sarah Colonna, Loni Love, and Kevin Hart, just to name a few. There are radio shows that have done a better job than Ray Peno at providing a stage for comics. Howard Stern can take some credit for Sam Kinison and a lot more for Greg Fitzsimmons and Artie Lange. *Bob and Tom* helped Frank Caliendo as well as Larry the Cable Guy, Bill Engvall, and Ron White from the Blue Collar Comedy Tour. *Opie and Anthony* brought Jim Norton to the forefront. Some have appeared on Leno's show but only after achieving their breakthroughs elsewhere.

Ironically, the most popular comic Letterman launched was Leno. But within the comedy community there have been so many more that he has helped, including nearly everyone from his early days at the Store, from Johnny Dark, Tom Dreesen, Richard Lewis, Jeff Altman, and Johnny Witherspoon to George Miller and a road comic named Jimmie Walker.

> *Designer colognes . . . they got Obsession, they got Passion. Now they've got a cologne for black men only, called Repossession—for the black man who thought he had everything, but it didn't work out that way.* (Jimmie Walker, *Late Show with David Letterman,* 1995 or 1996)

Letterman is not a "people person." Neither am I. Neither was George Miller, who in the early days roomed with Dave. Letterman and George became the closest of friends, and the three of us always got along. George and I traveled across America playing so many shows together.

When George was diagnosed with leukemia, Letterman made sure he was booked on his show enough times so he would qualify for his union health benefits (he would appear fifty-six times over two decades). When his condition worsened, Dave donated a million dollars to put him into an experimental medical program at UCLA. It saved his life for a while. And when George said, "I don't want to sit around and wait to die. I want to work," Letterman came through for him again.

He rarely called his agents at Creative Artists Agency (CAA), but for George he would do anything.

"Yes sir, Mr. Letterman, what can we do for you?"

Letterman proposed a tour called Classic Comics of Late Night, starring four old friends—George, Bobby Kelton, Gary Mule Deer, and myself. He told CAA he wanted the agency to book us into casinos and theaters around the country.

Miller, Kelton, Mule Deer, and Walker?

They told him, "We're agents, not God!" They could not book the tour.

What Letterman did next has never before been revealed: He paid the freight himself—paid for the whole tour. When a show did not sell-out, he bought the remaining tickets and had them given away. We played about twenty dates—the Foxwoods and Mohegan Sun casinos in Connecticut, Emerald Island casino in Nevada, Cerritos Performing Arts Center in Southern California, and elsewhere. We traveled first class and stayed at first-class hotels, and it was a great show too. Letterman did that for George.

Kelton had no idea what was going on; he thought we really were selling out. When Dave found out I told Kelton the truth about the tour, he was very upset with me. He didn't want everyone to know. He's that kind of guy. He will probably be pissed reading this now.

One day George and I were driving to a gig in Washington and we passed a cemetery. As if it was the most ordinary thing, George said, "Oh, that's where I'm going to put my ashes." The last thing he ever said to me was "You're gonna miss me when I'm dead!"

He worked until his last day. In March 2003 he collapsed in his hotel room at the Riviera in Vegas and was rushed to a hospital. I received an e-mail from Boosler saying, "Hi. How's your day going? Oh, by the way, George Miller died."

His memorial service at the Laugh Factory has gained legendary status. Assembled were Richard Lewis, Dreesen, Boosler, Mort Sahl, Johnny Dark, Charlie Hill, Kelly Monteith, myself, and many others. Of course, Leno showed up too. Letterman was unable to attend because he was dealing with his own medical condition at the time—shingles. Given the nasty breakup between Leno and Letterman, many of the comedians in attendance were grateful that a potential scene of discomfort and awkwardness was avoided.

Leno and others took the microphone to talk about George. The stories were rough, but as Boosler said, "Never has someone who hated so many been loved by so many." There was nothing but love in that room—comedian love.

It was the same when Landesberg, one of the nicest people any of us ever knew, passed away in December 2010. Brenner arranged for a memorial at a downtown LA theater, and those of us there, including Richard Lewis, Marty Nadler, and Hal Linden and Max Gail from *Barney Miller*, told Landesberg stories and jokes for two or three hours. I repeated his Laurence Olivier and Gabby Hayes story—and it killed.

Comedians can be strange and twisted and dark. Sometimes we are not nice people. But, dammit, anyone can make you cry. Only a few people in this world can make you laugh. George and Steve made me laugh. I miss them.

Not long ago I was once again on Letterman's show.

"Dave, thanks for putting me on, man," I told him during a commercial break. "I know you don't need me to come on. I do appreciate it."

"Hey," he said, "you're one of my dearest friends. As long as I have a breath, you will always be on my show."

Dave is not an emotional guy and neither am I. But after I finished my little skit, I went off stage and had to stop for a moment. Yeah, there were a couple of tears, people.

11

The N-Word

IN THE '60S THERE WAS A TV COMMERCIAL ABOUT AJAX LAUNDRY detergent, which was so good it supposedly turned dirty white clothes into sparkling white clothes. The character in the commercial was a knight on a white horse.

> *I only have one minor complaint about television, that is one commercial. The White Knight. You know, that nitwit on the horse that goes by, turns everything white. Lord, I hope he never passes me. I've got enough problems. Turn me white, I'll start running around feeling guilty all the time.* (Godfrey Cambridge, 1965)

Among the things white people feel guilty about is using the n-word—nigger. Political correctness is the opposite of truth and honesty, and I am all for truth and honesty. I would rather someone tell me the truth to my face than behind my back—and no ethnic group is more direct than Italians.

I loved working for them at private parties in their own resort area in the Catskills, called Monticello. Also, opening in Vegas for everyone from the Carpenters to Frankie Valli and the Four Seasons, I would often get asked to perform on an off day for groups of Italians. Every now and then I met the guy I was working for and the next day saw his mug shot next to a headline reading, "Johnny 'Three Fingers' Maragano Arrested."

An Italian guy would come up to me at a casino and say, "Eh, we fuckin' love you, man. We got some business we got to take care of, but we got the girls and the kids here and they want to see you. They want to see you do some of that nigger shit. So you do that, take care of that for a fuckin' half hour. We'll come back and give you a thou. But do that colored shit." He would yell to a friend, "Eh, Joey, come listen to the nigger. He's gonna do some shit here."

If one of his friends or family said to him, "Maybe you shouldn't use that word," he'd shoot back with "What fuckin' word? He's just doin' nigger shit. What word am I using that's so bad?" He honestly did not think he said anything wrong.

In 2010 Laura Schlessinger, aka Dr. Laura, said "nigger" several times on her radio show in response to a black caller asking if it was okay to use that word. Dr. Laura's answer was that it depended, but that black men seemed to call each other "nigger" all the time. She was right. Blacks love to use the n-word to each other. But usually when white people say the n-word, they know not to say it in front of us—even on the radio. Dr. Laura made that mistake, and soon afterward public pressure forced her to move her show to satellite radio.

Just like "dyn-o-mite," I do not say "nigger" in my act. After my early years in comedy it just no longer was part of my vernacular on stage. But when I hear others use it today, it does not bother me. Most black comics use it a lot. I loved when Paul Mooney said "nigger" a hundred times in his act. I can't stand that he has stopped.

"Come on, Mooney!" I told him. "That's your thing, man!"

I have known him since about 1969, and Mooney has always said "nigger." He is the godfather of that sort of comedy, the man who fed it to Pryor. For him not to say "nigger" is like a day without sunshine. Before he announced his prohibition, when people would tell him,

"You're so talented and funny, you don't need to say the word 'nigger,'" he answered, "I've been called it enough. I can use it whenever I want to!" Right on, brother!

What caused Mooney to stop was Michael Richards's rant at the Laugh Factory in late 2006. Responding to hecklers, Richards shouted "He's a nigger!" several times. The backlash was so severe that he retired from stand-up. Mooney was so distressed by the anger in Richards's voice that he reacted by saying, "We're gonna stop using the n-word. I'm gonna stop using it. . . . We want all human beings throughout the world to stop using the n-word." The next month he tried to give his first "n-free" performance. He made it through an hour before one slipped out. He apologized and has since kept to his pledge, suggesting that instead people substitute "Michael Richards" for the n-word.

For him to ban it from his act is just as wrong as "nigger" coming out of Cosby's mouth. If it fits who you are as a performer, then say it. If it doesn't, then don't. I can only hope that Mooney will once again say "nigger" on stage.

There are some things that are far more racially insensitive than the n-word. If blacks don't say or do them even among ourselves, then no one else ought to say or do them either. Such things go beyond political correctness and enter the area of just plain offensive.

One such thing happened when I opened for a week at the old school Fontainebleau Hotel on Miami Beach for singer Eddie Fisher and headliner comedian Jackie Mason. The audience was largely Jewish, but that had never been a problem for me. At the first show they applauded when I walked on. But that was it. There was not one laugh in twenty minutes. Not one. I could hear the ocean waves lapping against the shore outside the room. I could not use the excuse of "second show, Friday night" or that people were drinking and eating and talking and not paying attention. They sat there, they looked at me, they knew who I was, they heard what I said. When I was finished, I walked off to silence. Well, I thought, maybe everyone will have a bad show.

Out came Fisher, who had been a teen idol and one of the biggest stars in the world in the '50s. He was greeted by wild applause and the crowd loved him.

Near the end of his act he talked about how he grew up a Jewish boy in Philadelphia and about how he was discovered by Eddie Cantor at Grossinger's in the Borscht Belt. On stage was a full-length mirror with its back angled away from the audience. Fisher sat in front of it as he talked about Cantor, his mentor nurtured in vaudeville, and the other great Jewish singer of that day, Al Jolson. In his hands was a chunk of burnt cork and he began rubbing it onto his face. My mouth dropped open. Was this actually happening?

"I would now like to do a song for you dedicated to Eddie Cantor and Al Jolson."

Completely in blackface, just like his mentor had done in the early twentieth century, Fisher sang "My Mammy." He strolled into the audience, went down on one knee and, in front of an elderly Jewish woman, belted out, "I'd walk a million miles / For one of your smiles / My Mammy!"

The audience loved it! They gave him a standing ovation. The guy really with a black face bombed and the white guy who painted his face black was a hit. Go figure.

Mason followed him onto the stage.

> My grandfather always said, "Don't watch your money; watch your health." So one day while I was watching my health, someone stole my money. It was my grandfather.

The audience loved Mason too.

In an earlier time doing blackface minstrel shows was okay. I have no problem with presenting history accurately either. Mark Twain used the word "nigger" in *Huckleberry Finn* and no one should change that. But to recreate something such as a minstrel show for entertainment purposes, well, it's a free country—but be prepared for the consequences.

The review in the *Miami Herald* the next day noted Fisher's black-face routine but without any other comment. That morning I took a call from the local NAACP. "Did he really do that?" they asked. I told them it was true. The next night they picketed in front of the hotel. I believe that put a damper on Fisher ever performing again in blackface.

Once the public accepted black entertainers, there was no longer any excuse for having whites pretend to be black by putting on black-face. That acceptance, however, has taken some time. Just because *Good Times* and other black sitcoms were on the air in the '70s did not mean that all was well in race relations.

When Franklin Ajaye and I were the only black comics on the TV series *Playboy after Dark*, the director would have a camera only on the black people in the audience for reaction shots to our jokes. One time there was a black guy who would not laugh, and he was the one they kept going to. Finally, the director told the cameraman, "Fuck that black guy! Get me another black guy!"

For the *Dean Martin Celebrity Roast* series I was occasionally the only black guy on the dais—they had to have one. But Greg Garrison, from my *Rowan & Martin* experience, was the show's producer and director, and he still did not think I was funny.

"The only reason you're on the show," he said, "is that the network told me to put you on the show." Though the roasts were on NBC and *Good Times* was on CBS, my Q Score (which measures public appeal and is important to advertisers) was so high that even a competing net-work wanted me to make an appearance.

But Garrison made sure I rarely told many jokes. Instead, to fulfill his orders I was mostly shown sitting on the dais during the tapings. When viewers saw the shows, there I'd be, howling with laughter at a terrible joke from Charo. In fact, Garrison taped my reaction shots be-fore the roast. I had no idea what joke I would be laughing at!

The dictatorial Garrison also insisted that all of the men wear a tuxedo or suit and tie. But when we passed on the way to the set for the first show, I just had on my usual jacket.

"Where's your tie?" he asked.

"In my dressing room," I told him.

"Don't lie to your fuckin' idol!" he shouted.

He was right. I never did have a tie—and I never wore one on the show either.

The business of comedy continues to be segregated today thanks largely to another color: green, as in cash money. The bottom line is that black audiences, unfortunately, do not spend as much money at comedy clubs as white audiences.

As a result, most comedy clubs prefer white comedians. That may come as a shock to you if you believe we have become a color-blind society. But comedy clubs would rather have a white comic—or a black comic with a largely white audience—than a black comic who caters to a black audience. Because the black comic just doesn't bring in the paying customers who shell out the cash once they are inside the door.

> Black folks, we're much different than y'all. Y'all go out on an evening like tonight, spend thirty or forty dollars and say, "Hey, no problem at all." But black folks, we go out and spend thirty or forty dollars in the evening and we WILL turn over a table. Black folks like to take home souvenirs!

Because of the handful of high-profile black comedy stars, many people assume there is a long line of black stand-ups in the wings. In truth, there were not many black stand-ups at the Store or Improv back in my day. For a long time Pryor, Redd Foxx, Franklin Ajaye, and I would be the only ones to get on the marquee. And there are not many now.

The road to the top starts at the bottom. The education of a stand-up means having to be bad before you can be good. You need a place to learn and develop. But there were—and are—very few black comics in the showcase lineup at the LA Store hoping to rise up. To get noticed, black comics have had to succeed in other venues, from movies and TV to rap and even public parks.

Charlie Barnett found that outdoor stage out of necessity and his story is among the most tragic. Raised by his grandmother in West Virginia, he left home when he was eleven years old to live with his mother in Boston. The next year she kicked him out, and gangs, heroin addiction, crime, and reform school followed. At nineteen he made his way to New York City, where he became a street comic, which is a very hard gig. If you don't make folks laugh, they won't throw money in the hat, and you go hungry. But with his energy and his talent for physical comedy, he established himself at Washington Square Park. Unlike the other street performers, he was able to "fill the fountain," drawing crowds to the park's amphitheatre-like fountain area.

> I like Ronald Reagan 'cause he's gonna bring back the good ole days—slavery. But at least I'd be workin'. (Charlie Barnett)

Besides performing on the street, Charlie began to play clubs, which is where I first saw him. We worked together many times. He was screwed up and unreliable, but he was also a great guy, a nice guy. After Dave Chappelle was booed off the stage during the Apollo's Amateur Hour, Barnett was the one who helped restore Chappelle's confidence and get him going again.

The folks from *Saturday Night Live* heard about Charlie, brought him in for an audition, and were blown away. But on a show like *SNL* there is constant rewriting. New lines are immediately put on cue cards and fed very fast to the performers. The producers and writers noticed during rehearsals that Charlie was having trouble keeping up. I'm not sure that Charlie actually could read. If he could, his reading comprehension was very weak. The producers had to hold a last-minute audition to replace him. His spot was taken by a young kid named Eddie Murphy.

Charlie would appear in the comedy *D.C. Cab* and became a regular on the *Miami Vice* TV series. But in his personal life he was a lot like Pryor—if he made $500 that day, he would spend $500 that night. After *Miami Vice* went off the air, he was back living on the streets. In 1996, at age forty-one, Charlie died of AIDS.

The desperation that brought Charlie to Washington Square Park and was felt by many black stand-ups helped launch the Comedy Act Theater. Located in the Crenshaw district of infamous south central LA, the club was opened in 1985 by show business entrepreneur Michael Williams. The venue nurtured an entire generation of black stand-ups, from Robin Harris, who was a regular emcee, to Jamie Foxx, D. L. Hughley, Damon Wayans, Chris Tucker, Martin Lawrence, Steve Harvey, Bernie Mac, and on and on. In the early '90s a second club opened in Atlanta, where Cedric the Entertainer, Mike Epps, and Bruce Bruce worked, and another also opened in Chicago.

Few white people went to the Comedy Act Theater—especially not to that neighborhood in LA—and that was the point. These were black comedy clubs for black audiences. The comics could work "black" and not worry about offending white people or about having a wider audience. It was not surprising that many of the best acts that grew up at the Comedy Act Theater found their way into the Def Jam comedy machine and the Kings of Comedy tours. The Def Comedy Jam series on HBO in the '90s offered an enormously important springboard for black stand-ups, sending them into movies and their own TV shows. Most of those comics would never have had a shot, never been seen, if they had not first had the Comedy Act Theater stage to work.

A negative aspect, however, is that the style that the audiences encouraged there was what I call "Niggery Comedy"—gutter level, racial, laced with profanity, and solely for blacks. Let me be clear: I laugh at that too at times, and I admire many of those comics. Katt Williams might be the closest we have today to a Richard Pryor, both onstage and off. But there should be more black comics who want to do more. There should be some diversity.

In an *Ebony* article in 1975 I said, "I go for universality, to do what everybody can understand; black, white, green, whoever the hell it is. . . . A lot of people are getting hung up onto the black-white thing. . . . I'm not into any of that. . . . It's not relevant to the world as it is. And that's what I'm into, the world as a whole, full being. I'm not into just one little area because that's the way I grew up and I think that's a bad thing about little black kids now."

Sadly, the Balkanization of comedy has grown worse, not better, since then. "Funny is funny" is not a truism anymore. There's black comedy, black ghetto comedy, black woman comedy, Hispanic comedy, gay comedy, butch gay comedy, and on and on. Today, comics focus in on their own particular crowd with a laser beam. Comedians used to bring us together; now they separate us from each other.

> *Lot of stuff goin' on. On television now they have commercials that appeal to the ethnic group that is watching the show. If they have a Hispanic show, they have Hispanic commercials. If they have an Oriental show, they have to have Oriental commercials. I'm watching a black show the other day . . . the Pillsbury Doughboy comes on—and he's burnt!*

When the Store opened its room in Vegas at the Dunes, certain comics were packaged together—there was an all-woman group, a country group, and a black show. I usually led the latter, which also featured Finis Henderson, Joey Kamen, and Roxanne Reese. The Flabulous Henderson, as I called Finis (named by his mother because he was the "finest"), did impressions, usually musical, of stars like Sammy Davis Jr. and Michael Jackson. We nicknamed him the "Milkman" because when his act was going well, he would go beyond his twenty minutes and milk the audience for every second of applause.

One night Mooney came in to fill in for someone. He saw that the show was all black and proclaimed, "Oh, I see, it's the minstrel show, brother!" From that time on, during the several years we played there, that was what everyone called us—the Minstrel Show. I suppose we had made progress—at least we really were black.

Unfortunately, the black community has rarely fully supported black comics—including Cosby—who do humor a level above Niggery Comedy. Cosby's most dedicated audience has been the white audience. For my post-Panthers stand-up act that has been mine too. Thanks to my more traditional approach to joke telling, my lack of profanity, and the bad vibe in the black community the attacks on J. J. caused, my audience is largely white. I tell club owners who I have not worked with before not to even bother spending money on promoting my shows on local black radio stations or in black newspapers. I am not considered part of the black comedy thang. I am the Johnny Mathis of Black Comedians!

My stand-up has always been very different from Niggery Comedy. I try to have something to say about life, about politics, about society.

> More violence in Northern Ireland. Goes to show that in a country without any blacks, Jews, or Mexicans, people can improvise.
>
> Ever notice you never see any black suicide bombers? You ask a black guy to be a suicide bomber, he says, "Can't do it. I just put new rims on this car!"
>
> Economy is bad. People are willing to take a job doing anything. I know a guy with a master's degree in electrical engineering just got a job proofreading M&Ms.

Black stand-ups today rarely do political humor. There is truly no black equivalent to a Dennis Miller, Jon Stewart, or Steven Colbert. Having a black man as president has actually hurt political humor from black comedians. Very few—Larry Wilmore, the Senior Black Correspondent on Stewart's the *Daily Show* is a rarity—feel right about making a joke about one of our own. The black audience just might not like that. But even though I am black, I am a free man, and so . . .

> *Could be a little buyer's remorse after electing Barack Obama. How high were we that we elected a black guy as president? I mean, we like the guy. He's not a Flava Flav kind of black guy, but he is black. Now the country is $14 trillion in debt. I'm happy about that, to tell you the truth. Glad to see a black man can finally get credit.*

The black comic today who most reminds me of me is Chris Rock—his frequent use of the n-word aside. He works hard, is aware of all aspects of life, and knows not only comedy but also the history of comedy (which is why I think he cast me in his *Everybody Hates Chris* sitcom as his character's grandfather). Sometimes if you close your eyes and just listen to him perform, he has the same rhythm in joke telling as I do. More importantly, we both want to appeal to everyone; we strive for universality. That speech Brenner gave me at the African Room in the late '60s still holds true today: If you don't mind having a small audience, then only speak to blacks. If you want a large audience, you need to speak to whites: There are more of them than there are of us.

The problem is that white comics don't have to be white, but black comics have to be black. I took a lot of criticism about J. J. being ridiculous. What about Steve Martin and his wild and crazy guy? Was he any less ridiculous? If a black comic had done the same routine, he would have been crucified for "cooning it up." But Steve was white. He did not—nor did he have to—represent anyone or anything. He even made a movie about a white man thinking he was black. *The Jerk* opened with him saying, "I was born a poor black child . . . " It was stupid, and there is no problem with stupid in comedy—unless you are black and in front of a white audience.

Which is why white audiences rarely see Niggery Comedy. If you have seen Michael Epps, Earthquake, D. C. Curry, Adele Givens, Cheryl Underwood, and Joe Torry, you have been "ghettosized." None of these funny people have been seen on late-night network TV in any meaningful way. They have almost exclusively appeared on shows expressly aimed at black audiences.

There is a vicious circle: Because minority comedy acts are rarely seen on late-night, they find themselves on segregated venues—BET's *Comic View*, HBO's *Def Comedy Jam* and *Loco Slam*, and so on—and that labels them as comics for only a certain audience. Because of that, they do not get gigs at white comedy clubs, which means they are not booked on late-night TV. Afraid of losing their core audience, they stay with Niggery Comedy, which ensures that they will never broaden their act to include the white audience. They want to but they can't break out of the comedy ghetto. And so the cultural segregation continues—on TV we have BET and TV One for blacks, Telemundo and Galavision for Latinos, CMT for rednecks.

I received an invitation to the BET Awards. The information e-mail from Black Entertainment Television was a bit different from the invite to the TV Land Awards. I paraphrase, but not much:

> *Please let us know if you have a police record so we can clear you to get in. . . . If you have a posse, please only bring two of them. . . . If you have any weapons, please let us know in advance because everyone will be going through metal screening and searches.*

After the pat down I entered the lobby of the theater, ready to partake of the food. But there had been a problem and the caterer had yet to arrive. The organizers ordered an emergency fast food delivery—buckets of Popeyes fried chicken and biscuits. I was surprised they did not order watermelon too! When I stuck my hand into a bucket, a production assistant stopped me with "That's Snoop's chicken!"

I had been invited to the BET Awards because the rap world of Snoop Dogg had rediscovered J. J. thanks to late-night reruns of *Good Times* on TV Land. "Dyn-o-mite!" was sampled for various rap songs, from "Pass the Mic" by the Beastie Boys to "Dynamite Beats" by Bomb the Bass and "Going Postal" from Rhymefest. I'm still waiting for the checks, people!

Nas also name-checked *Good Times* in his 2001 track "Ether": "J. J. Evans gettin' gunned up and clapped quick." I didn't know what that meant or that the song dissed superstar rapper Jay-Z, but at least they remembered me. Years later I still did not realize there was a feud when rapper Cam'ron asked me to portray Jay-Z in his video for "Touch It or Not / Wet Wipes." It too dissed Jay-Z. All of a sudden the former Official Comedian for the Black Panthers in the East was in the middle of a gangsta rap war. Thankfully, peace broke out.

This is not rocket science, people. Black comics have had the most success when they have appealed to the most people.

Which brings us back, as always, to Cosby.

When Pryor first got on stage, he was doing nothing more than a Cosby impersonation. With help from Mooney, he would later find his own voice and style. But it says something that Pryor, who had very little in common personally with Cosby, thought Bill was the best stand-up comic there was.

No one has come close to what Cosby has done. Yes, nearly every black comedian today, from Rock to Chappelle—and many white ones too, like Dane Cook—tries to be like Pryor in terms of language and rawness. But you never see anyone try to follow in Cosby's footsteps—because they can't. You would have to work clean and work up observational routines, not just three-beat jokes. You would have to reflect real life, not a caricature of real life. You would have to command the stage effortlessly, so much so that you could sit down for an entire set of stand-up. Oh, and you would have to make everyone—black, white, whatever—laugh big time.

Ironically, the best stand-up in comedy has not changed stand-up comedy—because no one can follow Cosby. No one even tries. And he has succeeded without uttering a single "fuck" or "nigger."

Like Cosby, my act is not black—or blue. In other words, there is no profanity. James Brown, or Mr. Brown as he demanded to be called, had the same rule when I worked as the comic in his show late in his career. That even meant no "hell" or "damn." I don't go that far, but my feeling is that if you would not let your ten-year-old kid sit in the front row, then you are doing something wrong.

You might think that working clean would be a good thing. But these days it is not.

I was working in Corpus Christi, Texas, at the Crazy Times comedy club. I was fifteen minutes into my show when I saw a table being kind of restless. Finally, they all got up and walked out. I was stunned. That almost never happens and I feel guilty when it does because these people paid good money to see me and for some reason I had let them down.

I saw them in the back of the club having an animated conversation with the owner. After the show he told me, very unhappily, that "those people who left were regulars."

"What did I do?" I asked.

"They said you didn't do any dirty jokes, didn't use any cuss words. They had to think too much."

Oh. In that case, I can't say I'm sorry.

That is one reason why I insist that my opening acts also work clean. With a "blue" comic opening for me, people might expect that I will be the same, and then they will be disappointed.

I called one club a few days before my appearance and asked the assistant if I had a clean opening act. She said, "All of the comics stay at the same hotel, so I imagine they all take showers."

"No, no," I said. "Does the opening act use any profanity?"

I heard her ask a person nearby, "Do we have any acts who don't curse?" A moment later, she came back to me: "I'm sorry, but we've *never* had one of those here."

Sometimes I get an opening act that wants to negotiate. "Please! Can I just have two 'fucks'? That's all I need!"

There's a belief among most comics today that saying "fuck" makes any joke work better. Why then is it that most major comics have had the most success and made the most money not from their oh-so-hip "dirty bits" but from their clean projects? Chris Rock? *Everybody Hates Chris*. Eddie Murphy? *Beverly Hills Cop, Coming to America, Doctor Doolittle, Shrek*. Richard Pryor? His movies with Gene Wilder. It's not just a black thang either. Bob Saget has always had a very dirty stand-up act—but he made his cash with the oh-so-wholesome *Full House* sitcom and hugely successful *America's Funniest Home Videos*.

Dick Gregory, my first inspiration, had both black and white audiences. I finally met him for the first time a few years ago. I was anxious to know from a true groundbreaker for all black comedians how he came up with his material, about his life as a stand-up, and how he made the transition from comedy to activism.

"Naw, man, I don't deal with that anymore," he said. "None of that means anything. I'm all about love and feeling good. What's going on with your life?"

"Uh, but . . . "

"How do you feel? How's your health?"

I wish my only meeting with him had been more informative. But I will always admire what he did as a comic. He could have stuck to playing black clubs and the chitlin' circuit, but he wanted to perform in front of everybody.

So did I. I even went country. Renowned country radio and TV host Ralph Emery booked me on his *Nashville Now* show on what was then called the Nashville Network. There are not many black folks who are into country music, but I went on the show anyway. Apparently I did really well because he kept inviting me back and went so far as to arrange for me to appear at the Country Music Association's Fanfest in Nashville. I briefly thought about repositioning myself as the Charley Pride of comedy! Charley was the biggest black singing star in country music history.

In Vegas I opened for two other country stars, Trace Adkins and Randy Travis. You might think their audiences, completely white, would be put off by a black comic opening their shows. But they were not, and I was proud to be able to work those crowds. Both stars were great to be around too. Randy was especially supportive of me being on the bill with him at the MGM Grand, and I fit right in with his insistence on no profanity. He was very religious too and held a group prayer before every performance.

We did the room's early show, with me going on at 7:30 p.m. The showroom's late show began at 11 p.m. and was completely different, starring comic Sandra Bernhard, who loved to drop F-bombs and had a very controversial, sexually charged act.

One night, with his dressing room door open, Randy and his band and crew were doing their group prayer. A cross-dressing male backup dancer from Bernhard's act walked by in a mini-skirt and fishnet stockings and announced to no one in particular, "I gotta tape my dick in this goddamn mini-skirt!" Bet that was the first time Randy ever heard *that* sentence—at least I hope so.

As the rare performer who has worked completely white crowds at country concerts as well as completely black crowds at the Apollo, I believe the unspoken reality of American life is that black and white prefer "separate but equal." People who hope for a colorless world do not want to hear this but, despite civil rights legislation aplenty from the '50s until today, racism is part of the fabric of our society. I am not referring to public racism, which affects schools, employment, and housing for which the government demands integration. I'm talking about racism in our private lives. "Government cannot make us equal," black conservative Brian W. Jones has written. "It can only make us equal before the law."

Here's a simple test I have used for years. Go to your favorite bar after 6 p.m. Look at the groups of the same sex (not gay) hanging together. Those are the people they have chosen as friends. I'm talking

about a bar in a big city with lots of different ethnic groups, lots of in-
teraction with different races at work, at school, and so on. How many
of those groups are mixed in color? Very, very few. No one needs to feel
guilty about that. It just is what it is. There is a Tyler Perry movie and
there is *The Hangover*—and the characters in one do not hang out with
the characters in the other.

An exception to this antagonism between the races—and there are
always exceptions—is when people of different races date or marry. Sex
can overcome anything!

Pryor and Prinze used to tease me: "You and your white women and
your white posse!" It seemed whenever I went to the Store, I would
have at least a couple of my writers with me, and my girlfriend would
be white too. Brenner had a funny line when he saw black comic
George Wallace walk up to the Store with two white women: "George,
you are so lucky that there are so many white girls who want to hurt
their parents."

All but one of my serious relationships have been with white
women, something I never would have guessed when I was opening for
the Panthers!

When I dated Nancy, a secretary at Warner Brothers, she would
often stay at my townhouse. Once, while she was there alone, a man
with a deep Southern accent phoned.

"You got a nigga there?"

She was shocked.

He continued, "We don't allow niggas living with white women
'round here. We gonna come getcha!"

He hung up and a very distraught Nancy called me on the set.

She worked in the entertainment industry, but she did not know
comedians. We go right for the jugular. When she told me what happened and described the caller's accent, I knew immediately it had been
Landesberg playing a joke on her. I laughed. But I do not remember her
laughing. She was shaken.

The only black woman I was serious about was Edie. We met at some comedy event during the *Good Times* years. She was considerably younger than me and had been the only black to that date in the Rose Bowl Queen's Court. She was absolutely stunning and phenomenally poised and classy for a teenager. She reminded me of a young Lena Horne. When she gave me her phone number, I couldn't believe it. That I then dated her and we lived together was amazing to me. My lawyer, Jerry, would take her to lunch just so people would think she was "with" him.

She loved to go out and be seen. She loved to shop. She loved to tan by the pool (yes, black people tan). She slept most of the day and then spent most of the night partying with her friends. She was a black Paris Hilton before there was a white Paris Hilton. She loved doing talk shows and game shows and going to events with me, from awards shows to movie premieres. Otherwise, I was on the set during the day, with my writers in early evening and doing my act at the Store at night. The arrangement was clear: She would be stunningly beautiful and I would buy her almost anything she wanted. There were few guys on the planet who would not have traded places with me in an instant.

The only thing I would not get her was her own Mercedes. I gave her mine to drive and also paid to have her car fixed whenever she wanted. But she wanted her own—and did not like my refusing her wish. That argument was the only one we had, but it was the beginning of the end of our time together. It was the car or me! Obviously we are not talking about love in this situation. After about a year of a not-very-emotional relationship, we broke up, seemingly on good terms.

A month later Jerry received a lawsuit with my name on it for "alienation of affections." I was shocked and hurt. I decided to settle out of court. Almost immediately Edie apologized to me, saying that the lawsuit was her family's idea. She did not give me back the money, though.

I have not been seriously involved with a woman of color since. And I don't think black women across America are screaming, "Oh no, without Jimmie Walker, what are we going to do now?!" That's just a personal choice I have made. We are free in America to be politically incorrect.

> *People used to think we go around with fried chicken in a paper*
> *bag. But things have changed. Now, we carry an attaché case—*
> *with fried chicken in it. We ain't going to give up everything just to*
> *get along with you people.*

Who said that joke? Pryor in the '70s? Eddie Murphy in the '80s? Chris Rock in the '90s? Dave Chappelle in the '00s?

Answer: Godfrey Cambridge, 1965.

Any black comic in America could "adapt" that joke today and it would still kill—especially if he threw in a few F-bombs and a "nigger" here and there.

12

On the Road

I HAVE SPENT MOST OF MY ADULT LIFE ON THE ROAD. SURE, I STARRED on TV, but my life was always all about the stand-up. All I have ever wanted to do was get on stage and make people laugh. Not that doing almost three hundred shows a year in clubs across the country is easy. I have played bowling alleys where the stage is at the end of a lane and I had to wear bowling shoes. I have played Chinese restaurants— "Jimmie Walker *and* a Chinese buffet for $19.99."

* * *

I am booked at the Sahara in Atlantic City for a three-month gig in the lounge. I arrive at the airport and look around for the car that is supposed to pick me up. I see a limo with a Sahara sign on it and find the driver sleeping. I tap on the window and say, "Are you here to pick up Jimmie Walker?"

"J. J.?"

"Yeah."

"Oh, sorry. You know what's happening? We have WrestleMania in town." This was WrestleMania IV at the Trump Plaza in 1988. "I've been driving all day. I'm really tired. Do you know your way around Atlantic City?"

"Yeah, I've worked here a lot."

"Would you mind driving?"

"Yes, I would. That's your gig."

"Thought I'd ask."

At the Sahara the female desk clerk says, "Oh my God, J. J.! What are you doing here?"

"I'm working in the lounge. I'm going to be here for a while."

"Really? I never even heard. Where are you staying?"

"I'm staying here. Where else would I stay?"

"Uh, you know it's WrestleMania? We're booked."

"I'm supposed to have a room."

"We don't have any rooms."

I ask her to call Jay, the entertainment director.

"I'm sorry, Jay didn't get your reservation in on time. It's a little crazy. It *is* WrestleMania. But we'll figure something out." After an hour she wrangles me a room. I open the door and see a guy jerking off on the bed. I wince, close the door, and return to the reservations clerk. I tell her there is somebody still in the room.

"Oh, I guess they didn't clear it. Well, you know, it *is* WrestleMania."

She gets me another room, but it faces the Trump Plaza and the bright lights from that tower reflect right into my room. For someone who works at night and sleeps in during the mornings, this is a serious problem. I ask her for another room, but she shakes her head: "It's WrestleMania." Okay, fine.

The next day I go to the valet to pick up the car they usually lend to the entertainer playing the hotel.

"J. J.! I love that show, man!" he says. "What are you doing here?"

"I'm working the lounge. I'm here to get the club car."

He looks at me like I am insane. "You know it's WrestleMania? All the cars are taken." I ask him to call Jay, who tells him to send me down the street to a rental car place where I can get a car and that the hotel will pay.

I walk to the rental car place. The guy at the desk says, "Holy shit, J. J.? I love you, man! I used to laugh my ass off at that 'dyn-o-mite' thing. What are you doing in town?"

"I'm working the Sahara."

"So what are you doing in here?"

"I need a car."

"We don't have any cars. Didn't anyone tell you? It's WrestleMania."

"But I'm going to be here for three months. I need a car."

"Let me see what I can do. But keep in mind, it's WrestleMania." After an hour he locates an available rental and I drive back to the hotel.

The valet says, "Parking is full. It's WrestleMania." I give him the keys and let him figure out what to do.

I go to my room, but it has not been cleaned up. I see the maid, who is about to leave the floor, and I stop her.

"I think you forgot to hit my room," I tell her. "It's a little funky in there."

"I've been working since six o'clock this morning," she says sharply. "You know, it *is* WrestleMania."

I do my show that night and tell the tale of my trip so far. Jay comes up afterward and says, "Very funny, man. But we would appreciate you not doing that story. It makes the hotel look bad." I say, "No problem."

But when I go back to my room, it still has not been made up. I see the maid again and she gives me the same line: "It's WrestleMania." Okay, now I am getting annoyed.

I do my second show that night, and I tell the story again—and it absolutely kills. Jay says, "Didn't I ask you not to do that story?"

"Come on, Jay, what's going on? I can't even get a clean room!"

"We'll take care of it," he says, "as soon as WrestleMania is over."

The next day the valet drives my car to the pick-up area. It has a gash about a foot long in the side. "Hey man, what happened to the car?" I ask.

He looks at the damage. "Man, that is bad."

"It wasn't there when I checked it in yesterday."

"Well, you know, it *is* WrestleMania."

That night in the lounge I tell the story again. Jay waves me over to speak with him. "I've asked you twice not to do that story. I know you're getting laughs, but you're getting laughs at the expense of the hotel. We can't have that. Maybe it's best that you leave."

"Fine, I'm leaving."

The next day I board the plane to LA and settle into my seat. I turn to the guy next to me. It is the same guy I saw jerking off in the hotel room. I change my seat.

***

I am a road comic.

I spend a lot of time on planes and in airports. On the first day that planes could fly after 9/11 I went to the Las Vegas airport. I had a gig and it was time to help people laugh again. Everyone in the country was nervous, on edge, and a little bit scared too, especially if you were about to get on an airplane. I didn't know what to expect at the terminal. Inspectors searched my bags for what seemed like half an hour, but I finally made it through the checkpoint.

> *Security at airports is very tight. If your first name is Muhammad,*
> *your last name better be Ali.*

Walking through the concourse to my gate, an airline agent saw me and yelled, "Hey! Dyn-o-mite!" Not a smart move. She was hauled away by security guards, screaming, "Wait a minute! It's J. J., the 'Dyn-o-mite' guy!"

Please, if you see me at an airport, a simple "Hey Jimmie" will do.

***

After I work a club in King of Prussia, Pennsylvania, at 2 a.m. I drive the twenty minutes to a hotel in Philadelphia, where I get about five hours of sleep before I catch the shuttle to the airport so I can fly to Rochester, New York. The checkout clerk in Philly wants to know what it was like to be on *Good Times*. I tell him I'm late and can't chat right now. He tries to charge me for two nights. I tell him I've only been there for five hours—though it feels like two nights.

I'm five minutes late for the shuttle and have to grab a cab. I didn't have to hurry, however; the plane is delayed. So I call my agent. He's not in his office yet. When the plane is ready to board, I'm told I have to check my carry-on bag. No problem. I land in Rochester during the Northeast's worst snowstorm of the year. I head straight to a local TV show to promote my gig that night—but without my bag. The airline says it is not lost—they just can't find it. I suppose it must be hiding. They promise they will get it to my hotel as soon as they find what's not lost. I call my agent. He's gone to lunch.

The host of the talk show doesn't know who I am or why I am there. So I interview myself. I learn things about myself I never knew before. When I get back to the hotel, still no bag. I call Letterman's show to do a pre-interview for the appearance I'm scheduled for tomorrow. The talent coordinator is new. She doesn't understand why I'm on the show if I don't have a movie or TV show to promote. She asks me if I've ever met Dave. Then she gives me the Top Ten Reasons I Won't Be on the Show Again. I call my agent. He's still at lunch.

The Rochester gig sells out and the performance goes very well. I open with a joke about potholes in the streets:

> *Drove in from the airport. You have some potholes in your streets, Rochester! Saw one so big there was a Vietnamese family living in it!*

I kill. I sign autographs and hang out with the folks until 2 a.m., and I'm in bed an hour later. Have I mentioned that the airline still hasn't delivered my bag?

I'm up at the crack of dawn to do an early morning radio show with a local insult comic named Brother Wease. Apparently some people are bright-eyed and ready for insults at 7 a.m. I'm not, but the show must go on, so I stumble my way through it. Ellen DeGeneres has the best line about doing radio: "I knew I was a star when I didn't have to get up at 5 a.m. to do the *Rick & Rob Morning Zoo Show with Ike the Insane Intern*." Ellen is a star. I'm just a road comic, and the road is filled with potholes.

I remember years earlier receiving a call from a man with a very effeminate voice who said he was an assistant at a comedy club I was supposed to play in a few days.

"The talent booker is gone and I don't know our acts that well," he said in apology. "I mean, I know you used to be on TV and say 'TNT!' or 'Nitroglycerin!' or something like that. But I'm sorry to tell you that we can't sell enough tickets to your show. I'm afraid we will have to cancel."

Very disappointed, I quickly called my agent. He had no idea what I was talking about and called the club. They said my show was still on. I thought for a second about that voice on the phone. Landesberg!

I go to the Rochester airport to catch a flight to New York. I'm on time, but the plane is delayed, of course. I discover that the airline found my bag—and sent it to the hotel I just left. I arrive in New York without it.

Danny, the limo driver sent by Letterman's show, is a nice guy. He says he's also a comic. Isn't everyone? He's afraid to tell Letterman so he tries his jokes out on me. I'm glad he's a good driver.

We stop at Nathan's, the famous hot dog place in Times Square, and see one of the area's characters, Coupon Man. He never pays in cash; he uses coupons for everything. He buys me half a dozen hot dogs. In return I give him a ride around the block in the limo.

I tell Danny to wait for me while I walk down the street so I can buy some clothes because the airline still has mine. I pass a homeless man with two cups. I ask him, "Why two cups?" He says one is for his brother who is out sick. At the clothing store the salesman proceeds to give me a detailed description of two episodes of Good Times that I barely remember. Then he says, "What happened to you? Why aren't you on TV anymore?" I tell him I'll be on Letterman tonight. He says he only watches sports.

At Letterman's studio suddenly the talent coordinator knows that I first met Dave in 1975 and everyone treats me like a long-lost friend. The talent coordinator wants to know if Dave really had a beard. After the shot, Danny the limo driver tells me he thinks I did really well, but he has some jokes that would have been funnier.

We drive to the hotel so I can get some sleep before flying to Chicago tomorrow for a one-nighter. But there's a call waiting for me from Regis Philbin's show. A guest canceled and they would like me to fill in early the next morning. I'll be there. The young talent coordinator wants to know what Regis and I might talk about. She doesn't realize I have known Regis for decades and that we can do the interview in our sleep—which I may have to do. She has insisted on consulting Wikipedia and asks me not only about Good Times but Bustin' Loose. Really? She also wants to know about my wife.

I really need some sleep. But my hotel room faces the street. At 2 a.m. I hear: "Hey! Pick up the can, man! Just get the goddamn can!" The garbagemen are picking up the trash. I watch infomercials until 5 a.m.

Two hours later the phone rings. It's the Regis show saying the limo is on the way to pick me up. We get there only five minutes before air time. The talent coordinator is nervous because she still doesn't know what Regis and I could possibly talk about. I walk onto the set, Regis pulls out photos of me on a Perry Como special, and we are off and running. I plug my gig in Chicago that night and then I'm back in the limo headed for the airport.

Hope springing eternal, I ask the airline if they have rerouted my bag. I'm told I am "in the system." I call my agent. He's at a breakfast meeting. I ask his secretary if my agent saw my Letterman shot. She says he was at a B'nai B'rith dinner. I get a call from the airline. They assure me that they are on the case. They say my bag was last seen in Cincinnati.

I actually get in touch with Bob, my personal appearance agent. He once booked me into a farm convention where the farmers had to mow a clearing so they could set up lawn chairs for the audience. I helped them set up the chairs. Bob would sell rocks to the Palestinians and helmets to the Israelis. He tells me I'm booked for a date in Hot Springs, Arkansas, a hotbed of the Ku Klux Klan. I tell him, "Thanks."

At the Chicago gig I open with the pothole joke: "Drove in from the airport. You have some potholes in your streets, Chicago! Saw one so big there was a Vietnamese family living in it!" It kills. Every town has potholes. Every town will hear my pothole joke.

I arrive in Hot Springs at a dinner theater/country-western bar. The audience is rowdy, so I resort to audience participation mode: "Where are you from? What do you do for a living?" I talk to a blond woman in the front row: "You look a little nervous speaking to a black man." A guy who looks like an extra from *Mississippi Burning* jumps up and yells at me, "She's got good reason to be!" I don't ask for the details. We go on with the show—until a drunk woman stands up and shouts, "Women have half the money and all the pussy!" She then runs up on stage and says she wants to tell a joke. I have no choice. I let her. "What do you call a black test tube baby?" Pause. "Janitor in a drum!" The crowd loves it. I get her off the stage and move on.

This is not an audience I want to be confrontational with. I would not survive doing what Richard Belzer did one night at the Comedy Store in LA. I watched him as he walked on and a woman in front immediately yelled, "You suck! I've seen you before and you're horrible!"

"Big Dick" wasn't going to take that without a fight. He schmoozed her purse from her and went through it on stage. He took out marijuana joints and showed them to the crowd. She had a diaphragm, and he showed it to the crowd. Every time he took something out, Belzer ripped her apart and buried her. He destroyed her for half an hour. It was vicious and hysterically funny. The audience went wild.

The woman, not so amused, finally surrendered and said, "Hey, why don't you just do your thing."

Belzer hammered in the final stake: "My thing is fucking you in the ass!"

Somehow I live through my Arkansas gig and I'm back at an airport. The airline has my bag! But the handle has broken off. I look inside and there is the handle, with a note: "This must be yours."

My next stop is Greenville, South Carolina, where I deal with one of the scourges of comedy clubs today—the cell phone. People get calls during the show, hold conversations during the show, text during the show. I see a young woman in the second row who keeps looking down at the device in her hand. She does it over and over. Finally, I reach down and grab it from her. It's her insulin pump. Ouch. Sorry.

A couple of days later I'm in Buffalo. It's winter and it's snowing. What a surprise in Buffalo. I'm here to play the Comedy Trap, and local comic Air Force Eddie meets me at the airport. Eddie is obviously an optimist: He drives a '76 Gremlin with a burglar alarm. He tries to convince me that it is not *really* snowing—until we can't see the road anymore. We come to a stop in the middle of a field where two cows stare at us. Eddie calls a friend who pulls us out of the snow with his Jeep. At the hotel Eddie says with a straight face, "Buffalo doesn't get as much snow as people think."

The pothole joke kills again and the show goes well. The next morning I am at the Buffalo airport. The worst snowstorm the city has seen in years shuts everything down. No flights in or out. I sit in the airport café having breakfast. A woman comes up to me and says, "How are you doing?" I'm tired and I'm worried about making my gig the following night in Boston. I don't look up at her. I just say, "Okay," and wait to hear, "I loved your show. I still watch it. Do you ever talk to the cast anymore?" Instead, she talks about her mom, going on and on about mom this and mom that. I look up. It's my sister. She lives in Buffalo.

She tells me about my father, who was now about eighty years old. He had gotten sick and was in the hospital. He was getting worse. The doctors said he needed to be in a convalescent home, but my mother and his two other girlfriends fought to keep him out. They said they would help him return to his apartment. My mother also offered to take him to her place. After all, she had been a nurse. But the doctors said no; he had to go to the home.

My mother gave her okay. Then she stole a wheelchair and wheeled him out of the hospital. She kidnapped him! After half an hour, the hospital realized he was gone. She was nearly as old as he was, so they were still crawling down the sidewalk not too far away. The nurses started to chase her on foot! But she hailed a cab, put my father in with her, and escaped. They went to his apartment, and some time later he passed away.

So I call my mother. She reveals a secret she has been keeping from me for more than twenty years: Six months after Mr. Boyce died, she remarried my father. During the entire time since, she lived in two apartments, hers in the Bronx and his in Brooklyn. She was married to him the second time for over twenty years. At his funeral the other two women were also there, but she was officially the widow.

I am stunned. She never told me, her son. She doesn't understand why I am very angry with her. Instead, she gets angry with me for not understanding her feelings for my father.

"Why me?" I ask. "Why are you not angry with him? I didn't break your jaw twice! I didn't have two other women at my funeral! You should be upset with the person who did all that!"

"He was my husband and I loved him," she says. "He was your father."

I had moved on long ago. She never did.

I do what I do, and good or bad, I move on. That has been the mantra of my life. That is the mantra of the road comic.

Not too long ago I walked out of the London Hotel in New York and was blinded by the flash of what seemed like a hundred cameras.

The paparazzi had staked out the entrance. I stood there and smiled, wondering why they were so interested in me. I walked back into the hotel to ask what was going on. Answer: Justin Bieber, the hottest new teen singing star, was staying there. I guess the photographers figured they might as well take a few pictures of me while they were waiting for him.

At least I was upstaged by a teenager. I had already been upstaged by an eleven-year-old. I was booked for a gig at a civic center in Nampa, Idaho. Not Tampa, Florida. Nampa, Idaho. Outside Boise. Not even in Boise. But the place was sold out, and I saw more than a dozen media folks waiting—TV, radio, newspaper. I turned to the producer and said, "Wow, they all came out for this." By "this," of course, I meant "me."

"Oh, they're not here for you," he said. "They're here for Trevor Hattabaugh."

"Who?"

"He's an eleven-year-old comedian who works around here."

"Oh."

"He's opening for you."

"Oh."

The media rushed to a room backstage, where Trevor was with his mother. They asked him about the Funny Bone comedy club in Boise that had banned him because alcohol control officials said he was too young to perform there.

None of the media talked to me. As Trevor took the stage, all of the cameras and reporters followed him.

School used to be fun. Now all we do is study for standardized tests. I think it's because of this new law called No Child Left with a Mind. Yeah, it's working.

He was the best eleven-year-old stand-up comic I have ever seen.

As he exited I walked on stage—and all of the media left with him. So too did about a third of the audience. I could see the TV reporters in the back of the auditorium interviewing Trevor and shooting their set-up pieces for their nightly newscasts.

I'm on stage, people!

Show business is like a greased pole—even if you have climbed to the top, sooner or later you are going to slide back down. I still climb the pole every day. I may not reach the top again, but at least my butt is off the ground!

In 2011 *People* magazine published a special edition titled "1000 Greatest Moments in Pop Culture 1974–2011"—and J. J. saying "Dyn-o-mite!" was among them. That word has been woven into the fabric of American life, something I never could have imagined when it first came out of my mouth.

I will always be the guy in the floppy hat who said "Dyn-o-mite!" As Steve Crantz once said, "Your obit's going to read: 'Today the dyn-o-mite fizzled.'"

It hasn't all been "dyn-o-mite!" . . . but you should see the guy they sent to the ghetto.

Acknowledgments

Jimmie thanks Randie Gorbena, Diane Cantor, Kaye Morano, Harris Peet, Adam Chromy, David Brenner, Ben Schafer, Chuck Hurewitz, and Craig Glazer.